Sociology of Education Today

Also by Jack Demaine

BEYOND COMMUNITARIANISM: Citizenship, Politics and Education
(*with Harold Entwistle*)

CONTEMPORARY THEORIES IN THE SOCIOLOGY OF EDUCATION

EDUCATION POLICY AND CONTEMPORARY POLITICS

Sociology of Education Today

Edited by

Jack Demaine
Department of Social Sciences
Loughborough University
England

palgrave

First published 2001 by
PALGRAVE
Houndmills, Basingstoke, Hampshire RG21 6XS and
175 Fifth Avenue, New York, N.Y. 10010
Companies and representatives throughout the world

PALGRAVE is the new global academic imprint of
St. Martin's Press LLC Scholarly and Reference Division and
Palgrave Publishers Ltd (formerly Macmillan Press Ltd).

ISBN 0–333–77828–6 hardback
ISBN 0–333–77829–4 paperback

This book is printed on paper suitable for recycling and
made from fully managed and sustained forest sources.

A catalogue record for this book is available
from the British Library.

Library of Congress Cataloging-in-Publication Data
Sociology of education today / edited by Jack Demaine.
    p. cm.
  Includes bibliographical references and index.
  ISBN 0–333–77828–6 — ISBN 0–333–77829–4 (pbk.)
    1. Educational sociology. I. Demaine, Jack.
  LC191.2 .S634 2000
                                            00–048353

10 9   8   7   6   5   4   3   2   1
10 09 08 07 06 05 04 03 02 01

Printed and bound in Great Britain by
Antony Rowe Ltd, Chippenham, Wiltshire

Contents

Acknowledgements

As editor, I would like to thank the following people for their contributions, encouragement, support and hard work: Madeleine Arnot, Linda Auld, Stephen Ball, Alastair Bonnett, Bruce Carrington, Lorraine Culley, Roger Dale, Lynn Davies, Jo-Anne Dillabough, Tim Farmiloe, Sharon Gewirtz, Heather Gibson, Dave Gillborn, Peter Kelly, Jane Kenway, Anoop Nayak, Sally Power, Larry Saha, Geoff Short, Fay Smith, Richard Tomlin, Christine Skelton, Carol Vincent, Geoff Whitty, Sue Willis, Pat Wiltshire and Deborah Youdell.

Notes on the Contributors

Madeleine Arnot is Fellow of Jesus College and Reader in Sociology of Education at the University of Cambridge. Her publications include *Feminism and Social Justice in Education* (with Kathleen Weiler) (1993), *Educational Reforms and Gender Equality in Schools* (with Miriam David and Gaby Weiner) (l996), *Recent Research on Gender and Educational Performance* (with John Gray, Mary James and Jean Rudduck) (1998) and *Closing the Gender Gap: post-war education and social change* (with Miriam David and Gaby Weiner) (1999). She is a member of the editorial board of *International Studies in Sociology of Education* and an executive member of the editorial board of the *British Journal of Sociology of Education*. She is an international consultant for *Gender and Education*.

Stephen Ball is Karl Mannheim Professor of Sociology of Education at the Institute of Education, University of London. His publications include *Politics and Policy-making in Education* (1990), *Education Reform* (1994) and *Markets, Choice and Equity in Education* (with Sharon Gewirtz and Richard Bowe) (1995). He is managing editor of the *Journal of Education Policy* and a board member of a number of other journals including the *British Journal of Sociology of Education, Discourse*, and the *International Journal of Inclusive Education*.

Alastair Bonnett is Reader in Human Geography at the University of Newcastle upon Tyne. His publications include *Radicalism, Anti-racism and Representation* (1993), *Anti-racism* (1999) and *White Identities: Historical and International Perspectives* (1999).

Bruce Carrington is Professor of Education at the University of Newcastle. His publications include *Children and Controversial Issues* (with Barry Troyna) (1988), *'Race' and the Primary School: Theory into Practice* (with Geoffrey Short) (1989) and *Education, Racism and Reform* (with Barry Troyna) (1990).

Roger Dale is Professor of Education and Associate Dean of Arts at the University of Auckland. His publications include *The State and Education Policy* (1989) and *The TVEI Story: Policy, Practice and Preparation for Work* (1990). He is a member of several editorial boards including the *British Journal of Sociology of Education, International Studies in Sociology of Education, Discourse* and *Educational Research*.

Lynn Davies is Professor of International Education and Director of the Centre for International Education and Research at the University of Birmingham. Her publications include *Pupil Power: Deviance and Gender in School* (1984), *Equity and Efficiency: School Management in an International Context* (1990), *Beyond Authoritarian School Management: the Challenge for Transparency* (1994) and *School Management and Effectiveness in Developing Countries* (with Clive Harber) (1998). She is an executive editor of *British Journal of Sociology of Education* and a member of the editorial board *of International Studies in Sociology of Education.*

Jack Demaine is Senior Lecturer in the Department of Social Sciences at Loughborough University. His publications include *Contemporary Theories in the Sociology of Education* (1981), *Beyond Communitarianism: Citizenship, Politics and Education* (with Harold Entwistle) (1996) and *Education Policy and Contemporary Politics* (1999). He is an executive editor of *International Studies in Sociology of Education.*

Jo-Anne Dillabough is an Assistant Professor at the Ontario Institute for Studies in Education, at the University of Toronto and was formerly Research Fellow in the School of Education at the University of Cambridge. Her publications include *Challenging Democracy: International Perspectives on Gender, Education and Citizenship:* (with Madeleine Arnot) (2000). She has contributed to journals including the *British Journal of Sociology of Education, Curriculum Inquiry, British Journal of Educational Studies* and *Theory and Research in Social Education.*

Sharon Gewirtz is Lecturer in Social Policy at the Open University. Her publications include *Specialization and Choice in Urban Education* (with Geoff Whitty and Tony Edwards) (1993), *Markets, Choice and Equity in Education* (with Stephen Ball and Richard Bowe) (1995), *Rethinking Social Policy* (with Gail Lewis and John Clarke) (2000), *New Managerialism, New Welfare?* (with John Clarke and Eugene McLaughlin) (2000) and *The Managerial School* (2001). She is a member of the editorial boards of the *Journal of Education Policy,* the *British Journal of Sociology of Education,* and *Education and Social Justice.*

David Gillborn is Professor of Education and Head of Policy Studies at the Institute of Education, University of London. His publications include *Racism and Antiracism in Real Schools* (1995), *Recent Research on the Achievements of Ethnic Minority Pupils* (with Caroline Gipps) (1996) and *Rationing*

Education: policy, practice, reform and equity (with Deborah Youdell) (2000). He is founding editor of the journal, *Race, Ethnicity and Education*.

Peter Kelly is a Lecturer in Social and Behavioural Studies in the Faculty of Social and Behavioural Sciences at the University of Queensland, Australia. He recently completed a PhD titled 'Risk and the Regulation of Youthful Identities in an Age of Manufactured Uncertainty' and he has written for the *Journal of Youth Studies*, the *Journal of Adolescence* and the *British Journal of Sociology of Education*.

Jane Kenway is Professor of Education in the Language and Literacy Research Centre in the School of Education at the University of South Australia. Her publications include *Marketing Education: Some Critical Issues* (1995), *Gender Matters in Educational Administration and Policy: A Feminist Introduction* (1994) (with Jill Blackmore), *Critical Visions: Policy and Curriculum Rewriting the Future of Education, Gender and Work* (1995) (with Sue Willis), *Answering back: girls, boys and feminism in schools* (1998) (with Sue Willis, Jill Blackmore and Léonie Rennie), and *Economising Education: the Post Fordist Directions* (1994). She is on the editorial boards of *International Journal of Inclusive Education, Discourse, International Journal of Cultural Policy Studies* and *Australian Educational Review*.

Anoop Nayak is Lecturer in Social and Cultural Geography at the University of Newcastle upon Tyne. His publications include *Invisible Europeans? Black people in the New Europe* (1993) (with Les Back). He is editor of the special issue of the journal *Body & Society* on 'racialized bodies'. His research interests include masculinities and education; youth subcultures; race, ethnicity and whiteness.

Sally Power is Professor of Education at the Institute of Education, University of London. She is co-author of *Grant Maintained Schools: Education in the Market Place* (with John Fitz and David Halpin) (1993) and *Devolution and Choice in Education: The School, the State and the Market* (with David Halpin and Geoff Whitty) (1998). She is a member of the editorial board of *International Studies in Sociology of Education* and the *Journal of Education Policy*.

Lawrence Saha is Reader in Sociology at the Australian National University. His publications include *Education and National Development: A Comparative Perspective* (with Ingemar Fägerlind) (1989) and *Schooling* *and Society in Australia: Sociological Perspectives* (with John Keeves) (1990). He is an editor of *The International Encyclopedia of the Sociology of Education* (1997). He is associate editor for the *Social Psychology of Education*, advisory editor for the *International Journal of Educational Research* and a member of the editorial board of *The Australian Monitor.*

Geoff Short is Reader in Educational Research at the University of Hertfordshire. His publications include *Race and the Primary School: Theory into Practice* (with Bruce Carrington) (1989). He has written widely on ethnicity and education and is currently working on Holocaust education and on the question of citizenship.

Christine Skelton is Director of Undergraduate Studies in the Department of Education at the University of Newcastle. Her publications include *Whatever Happens to Little Women? Gender and Primary Schooling* (1989) and *Schooling the Boys: Masculinities and Primary Schools* (2000). She is a member of the editorial board of *Gender and Education.*

Fay Smith is Lecturer in Education in the Department of Education at the University of Newcastle. Her PhD was on the relationship between teaching methods and student learning style, and her research interests are in language and communication and in lifelong learning. She has written for the *Journal of Vocational Education and Training*, the *Cambridge Journal of Education* and *Studies in Teaching and Learning.*

Richard Tomlin is Managing Director of *Community of Science Incorporated*, Baltimore, United States of America and Visiting Lecturer in the Department of Education at the University of Newcastle. His publications include *A Study of the Impact of the 1992 RAE* (with Ian McNay) (1995), *Developing a Strategic Role for Technology Transfer* (1996) and *Research League Tables: is there a better way?* (1997). He is an adviser to the European Commission on research management and related issues.

Carol Vincent is Senior Lecturer in Policy Studies at the Institute of Education, London University. Her publications include *Parents and Teachers: Power and Participation* (1996) and *Including Parents? Citizenship, Education and Parental Agency* (2000). She is a member of the editorial board of the *International Journal of Inclusive Education*, the *British Journal of Sociology of Education* and the *Journal of Education Policy.*

Geoff Whitty was formerly Karl Mannheim Professor of Sociology of Education and is now Director of the Institute of Education, University of London. His publications include *The State and Private Education: An Evaluation of the Assisted Places Scheme* (with John Fitz and Tony Edwards) (1989), *Specialization and Choice in Urban Education: The City Technology College Experiment* (with Sharon Gewirtz and Tony Edwards) (1993) and *Devolution and Choice in Education: The School, the State and the Market* (with David Halpin and Sally Power) (1998). He is a member of the editorial board of *International Studies in Sociology of Education* and the *British Journal of Sociology of Education*.

Sue Willis is Professor and Dean of the Faculty of Education at Monash University, Australia. Her publications include *Real girls don't do maths: gender and the construction of privilege* (1989), *Being numerate: what counts?* (1990) (with Jane Kenway), *Hearts and minds: self esteem and the schooling of girls* (1990), *Telling tales: girls and schools changing their ways* (1993), *Critical Visions: Policy and Curriculum Rewriting the Future of Education, Gender and Work* (1995) (with Jane Kenway), *Critical visions: rewriting the future of work, schooling and gender* (1996) and *Answering back: girls, boys and feminism in schools* (1998) (with Jill Blackmore, Jane Kenway and Léonie Rennie).

Deborah Youdell is Research Associate in the Faculty of Education, University of Sydney. Previously, she worked as a researcher at the Institute of Education, University of London. Her publications include *Rationing Education: policy, practice, reform & equity* (2000) (with David Gillborn).

Introduction: Research in Sociology of Education Today

Jack Demaine

In the two decades since my *Contemporary Theories in the Sociology of Education* (Demaine 1981) sociology of education has continued to develop and indeed thrive. In the first chapter of this new book Roger Dale offers an account of developments in the sociology of education over the last half century. He argues that much of the subject matter, theoretical inclinations, meta-theoretical assumptions and methodologies that characterize the sociology of education emerged from the operation of what he refers to as a 'selection principle'. He suggest that during the period from the end of the Second World War three factors – context, purpose and location – combined to create the selection principle that framed the focus and approaches of the sociology of education. He argues that the selection principle took different forms at different periods of time as the relative weight and the relationship of the component parts altered.

In the chapter that follows, 'Feminist Sociology of Education: dynamics, debates and directions', Jo-Anne Dillabough and Madeleine Arnot discuss the impact of feminist research especially on girls' and women's education. They argue that feminist research is characterized by its flexibility – its power lies in its ability to keep up with changing circumstances and to adapt its research agenda to engage critically with social democratic ideals as well as with neo-conservative reform programmes. Current research offers rich data on the relationship between government-led educational reforms and the processes of gender identification, and on the consequences of gender change on the patterns of educational performance. Jo-Anne Dillabough and Madeleine Arnot argue that through the strength of its policy analysis and research, feminist sociologists have been able to use their own yardstick of social justice to question and challenge the implementation of government programmes in relation to male and female patterns of education.

Sharon Gewirtz addresses concepts at work in discourse on social justice in Chapter 3. She argues that given the centrality of issues of social justice to policy–sociology research in education, further conceptual work is needed to extend the boundaries of what is usually thought of as social justice. She draws on Iris Marion Young's sophisticated conceptualization of social justice to delineate a social justice agenda that education policy–sociology might pursue.

In Chapter 4, David Gillborn and Deborah Youdell are also concerned with social justice in relation to education. They explore the school-based processes 'that might explain why, at a time of rising overall achievement, there has also been a consistent increase in relative inequalities of attainment, especially in relation to social class and ethnic origin'. They focus on one particular aspect of the processes, namely, the role of 'ability' in the dominant discourses, arguing that ability has come to be understood by policy makers and by practitioners as a proxy for common-sense notions of 'intelligence'. They argue that 'ability' is constituted in ways that provide for the systematic disadvantaging of particular socially defined groups, especially children of working-class and Black/African-Caribbean heritage, allowing discredited and abhorrent ideologies of hereditarian IQism to exercise a powerful influence on the realities of contemporary education.

There is much work to be done in the field of ethnicity, racism and education. In Chapter 5, 'New Teachers and the Question of Ethnicity', Bruce Carrington, Alastair Bonnett, Anoop Nayak, Geoff Short, Christine Skelton, Fay Smith, Richard Tomlin, and Jack Demaine report on part of their two-year research into ethnic minority recruitment to teaching. In this chapter, the focus is on research undertaken in 15 English universities and an institution providing 'school-centred' initial teacher training. The chapter reports on measures taken to attract ethnic minority trainees to teaching, and examines strategies employed by training institutions and their partnership schools to support ethnic minority students during the course of their training.

In Chapter 6 we turn to another, rather different, arena of vocational training. Jane Kenway, Peter Kelly and Sue Willis report on their research in Western Australia into how a vocational education and training programme in a local secondary college was 'manufactured' to fit its location and how youthful identities too are manufactured. Their research elaborates on the ways in which 'regional entrepreneurs' both in the school and in the locality customized the vocational education and training programme in order to 'design' young workers in response to their globalized context.

In Chapter 7, Lynn Davies develops a range of arguments around the theme of the globalized context of education. She argues that three of the most important strands in sociology of education today are sociology of development, sociology of democracy and sociology of deviance. 'They are not often put together, but global trends suggest a new combination of thinking which would lead to a more proactive role for sociologists of education.' Her chapter provides a way of reconceptualizing the macro and micro, structure and agency, drawing on the newer fields of chaos and complexity theory, and contextualizing the systems approach through human rights theory and practice.

In Chapter 8, Lawrence Saha also discusses the influence of global social and economic tendencies, arguing that the comparative study of education has shown how varied are the roles and structures of education in different cultural settings. He concludes that the field of comparative education has provided sufficient evidence to dispel any assumptions about there being a single model of education appropriate for all countries. Education is a major agent for the economic, social and political improvement of society, but only if it is adapted and used in a manner appropriate to the cultural context of a particular country.

In Chapter 9, Stephen Ball and Carol Vincent are concerned with Britain and, specifically, with new class relations in education and the strategies of what they refer to as 'the fearful middle classes'. As with the following Chapter 10, their work is part of a broader effort within the sociology of education to write social class back into the analytical problematic of the discipline. Ball and Vincent show how current social and economic conditions underpin the reworking of the sociology of class differentiation in education. They conclude that despite the increasing fluidity and complexity of social relations in high modernity, and the decline of traditional class politics, social class position still goes a long way towards determining life chances, although societal fragmentation may render this more opaque.

In Chapter 10 Sally Power also addresses the question of the middle class. There is a general absence of a sociology of the middle class and of a sociology of educating the middle class in particular because, traditionally, the social scientific 'gaze' has been directed towards the working classes, the poor and the dispossessed, and also at the wealthy and powerful. This is particularly so with respect to education, but examination of the intimate relationship between education and the middle class and the complex way in which schools foster differentiated middle-class identities can illuminate how 'success' is constructed and distributed, and how this success contributes to social and cultural reproduction.

In Chapter 11, Geoff Whitty discusses recent reforms that have sought to dismantle centralized bureaucracies and create in their place devolved systems of schooling with an emphasis on consumer choice. Sometimes, alongside these elements of deregulation, there have also been new systems of inspection and accountability. He suggests that, although these developments are sometimes described as privatization, it is difficult to argue that education has actually been privatized on any significant scale. In most countries, marketization is a better metaphor for what has been happening in relation to education. The development of 'quasi-markets' in state-provided services has involved a combination of increased parental choice and school autonomy, together with a greater or lesser degree of public accountability and government regulation. He notes Chris Woodhead's call for a 'third way' for the sociology of education involving, among other things, a return to its 'classical terrain' in an effort to regain the 'intellectual high ground it occupied' in Karl Mannheim's time. But, as Whitty correctly concludes, the application of Mannheim's legacy to the contemporary educational scene would not necessarily lead to research findings that Woodhead himself would wish to see, any more than it would necessarily lead to the policies of New Labour, for that matter.

Of course, the chapters in this book represent but a fragment of the work of sociologists of education around the world, but they demonstrate some of the diversity and complexity of their research. This evidence of diversity leads to the conclusion that there is no single 'way forward', no royal road, no shining path to ultimate truths about education and its processes. Rather, there is a lot of interesting work in progress and much more still to be done.

1
Shaping the Sociology of Education over Half-a-Century

Roger Dale

In this chapter I want to argue that much of the subject matter, theoretical inclinations, meta-theoretical assumptions and methodologies that characterize the sociology of education can be seen to emerge, not so much from a conscious process of academic or intellectual deliberation, as from the operation of what I will refer to as a 'selection principle'. This selection principle has three components: the wider political contexts within which the sociology of education has operated; the nature of what I will suggest is its dominant project; and the circumstances and conditions in which it has been practised. I shall suggest that over the 50 years following the end of the Second World War, which is the time span I shall cover, these three factors, that can be presented in a shorthand if not comprehensive way, as context, purpose and location, combined to create the selection principle that framed the focus and approaches of the discipline. This selection principle took different forms at different periods as the relative weight and the relationship of the component parts altered. I shall especially consider how these different forms of the selection principle influenced the discipline's focus and its theoretical approaches, and the consequences of their relationship for the nature and strength of its theoretical output.

The basic argument is far from new or novel. It was put relevantly and succinctly by Karabel and Halsey in one of the defining texts of the sociology of education in the 1970s, when they argued that 'sociology has been influenced more by its social context than by any "inner logic" of the development of the discipline' (1977, 28). However, my aim in this chapter is to elaborate that idea somewhat and to give it some substance and specificity in the context of an account of the changes in the sociology of education. To advance this, I shall seek to outline the nature and operation of the selection principle across three distinct periods in the last 50 years, to show how the parts of the selection principle combined over those periods and with what consequences for the discipline.

Elaboration may proceed by considering some objections to this argument. An especially useful critique of the 'sociology of sociology of education' approach is provided by Geoffrey Walford in the introduction to a collection of chapters describing the research process in sociology of education (Walford, 1987). Walford begins by criticizing, quite rightly, accounts of the history of the sociology of education that view it 'as a fairly linear process with a succession of new theoretical perspectives, problems and methods supplanting the old' (p.2). However, his grounds for this criticism are not that such accounts decontextualise the discipline and tend implicitly to tie its 'development' to an unexplicated evolutionary principle, but that they are inadequate empirically; 'quite simply (these accounts) do not cover the majority of research and publications in what most people (sic) would accept as the sociology of education' (p.3). And while accepting that the model is 'a fairly reasonable indication of how the discipline has been presented to others at various historical periods since the war' (p.3), he puts the shifts down to changes in theoretical fashion. Walford goes on to suggest that while these 'changes in fashion can be newsworthy...the majority of researchers do not follow changes in fashion.' (ibid). These people just get on with their work; they 'usually go on wearing their old clothes, watching each succeeding generation don the current fad. They are aware that if they wait long enough their old clothes may come back into fashion and that few of the new innovations are new anyway.'

The basis of this cynical and 'commonsensical' reaction seems to be Walford's belief that sociology of education is not just 'What "most people" think it is', but 'what sociological researchers do', in a very literal sense. He emphasizes that 'doing research is a profoundly pragmatic and down-to-earth activity' and points to the numerous problems involved in that activity; not surprizingly, first among these problems are finance and time. The difficulty with this view of the sociology of education is that it reduces its focus to an unproblematic 'what most people think it is', and its approach to a preference of research method, apparently uninformed by any theoretical or methodological 'fads or fashions', and able to ignore the wider political and locational factors that *generate* the 'practical' problems of time and money. This kind of voluntarism turns the study of the discipline into a search for the weight of personal preference, periodically disturbed by mercurial changes in fashion. That is to say, it is a sociology of education that excludes itself from the possibility of being the object of sociological study. And that, really, is the key point; isolating a selection principle and reflecting on its effects enables us to do for our discipline what we claim to do for others.

Three important and useful points that can be extracted from the critique of Walford's approach. The first is that it is not necessary for the selection principle, or any of its component parts, to be consciously recognized for it to be effective; quite the opposite on occasion, as Walford seems to be telling us when he alludes to the resistance shown to what are seen as changes in fashion. The second is that the selection principle is not confined to one particular set of approaches, those that may be classified as theoretical fads and fashions. For instance, other means than 'theoretical understanding' or public advocacy may be employed to achieve a purpose; demonstration, various kinds of action and collaboration with practitioners and policy analysis are examples of combinations of focus and approach that the selection principle may promote.

Finally, it is no part of the argument to suggest that all sociologists of education are similarly affected by changes in the selection principle. The selection principle is just that; it is a principle not a formula. It acts as a filter, rather than moulds, still less determines. It does not have an homogenizing effect on the discipline because its impact varies according to the precise local valuations of its component parts.

The form of the paper will be as follows. In the next section I shall elaborate on the components of the selection principle. I will then discuss how they have combined at three different periods in the discipline's postwar history and how the selection principle based on these elements influenced the focus and approaches of the sociology of education in those periods.

Purpose: the dominant project

The importance of focusing on the 'purpose' of the discipline is made clear by Karabel and Halsey, (1977). While they do not address the nature of the social context systematically, they do give some prominence to the notion, taken from Alvin Gouldner, of the 'infrastructure' of social theory. This is composed of 'the sentiments, the domain assumptions, the conceptions of reality accented by personal experience' that 'constitute its individual and social grounding' (Gouldner, 1971, 29–49, 396–7, quoted in Karabel and Halsey, op. cit., 29). And the authors have earlier – 'because of our belief that personal background is an important factor in shaping the interpretation of a field, its significant theories, and relevant methods' – declared that what brought them together was 'not only a common sociological interest in education but also a shared political vizion of a classless education system dedicated to the pursuit of what Raymond Williams has called a common culture' (op. cit., vi). This is a very clear and explicit statement of what I mean by purpose.

I want to suggest that the substance of the sociology of education's purpose in the period under review has been essentially redemptive and emancipatory. Education has been seen as both the dominant symbol and the dominant strategy for that mastery of nature and of society through rationality that has characterized the project of modernity from its origins in the Enlightenment. On the other hand, it has been a keystone of attempts to extend the benefits of progress to whole populations, indeed to the whole of humanity. It has come to stand for the possibility of individual and collective improvement, individual and collective emancipation. Since it really began to develop as a discipline in the 1950s, almost all of the sociology of education in Britain has, however implicitly, taken that project of social redemption/emancipation through universal provizion as a central normative guideline and has concentrated its energies, in rather diverse ways, on identifying and removing the obstacles to the attainment of that unproblematic and rarely questioned goal. That basic purpose has, of course, been interpreted in a wide variety of ways in the past 50 years, but what it is crucial to note here is that those variations in interpretation themselves have their basis in the relationship between purpose and the other two components of the selection principle. For instance, as we shall see, the almost symbiotic relationship btween sociology of education and the burgeoning KWS settlement in the late 1950s and early 1960s was important not just in itself but in the model it provided for future sociologists of education; the viability of the redemptive/emancipatory purpose was clearly demonstrated.

However, the purpose of the sociology has tended to be tempered by some of the assumptions that derive from that early positive climate. In particular, it means that as John Meyer argues, 'the sociology of education stays rather close to the scientific theorizing built into the educational system.... The main lines of thought in the sociology of education...arise as sociological *commentary* on the institutionalized science of education. They parallel the system at every point, asking the sociological questions and expressing sociological skepticism about it...they tend to accept the assumptions and explanations built into the system itself and then to question whether they are *real* in actual social life' (Meyer,1986,341,343, emphases in original). In particular, the sociology of education has as its central questions the two main purposes of modern education systems, progress and inequality. The former is based on the idea that 'the educational reconstruction and expansion of individuals will produce social development', the latter on the idea that 'Education is to create an equal citizenry and to legitimate any inequality on meritocratic grounds.' (ibid. 344) Sociological commentary on these issues is almost all '*pro-education*, that is, in support of the official theory if this theory could be made to work.... Most critics dream of the improvement, not the elimination, of education' (ibid., emphasis in original).

Meyer argues that this produces a sociology of education that is deeply functionalist in character, due to its inability to transcend the legitimacy of the rational and purposive nature of education as an ideal. He suggests that whether in studying individuals, organizations or macro-sociological questions the styles of explanation leave something to be desired, leaving many areas of education unnoticed or little discussed. It might be suggested that this relationship to the education system treats it as resource rather than topic, and takes it for granted as the means to deliver redemption rather than as itself an object of enquiry. Further, and for Meyer most important, the failure to question the fundamental nature and claims of the education system leads to an almost total neglect of any alternative to the official conception of what education systems are for. To put it more starkly, 'education' becomes unproblematic for the sociology of education. And further it might be suggested that this fundamental stance has persisted across the period under review and that it may have constituted a major, but unrecognized, obstacle, to the development of new types of theoretical approach in the discipline.

The point I am trying to make about the importance and place of the prominence of its purpose in shaping the focus and approach of the sociology of education can be amplified if we compare the situation that Meyer describes in the discipline with that in other 'specialist' areas of sociology. Consider, for instance, the sociology of religion and the sociology of the family. In neither of these cases is the promotion of a particular view, whether official or unofficial, of a desirable set of arrangements for the area of social life or activity involved. This is not to say, of course, that there are not sociologists in both these fields with committed and clear views of the proper role and nature of the family or of religion. It is, though, to say that these views do not influence the focus and approach of the field in the same way as I am suggesting that the 'redemptive project' has influenced the sociology of education.

Location: the conditions of academic work

What equally importantly differentiates the sociology of education from other sub-areas of sociology, such as the sociology of religion or the sociology of the family, is that neither of them is as closely involved in professional training as the sociology of education. And, possibly as a consequence of this, sociology of education has never been a high status branch of sociology. Whatever the reason, this has increased the importance of its relation to teacher education as the key institutional location of sociology of education.

There are a number of very important features of this institutional location. Before I discuss them in more detail it is necessary to make two important points. First, nothing that is said about the effect on the sociology of education, its theoretical orientations or the outcomes of its location in institutions where teacher education is the main or a very significant sustaining activity should be read as implying that these effects are inevitable results of either that location, or of the kinds of academic work that goes on there, or of the interests of people who are attracted to work there. There is nothing inherently less 'academic' about what goes on in 'professional' departments. Second, the nature of the institutional location was dramatically altered in the 1980s and 1990s by reforms of the political control over teacher education. This meant a conspicuous and massive increase in political monitoring and control of the work of departments of teacher education. However, while this has had a major effect on the issues I am discussing, the point I am trying to make is neither stimulated by that new regime nor dependent on or confined to its effects.

Among the most important features of the institutional location are the following:

(i)   It implies, and possibly requires, some level of commitment on the part of those working there to the system for which they are preparing their students. That this may be a critical commitment does not alter the fact that it is the system as it exists that is the focus of critique (or commentary, as Meyer (1986) would have it).

(ii) It involves some minimal level of contribution to the development of professional practice. And though teacher educators, including sociologists of education, may be very influential definers of professional reality for teachers, the professionals themselves clearly have an influence on that definition, which may not be wholly compatible with the academics'.

(iii) It ensures that academics are kept aware of what is happening in schools and other educational institutions. It did not require a ministerial directive on the necessity of 'recent and relevant' classroom experience to ensure that teacher educators were kept in touch with the practicalities of school life.

(iv) In addition to these institutional factors themselves, the fact of their being the basis of the shared experiences and understandings of a large proportion of sociologists of education is also very significant. This experience provides a key joint problematic around which we might expect a professional culture to develop.

(v) The very institutions in which they work are themselves founded on, and to a degree dependent on, particular assumptions about the proper and possible role of teacher education and of the place of sociology of education within it. Central to these assumptions are two that have a clear affinity with the purpose of the sociology of education, collective (through the banishment of inequality) and individual (through the application of progressive methods) redemption.

These features have a range of consequences which may shape the focus and approaches of the sociology of education in crucial ways. They place a premium on the immediacy and 'practicality' of the analysis. They contain a bias in the direction of repairing, restoring and maintaining the system as it exists for those who work in it.

Another very significant facet of the institutional location of the sociology of education is its view of teachers. This varies considerably across different approaches in the discipline. In some accounts teachers have been seen as mere dupes of the system who unwittingly act as social selectors and arbiters of children's careers and are powerless to do anything to change it. In others they have been seen almost as the shock troops of the revolution to be brought about by means of the education system, or at least as the critical pedagogues who have it in their power to demystify the world, to undermine the hegemony perpetuated through schooling. In yet others they scarcely merit a mention. Some approaches stress the nature of teaching as work, or as a career. Others focus on who become teachers, on their social background. One major strand of work in the sociology of education, classroom ethnography, has teachers as its central focus.

Overall, however, sociology of education has been characterized by a kind of 'hands off' approach to the work of teachers. That is to say, there is a tendency, which is exemplified particularly in the approaches that see teaching as what teachers do, not only to avoid criticism of teachers but to avoid getting into situations where criticism may be called forth. Teachers may be seen as exhibiting false consciousness, or as having their autonomy seriously curtailed by external structural forces, but rarely if ever are they submitted to systematic criticism on the basis of their performance. Instead, the response, for instance when an industrialist publishes an article 'blaming the teachers', is to deny the charge and to defend the teachers and to point to the interested location of the comment. Similarly, denial rather than discussion has been the response to the charges of 'provider capture' that have been levelled at teachers in several countries since the mid 1980s. The point is not whether or not the charges can be sustained but the assumption that they are necessarily politically motivated attacks on teachers – and nothing else – and hence can be ignored. Part of the problem is that in terms of the selection principle hardly any other response is possible; in terms of both purpose and location teachers have to be seen as effectively beyond criticism, on the one hand because practitioners are dependent on them to bring about redemption, on the other because they are the bread and butter of the discipline, which, moreover, helped train them. In neither case does this lead to the theorization of teaching, which might form a basis of critique of teaching practices, becoming a high priority.

Three other aspects of the institutional location require mention. One is the career structure within the discipline and its effect on its focus and approaches. I have no firm statistical evidence on this, but impressionistically, it seems that two categories of achievement are associated with progress in the career, publication record and administrative experience in teacher education. The second aspect is important in linking location and purpose. It concerns the generational nature of British sociology of education. For a number of contextual reasons – that on the one hand saw its numbers peak very early, and on the other saw a planned decline in the opportunities available to later generations of sociologists of education in teacher education – a single generation, that recruited at relatively young ages in the late 1960s and early 1970s, is still the largest and most influential in the discipline. Evidence of this is the fact that the editorial board of the *British Journal of Sociology of Education* is still dominated by members of that generation. For instance, membership of the Executive Board has remained almost static throughout the journal's 20 years of publication, while relatively recent additions to the Advisory Board have scarcely reduced the large majority of 'first generation' members. Third, and most important, in the last decade the institutional location has been augmented by expectations relating to research performance. Great pressure is put on all departments to maximize their academic output and their research income. I have suggested elsewhere (Dale 1994) that these pressures lead to 'premature application' (and, we might add, sometimes premature publication) of the outputs of research. In the particular area of interest, much of the research funding available to sociologists of education is controlled by sources with interests in and commitments to the education system. It does not necessarily follow that research funded from such sources cannot be critical, or go beyond the expectations of the funders. Nevertheless, it is not unlikely that sponsored research undertaken by sociologists of education may (be required to) assume the 'official' parameters of the education system and hence require conscious and special efforts to transcend these parameters. And when this is placed alongside the tendency not to make 'education' problematic, there is a serious danger – in terms of both its likelihood and its consequences – that sociologists may find themselves, unwittingly, confirming 'official' definitions of 'education'.

Context: opportunities and constraints

In a rather loose sense, context could be seen as the independent variable in this analysis, and most of the discussion of it will focus on the details of the contexts under which sociology of education operated in each separate period. However, it may be worthwhile to point out how the sociology of education's perception of the context in which it was operating was framed, and at some of the ways the nature and scope of 'context' may be taken for granted. Essentially, the political context of the sociology of education was on the one hand interpreted through the prism of the dominant purpose, while on the other hand its impact was defined very largely through its effect on its institutional location. Separately and together, these perceptions produced a partial, not to say distorted, picture of the nature and significance of the context for the discipline. While reducing the effect of political context to its effect on the institutional locations in which sociologists of education work tends to produce a somewhat muted and narrow conception of its scope and impact, judging it largely on the basis of how propitious it might turn out to be for the promotion of the dominant purpose tends simul-taneously to inflate the significance of its ideological aspects and typically to restrict the recognition of those aspects to changes of governing party or political emphasis. That both these perceptions have often been accurate should not blind us either to their own partial nature or to other ways that political context impinges on the focus and approaches of the sociology of education. Two of these merit brief mention. One is the danger of neglecting the importance of 'institutional' changes, for instance in the mode of policymaking or implementation. The other is the danger of seeing context as offering only constraints and ignoring its effect on the channels through which the discipline's message could be delivered, how it could have an effect, and new opportunities that context changes may enable.

The selection principle and the focus and approaches of the sociology of education in Britain, 1950–95

I will now examine, briefly, the relationship between the selection principle and the focus and approaches of the sociology of education at three phases in Britain since 1945. In each case I will set out how purpose, location and context combine to form the selection principle and consider how they relate to the focus and approaches that characterize the discipline.

Before doing that I should note the basis of the periodization I shall use. Since it is central to my argument that it is the external political context, rather than internal, 'discipline-driven' shifts, that underlies changes to the focus and approaches of the sociology of education, that context is used as the basis of periodization; this also removes any suggestion of a *post hoc* mapping of the one on to the other. Any periodization is relatively arbitrary and no doubt the period under review could be divided up in many finer, or even coarser, ways. However, I think it is possible to distinguish three relatively distinct periods, though of course the precise transition points vary across different parts of the public sector. They are the period of what is commonly known as the Keynesian Welfare State settlement, which ran from the end of the war and began eventually to crumble definitively in the middle of the 1970s: the period that followed this, which completed the transition from the KWS but without there being a definitive settlement in respect of the political context of education until the third term of the Thatcher government in the middle of the 1980s: this may be seen to have been in retreat since the election of the Blair government, which I will take as the end of the third period.

1950–75

The purpose that guided the sociology of education over at least the first-half of this period had its roots in the widespread determination to rebuild the world in ways that would overcome the social evils of the 1920s and 30s. This had three main aspects: an emphasis of the role of education in creating a technologically based society, a desire to make education the central component of the attack on social inequality, including inequality in education itself; and its role in easing the adjustment to a rapidly changing society. In his fine analysis of the sociology of education in this period Bill Williamson suggests that '(The) basic demand is that policies in the field of education should be grounded in a knowledge of the social facts of unequal provizion and inequality. Their work made a wide appeal to a wide audience, but its basic orientation was dictated by a desire for social democratic change to a more equal society' (Williamson,1974,6). And while, by the middle of the period, affluence had increased and by the end of it unemployment had begun to reach serious levels, the purpose remained fundamentally the same, though rather differently interpreted and pursued by rather different strategies.

There were two main locations from which this purpose was to be achieved; departments of sociology, especially the London School of Economics, which had given birth to the political arithmetic tradition in which the purpose was based, and government statistical research, which was carried out in connection with the major postwar reports on education – 'Early Leaving' and the Crowther Report were prominent examples, but the use of such reports as a major means of setting education policy continued throughout the period and all of them made some use of sociological expertise.

The political context was, as noted above, dominated by the KWS settlement. The constraints on the sociology of education were few and the opportunities presented to the sociology of education were many and powerful. That context had a clearly defining effect on the possibility as well as the orientation of the sociology of education. It was benign and encouraging in that the social democratic welfare state reforms set in place by the Labour government from 1945–51 almost required a sociology of education to assist in its development and growth. It provided a positive external context and ample opportunities for advocacy. These reached their peak with the close links between the leading sociologist of education, A.H. Halsey, and Anthony Crosland, the Labour minister of education.

The three elements combined in a selection principle that was clear and quite explicit. Sociology of education should focus on *understanding* the structures and institutions of inequality on the role of education in the persistence of that inequality and the relationship between education and the economy. This focus is well represented in the first reader in the sociology of education, though with what may now seem a surprizingly strong emphasis on the relationship between education and the economy. For instance, the Preface states that the volume is 'narrowly focused on the connection of education in modern society with the economic and class structure' (Halsey, Floud and Anderson, 1961, v.) while the first sentence of the Introduction reads, 'Education is a crucial type of investment for the exploitation of modern technology' (ibid., 1).

However, by the end of the period, major and radical changes had become evident in the sociology of education. The indications of the demise of the KWS were already evident before what is generally taken as at least the symbolic closing of that settlement, the OPEC price rise in 1974. What was to be a fight to the death between the Conservative government and the miners had begun and there was a widespread feeling that an era had come to an end. The events of 1968 had brought many educational practices into question. One key factor precipitating the changes in the sociology of education was the apparent failure of the introduction of legislation requiring local authorities to introduce comprehensive secondary schooling, which could be seen as the high water mark of political arithmetic tradition in the sociology of education (though it has to be said that the eventual legislation owed rather little to the arguments of sociologists of education and rather more to the political pragmatism that was necessary to bring it into being). Not only was the legislation a long way from being universally implemented, but it was rapidly becoming clear – through the work of sociologists of education like Julienne Ford (1969), for instance – that it was doing little if anything to increase equality of opportunity in, and through, education. These contextual changes were accompanied by significant changes in location. Particularly important here was the changes in the pattern of teacher education. In large part through the introduction of the BEd from the second half of the 1960s, it became both longer and more academic. This shift provided major new opportunities for sociologists of education; from that point on, this institutional location, in different ways at different times, changed the nature of the selection principle. One other consequence of this growth in the demand for sociology of education was to strengthen the importance of the courses on the sociology of education produced in the Open University from the early 1970s. Though these courses were not directed at teacher education their public accessibility was to make them useful and convenient sources for people required to teach the sociology of education in a wide range of institutions for much of the next decade-and-a-half.

These major changes in the political and educational context and the institutional location served to modify the purpose of sociology of education and led to major changes in its focus and approaches, that took a range of rather disparate directions, in the early and middle 1970s. The failure of attempts to realize the purpose through structural change at macro level had two important consequences; they revealed the ineffectiveness of the 'structural reform' strategy for bringing about greater educational equality and they implied that the problem may not lie at the structural level. This led to approaches that focused on the content and processes of education rather than its structure, on how these affected the realization of the purpose and on how they might be transformed. The best known example of this shift in focus and approach is, of course, the New Sociology of Education. An enormous amount has been written on the NSOE and I do not intend to traverse that literature here. I merely wish to suggest that its emergence is more effectively explained by the selection principle than by a spontaneous embrace of new theoretical fashions.

According to Michael Young, there were three aspects of the NSOE that relate to its claim to be offering 'new directions'; its relation to the question of educational inequalities; its prioritizing of curriculum as a topic for the sociology of education; and its emphasis on teachers and teacher educators as 'agents of progressive change'. And he goes on, 'what was not recognized at the time but is striking in retrospect, was the extent of the similarity of political concerns between those identified with the NSOE and those whose work it criticized, for example Halsey, Floud, J.W.B. Douglas and Glass. For both these groups the primary political question in English education was the persistence of social class inequalities' (Young, 1988,9). The NSOE, then, represented not so much a replacement of the redemptive purpose of the sociology of education, as a challenge to the existing interpretation of it. And that challenge was enabled and encouraged by changes in the political context and in the institutional location of sociologists of education. The NSOE, then, sought to realize the purpose of the sociology of education by means of radical changes to educational practice based on understanding the content and processes of schooling, in place of the 'old' sociology of education's aim of improvement of structures based on an understanding of the relationship between education and the wider social structure.

1975–85

The purpose of the sociology of education had already begun to be interpreted in different ways before the OPEC price rise, and those interpretations continued to multiply over the course of the next decade, as the political context remained unstabilized and the institutional location became subject to new pressures, until the outlines of a new settlement in education began to emerge in the third term of the Thatcher government. But while the central core of the purpose remained strongly in place, and education was still seen as the central key to equalizing life chances, the interpretations and implications that developed especially over this decade were sufficiently diverse that they came to challenge the unity of the discipline.

The outstanding change for the sociology of education over this decade was the transformation in the attitude to education on the part of governments of both parties. James Callaghan's Ruskin College speech in 1976 signalled the beginning of a continuing loss of faith in education; education had lost its place in the sun and it has not since been awarded the automatic respect and importance that it had enjoyed in the 20 years after the war. This took the form of a change not just in discourse but in the institutional structure of the education system, with the creation of the Manpower Services Commission, for instance, partially in recognition of the inability of the education system to produce an adequate response to the increasingly serious problem of youth unemployment. Both the 'traditional' discourse and institutional structure of the education system had been central to the purpose and the location of the sociology of education and it was inevitably threatened by those changes. However, the discipline was to suffer not just the general consequences of that shift, but measures quite specifically targeted to reduce its influence and status, such as the denial of entry into teaching to sociology graduates and the effective removal of sociology of education from the curriculum of teacher education. The context became a powerfully constraining one and offered few if any opportunities to sociology of education.

Many of the effects of those changes in context were mediated through the changes to its main institutional location, teacher education. These saw a very considerable tightening of central control over teacher education, through the Council for the Accreditation of Teacher Education in particular, one of whose requirements was that all teacher educators should themselves be able to demonstrate 'recent and relevant' classroom experience. This was of a piece with the main thrust of the control of teacher education, ensuring that it was more 'relevant' and placed more emphasis on practice than on theory, especially sociology of education. All this led, as it was intended to, to a contraction not an expansion of the scope of teacher education and a reduction in the breadth and depth of its curriculum. The focus was strongly on studies of educational processes and this was reflected in what was becoming a more significant component of the location of sociology of education, research funding. By the end of this period, funded research was becoming a significant alternative means of sociologists of education maintaining themselves, and its control and distribution were becoming much more significant than they had been in the first period.

The consequences of these shifts were not immediately apparent. The first distinct change in focus and approach in this period, from the NSOE to a neo-Marxist analysis, suggested that little had changed; indeed, it could be seen as a significant strengthening of the purpose. Furthermore, this shift is one example of a shift occurring *within* the selection principle (and one that thereby shows its flexibility). I am indebted here to an argument advanced by Rob Moore. He suggests that the impact of *Schooling in Capitalist America* (Bowles and Gintis, 1976) (the key text of the neo-Marxist sociology of education and an Open University set book) 'has to be seen . . . within the context of the radical sociology of education at the time of its publication' The NSOE, he argues, was confronted by three fundamental problems:

(i)   how to achieve a non-positivistic conceptualization of social structure which preserved the radical humanism of the phenomenological critique but which did not entail its rejection of social structure (and class in particular) as an ontologically effective category;

(ii)   how to construct a methodological procedure whereby the class form of social structural relationships could be revealed within the power relationships of the educational system and classroom interaction;

(iii)   how to retain the possibility of radical action and change, both within education and in society at large, within a theoretical framework in which the principle for analysing social interaction was derived from an assumption of the determining power of social structure'

(Moore,1988,3)

and, crucially for the argument here, he suggests that 'the correspondence principle supplied an apparent resolution of some of the tensions within these three critical areas' (ibid. p.2) He goes on:

> What both Bowles and Gintis and Althusser provided were powerful articulations of a principle already implicit within a field dominated by the requirement to conceptualise the notion of social structure relative to particular concerns with the issues of situational analysis and radical intervention. . . . However, because of the pre-eminence of the concern with *action* . . . the problem *of conceptualising social structure* has dominated the development of the field.
>
> (ibid. p.5, emphasis in original)

Here, no elements of the selection principle have altered; the change in focus and approach is a response to issues internal to the focus and approach. However, it may be argued that the embrace of a neo-Marxist perspective, important though it was at the time, may have been a factor in the marginalization of the discipline. (It may be worth remarking here that this was possibly the only time when the sociology of education moved outside the parameters and assumptions outlined by Meyer.) I have referred elsewhere to this phase as 'a Pyrrhic victory . . . (where) sociology of education . . . proved its point but at potentially crippling cost that may ensure, through dissipation if by no other route, a prolonged impotence to accompany its marginalization' (Dale, 1992, 203). The evidence for that dissipation is plentiful. It had its basis in a 'rebranding' strategy that saw 'sociology of education' disappearing from the curriculum to be replaced by 'multicultural education', 'gender and education', 'education and work', 'school organization', 'education policy', 'classroom studies' and so on. It was also the case that the 'professional' audience continued to take precedence over the 'public' and academic audiences. One result of these factors was a series of significant bifurcations in the sociology of education between what were regarded as 'micro' and 'macro' approaches; between emphases on agency and structure and between the problematics of redistribution and recognition. There were some exceptions to this, notably some lines of feminist research, and education policy, which began to emerge towards the end of this period and bridged across to the next one.

The subsequent career of education policy study illustrates well some of the effects of the selection principle in the second-half of this period. A key aspect of its importance is that it was associated with the development of funded research as a more attractive and flexible dimension to the teacher education dominated location for sociology of education (and it should be noted that most of the research on education policy since this time has been carried out by sociologists of education). Ironically, perhaps, two of the major sources of funding for these activities were the evaluation of local TVEI schemes (required and funded by the Manpower Services Commission, which set up the scheme), and the study of the early reforms introduced by the Thatcher government in the provision of secondary education, both of which conflicted quite strongly with many of the principles of the redemptive purpose. However, these research activities could also be seen as attempts to pursue the 'traditional' strategy of understanding, if not to improve or change, at least to reveal the nature and consequences of the reforms. Nevertheless, as became clearer in the next period, these activities by no means 'neutralized' the effects of location on the focus and approaches adopted by sociologists of education. That is to be expected in the case of the focus – the topic of research is determined by the funder, though the 'contractors' may be able to interpret it in various ways – but approaches also are constrained by the expectations of the funder, who may also retain control over publication of results and findings. Indeed, Stephen Ball (1998, p.72) has suggested that the new opportunities were those for ' "new identities" as "school effectiveness researchers" and "management theorists". Around this latter kind of work, a new relationship *to* policy, or rather *inside* policy, was formed. Issues related to system design, analysis of provision and social justice were replaced by implementation studies focused on issues like "quality", "evaluation", "leadership" and "accountability".' (emphases in original). That is to say, 'policy', like 'education' was taken unproblematically by those who studied it; and as in the case of education, there has been a tendency for that stance to persist.

Towards the end of this period the importance of the state in education policy came to be more widely, if over-simply, recognized. Its appeal was that it linked the neo-Marxist aspirations of the first half of the period with the education policy focus of the second half. A focus on the state was taken both as a basis for understanding what was going on in education and as the means through which change might be brought about, or, at least, undesirable change obstructed. However, the value of this approach, too, was vitiated by its *ad hoc* application in the pursuit of immediate application (see Dale, 1992); and the failure to problematise the concept of the state was to lead to distinct difficulties in coming to terms with the changing conditions of the next period, many of which centred around its changing role.

The experience of this period also highlights the importance of two other features of the selection principle. The first comes from a more recent article by Rob Moore. Essentially, in the terms used here, he argues that the selection principle operates to make invisible research findings that fall outside the approaches it underlies. His focus is how the evidence of the academic success of black girls is accounted for in approaches that emphasize factors that would deny that success. He suggests that it is rendered invisible, because

> it reflects the problem of pupils performing in ways counter to the positions assigned them by reproduction theories of education. The success of girls and blacks is a difficulty for paradigms constructed around meta-narratives of education as an agent of patriarchy or racism.
>
> (Moore,1996,148)

He points also to the reception of Maureen Stone's book, *The Education of the Black Child in Britain*. 'Few studies', Moore claims, 'have been so right about so much. Yet it cannot be seen as having acquired the central position it deserves. The reason for this is clear. The one thing that Stone did *not* do was to endorse progressivism and its EO variants.' (ibid, 159, emphasis in original).

However, he does not see this as a matter of selection or preference *within* approaches but as resulting from the dominance of what he refers to as 'sociology *for* education', a 'sociology of weak effects ... (that) focusses on internal features of the system ... (is) limited by its field location (teacher training), tending to "take" its problems rather than "make" problems through the external criteria of critical social theory.' (ibid, 158) As he puts it, 'Stone's (Gramsci-inspired) view that 'traditional' academic education best suits the interests of black and working-class pupils problematises the standpoint of sociology *for* education ... (ibid 159, emphasis in original). Moore clearly identifies location as the main reason for the 'blindness' to which he draws attention. He elaborates and embeds a point made above;

> Sociologies for education are oriented towards the interests of practitioners. A typical feature of EO writing is its claim to a special relationship with teachers – celebrating, for instance, the alliance between the feminist researcher and the feminist teacher ... The major problem with taking the standpoint of the field in this way is that the structure of the field comes to be reproduced in the theory,

for instance in the way the traditional/progressive dichotomy has come to be reproduced within the sociology of education.

(ibid, 158)

This example illustrates very well how the context-imposed framing of location combined – and may still do so – with particular interpretations of purpose to set very clear theoretical parameters for some sociologists of education.

The other example of the effects of the selection principle on the approaches adopted in the sociology of education is drawn from a recent article by Francis Schrag, entitled 'Why Foucault Now?' (1999). Schrag is baffled by the apparent appeal to educationists of Foucault's work, the logic of which he considers bears a strong resemblance to structural–functional accounts. In a nutshell, his explanation is that appealing to Foucault enables scholars who wish to maintain their commitment to egalitarianism in the face of schools' apparent immunity to change

> to give expression to both the aspiration for transformation and to the despair regarding this possibility.... To put my point in a more Gallic manner; by embracing Foucault, scholars can announce their resignation to the status quo while appearing to protest it. (381)

Schrag is writing of the situation post-1989, but his comments have clear relevance to the period of confusion that followed the demise of the neo-Marxist sociology of education.

These examples suggest that the main elements of the *focus* of the sociology of education in the latter half of this period may be captured in the following; they are not presented in any order of priority.

(i)   An emphasis on curriculum rather than pedagogy. Curriculum is much more visible, anonymous, explicit, codified and 'political' than pedagogy – and hence more accessible, relevant and apparently, quickly and politically acceptably, mutable.

(ii) Associated with this is an underemphasis on learning. The field of learning seems to have been almost entirely evacuated to the psychologists. This seems to be a result of the selection principle directing attention away from the theorization of the sociology of teaching towards recording what teachers do.

(iii) An emphasis on economic success rather than other outcomes of education.

(iv)   An emphasis on access rather than outcomes. Again, the ready manipulability of access is important here, as well as the greater ease of, and immediate payoff to, theorising access than outcomes.

(v)   An emphasis on streaming rather than discipline. Streaming obviously impinges more directly on the allocation of life chances through education and on its immediate effects on pupils' experience of schooling. Discipline, on the other hand, does contain elements of criticism of teachers, has little resonance with either the redemptive or the progressive project, and has been traditionally linked to a conservative political stance.

(vi)   At a different level a tendency to focus on policy rather than politics (see also Dale, 1994).

(vii) A matching tendency to focus on government rather than the state. The greater visibility and accessibility again appear to be major influences.

(viii) A greater stress on 'liberation' than democracy as once again something that it is apparently more feasible and recognizable for education to bring about in the short term.

In terms of the theoretical and methodological *approaches* adopted over the period, it could be argued that they followed and were shaped by the main elements of the focus, where the effect of the dominant purpose was most evident. In respect of the approaches used, then, the selection principle worked on the one hand to narrow the range of what was considered theoretically problematic and on the other to set the level of theoretical abstraction at a level oriented to informed commentary or political hostility rather than more extended conceptual analysis. This may be seen to result in approaches whose parameters are national, pragmatic, professional, problem-taking, solution-oriented, 'intra-institutional', meliorist, 'relevant' and immediate.

This period, then, saw major shifts in the sociology of education, from what seemed the peak of its influence to divergence internally and marginalization externally, that simultaneously increased the breadth of its focus and narrowed the range and reduced the strength of its approaches, to the point where its coherence was seriously threatened.

1985–97

The start of this period is taken as 1985, because it approximately marked the beginning of the qualitative shifts in public sector management in general and the most profound changes in education, in particular brought about by the Thatcher and Major governments, while the election of a Labour government in 1997 marks the beginning of a self-consciously 'new' period. Over this period the political context dominated the nature of the location of sociology of education and together they had major effects on the purpose of the sociology of education. Indeed, the changes to the political context in particular represented the first challenge in the whole period under review to the dominance of the redemptive purpose of the sociology of education. Three aspects of that context underlay that challenge to its sustainability. First, the period witnessed an accelerating shift in political priorities, that may be summed up as a shift from the notion that the economy was to serve social policy to the opposite view. Second, the means by which it had been assumed the project could be brought into being, a policymaking social democratic state, had also been almost totally eroded. And third, was the collapse of the eastern bloc. Though the substance of the claims to an alternative route had never been realized, the existence of a claim that a state-led redemptive strategy in education was possible had, however implicitly, provided some support for the redemptive project.

It is worth elaborating briefly on the second of these as it may be seen as having had the most effect on the selection principle. (For further elaboration, see Dale, 1999c and 1999d and Robertson 1999 and 2000.) Its essence may be captured as a shift from a system of governing based on 'tax, spend, policy, consult' to 'liberalise, monitor, regulate, juridify'. Very briefly, the changes to public sector management over this period brought about a heavy emphasis on accountability, the reduction of influence of all partners in the education service outside the central state, placing education on a quasi-market basis, reductions in, and centralization of control over funding, and the introduction of control by quango (the Teacher Training Agency was especially significant for sociology of education). What these measures added up to was effectively a replacement of policy by a regulatory framework, within which the role of policy was restricted to repairing the holes in the framework, accompanied by a general 'de-democratization' of educa-tion (see Dale, 1999a and b), thus eroding the mechanisms through which it had been implicitly assumed change would be brought about. The effect of this was not just to impose notably greater constraints on the locations of sociology of education, but to remove almost all bases outside the academy through which it could make its voice heard.

The implications of this changed context on location were profound. The TTA introduced much tighter and much more practice-based rules for teacher education that reduced the amount of 'academic' input and discretion considerably. Ofsted's audit regime also helped reduce the scope for innovation and set tight and exclusive standards for the processes of schooling. Outside teacher education, and at least as important in its effects, the increasing importance of a research based component to university funding put very great pressure on sociologists of education to maximize their number of publications. The pressure to publish did have some positive effects. It raised the profile of academic approaches within the discipline and it did open up new possibilities of support from within the institutions, though it did also put sociologists of education into competition with each other.

These changes in the context and location of the sociology of education had evident effects on its purpose. Coming alongside the collapse of the state socialist alternative, they represented the final confirmation of the impossibility of a structural response to the problem of inequality, which had been a central plank of the redemptive project. Where it was maintained, the focus of that project turned in the direction of the individual and identity, and to the possibilities of agency rather than structure as the key to change. At the same time, the pressure to publish was essentially indifferent to what was published, and this inevitably led to moves outside the now somewhat discredited 'traditional' purpose for topics of research.

The effects on the focus and approaches of the discipline can be set down very briefly. The changes to the selection principle did little to turn back its increasing diversity and dissipation. But while the TTA's control over teaching related research did narrow the range of possibilities somewhat, the search for sources of research funding may have restored the balance.

Conclusion

I have tried to do two things in this chapter. The first was to provide an account of the changing focus and approaches of the sociology of education that related them to a selection principle made up of changing combinations of the discipline's purpose, location and contexts. In doing that I have outlined a brief and necessarily partial history of the sociology of education in England over the past half century. The second, equally important, aim has been to understand the conditions of theory production in the sociology of education and in particular what makes it less productive and effective than it might be (which has been a lament common to almost all sociologies of sociology of education – see, for example, Ball, 1998, Brehony and Deem, 1999, Shilling, 1993). This does not imply either a relativism towards theory or a commitment to theory for its own sake.

I have suggested that the discipline's focus has been shaped largely on the basis of it taking for granted the existing framework of assumptions within the education system; in particular, the purpose of the sociology of education was tied to the possibilities of the education system as they were known and understood. This entailed a substantial, if unacknow-ledged, or unrecognized, narrowing of the possible scope of the sociology of education, which might be seen as formed by four sets of questions; 'Who gets taught what, how, by whom, and under what circumstances, conditions, contexts and resources?'; How, by whom and through what structures, institutions and processes are these matters defined, governed, organized and managed?'; What is the relationship of education as a social institution to other social institutions of the state, economy and civil society?; and 'In whose interests are these things determined and what are their social and individual consequences?' And the limiting of the focus to issues that fit with the existing frameworks of provision, practice and control has affected not only what questions get asked, but how they are asked and what counts as an acceptable answer.

I have suggested that the main theoretical and methodological approaches have been not only directly influenced by the selection principle but that the operation of that principle has meant that the approaches have been shaped by the focus rather than vice versa and that together these factors have contributed to a curbing and curtailing of theoretical ambition. The nature of the approaches has been affected in particular by the nature of the dominant purpose. That purpose has been to bring about change in one key area of the social world. In conjunction with the main institutional location of the discipline, in teacher education, it formed a selection principle whose focus was exclusively on that particular area of the social world; this focus largely ignored other aspects of its wider context, whose significance was itself interpreted through the prism of the dominant purpose. As I have pointed out above, it also took as unproblematic the education system as the means to attain the purpose. Here the influence of location was crucial in linking together the confines of the focus with those of the approaches.

It should, finally, be noted that these comments about the nature of theoretical development in the sociology of education carry no implications about the quality and ability of its practitioners. Indeed, the very suggestion that that might be the case is somewhat ironic, given that a leading sociological theorist has argued that the sociology of education represents the cutting edge of sociological theory (Collins, 1986). However, the fact that this claim is based entirely on the contributions of Basil Bernstein and Pierre Bourdieu adds to the argument presented here, since it can be argued that the work of neither of these theorists has been significantly influenced by the selection principle outlined here. Few would doubt that Bernstein has been the outstanding theorist in the sociology of education over the greater part of the period covered here. It is also clear that his work is at some distance from that of most that has been discussed here; indeed, it might be argued that it is the differences between the assumptions of the selection principle and those that inform his work that have underlain at least some part of the misunderstandings and the difficulties with which that work has often been received. However, it seems to me that Bernstein's work differs from that influenced by the selection principle in the ways described in this chapter along one crucial dimension in particular, the relationship between the dominant purpose and the nature of the theoretical approach.

In a nutshell, his work inverts that relationship, so that theory frames focus rather than vice versa and, while he is very clearly sympathetic to the redemptive purpose, he takes that not so much as requiring a focus on educational practice but a different level of theoretical abstraction that seeks understanding well beyond those immediate conditions. It is difficult to exemplify this briefly, but the following quotations from the introduction to a chapter, 'Pedagogic Codes and their Modalities of Practice' may help (Bernstein, 1996). In this chapter he

> make(s) a very deliberate choice to focus sharply upon the underlying rules shaping the social construction of pedagogic discourse and its various practices. I am doing this because it seems to me that sociological theory is very long on metatheory and very short on providing specific principles of description. I shall be concentrating very much on being able to provide and create models, which can generate specific descriptions. It is my belief that, without these specific descriptions, there is no way in which we can understand the way in which knowledge systems become part of consciousness

and he summarizes the problems with which he will be concerned as

> how does power and control translate into principles of communica-
> tion, and how do these principles of communication differentially
> regulate forms of consciousness with respect to their reproduction
> and the possibilities of change? (ibid, 17, 18).

There is of course no suggestion that inverting the relationship between
theory and purpose necessarily leads in the directions that Bernstein has
followed; but though it is obviously not a sufficient condition of productive theory, the argument of this paper suggests that it may well be a
necessary one.

In conclusion, if we ask how the arguments outlined here might assist
theory production in the sociology of education, the brief answer would
be that what is required is a realignment of the relationship between
purpose and theory of the kind just sketched out. One reason for this is
that the purpose component of the selection principle is much more
negotiable than either the location or the context; not only that, but it is
the medium through which the meaning of context is understood. That
is why the crucial relationship is that between purpose, focus and
approaches. As long as the purpose is perceived as being most successfully achieved through changing the focus of the discipline, theoretical
production will be under threat. Only when it is realized that purpose is
attainable only through changing approaches as well as, and prior to,
changing focus, will the conditions be such as to allow theoretical
production in the sociology of education to flourish.

Acknowledgement

I would like to thank the following friends and colleagues for their
generous and very helpful comments on an earlier version of this
chapter; Basil Bernstein, Andy Green, Tony Green, Maeve Landman,
David Livingstone, Rob Moore, Terri Seddon, Geoff Whitty, Michael
Young and Lynn Yates. I would also like to thank Sara Delamont and
Paul Atkinson, and Kevin Brehony and Rosemary Deem for allowing me
to see their unpublished papers on the sociology of sociology of
education. Finally, I must thank Susan Robertson both for her
contributions to this discussion and for allowing me to draw on her
extensive study of teachers' work (Robertson, 2000). None of these
people will agree with everything that I have written here, but they have
all helped to make the chapter better than it might otherwise have been.

2

Feminist Sociology of Education: Dynamics, Debates and Directions

Jo-Anne Dillabough and Madeleine Arnot

Feminist sociology of education is one of the richest veins within the discipline today. Although its specific contribution is the analysis of gender relations in education, it has added substantially to an understanding of the broader relationship between education and society. Within the feminist project, history, structure and biography join hands in imaginative theoretical and empirical ways. Bearing many of the hallmarks of the postwar social democratic period in which the women's movement gathered pace, feminist sociology of education has engaged vigorously and with some success in the analysis of, for example: educational inequality and social stratification; the hierarchies of knowledge and the arbitrary values underlying the curriculum; and the role of the state, economy and the family in modern education systems. At the same time it manifests many of the illusions and disillusionments of the era – recognizing, for example, the forms of economic and social determination which are pitted against the goals of personal or collective liberation. What characterizes the development of feminism as a major political force in the postwar period in the United Kingdom and therefore what accounts for its impact on the educational system and academic research (especially in relation to women's education) has been its flexibility. It has kept up and adapted its academic agenda to engage critically with social democratic ideals as well as with neo-liberal and neo-conservative reform programmes (Arnot *et al.*, 1999). With its strong tradition of policy analysis and research, feminist sociologists have used their own yardstick of social justice to question and challenge the implementation of government programmes in relation to male and female patterns of education, and the gendered premises of the liberal democratic project (see Arnot and Dillabough, 1999). The record of feminist sociology of education, therefore, is a particularly strong one.

The fundamental presupposition of feminist sociology of education is that gender is a social category, hence a social construction. Ann Oakley (l972), an anthropologist, argued that if gender (rather than sex) could be used as a theoretical construct, then it could be applied to the study of socialization and society. The concept of 'gender' therefore became analytically, as well as politically, preferable to the concept of 'sex' (that is, biological distinctions between men and women) in sociological studies of education. Through the critical application of the social category of gender to the study of education, gender patterns in schooling were linked to broader social inequalities. For example, in 1978 Eileen Byrne and Rosemary Deem separately documented the myriad ways in which sexual discrimination was entrenched in the UK education system, while Dale Spender's (1980, 1982 and 1987) polemical accounts of the 'patriarchal paradigm of education' added new political concepts such as girls' 'oppression', 'female exploitation', and 'male domination' to the study of schooling. The outcome of this work was a body of scholarship now commonly identified as the 'sociology of women's education' (Arnot, 1985).

By the 1980s, liberal feminism had become part of mainstream sociology of education (Arnot l982), bringing with it an emphasis on individual socialization and educational outcomes which had derived from, on the one hand, Parsonian structural functionalism and, on the other, from the empirical and indeed rationalistic assumptions of the natural sciences in relation to causal relationships. Paradoxically this tradition, when applied to gender, had a radical politics in terms of access, while at the same time leaving unchallenged the roots of liberalism in male epistemologies of knowledge. Drawing largely upon the 'European structuralist tradition' (Sadovnik, 1995), critical feminist sociologists challenged such micro-level academic thinking about gender inequalities by arguing for a broader and more politically driven conceptual frame through which to examine the manifestation of gender politics in educational environments (for example Barrett, 1980; David, 1980; Deem, 1980). They drew upon Durkheimian concepts of the moral order and Marxist concerns with conflict, consciousness and social change. Fundamental to this analysis was the understanding of gender as a historically and culturally specific category that forms part of the economic and material, social (sexual) division of labour. The gender order thus described was clearly linked to theories of social order and to the mainstream (and often male centred) theoretical and empirical concerns in the sociology of education.

Early feminist interventions in the sociology of education attempted to establish a new critical, but also liberatory, agenda for education. This attempt was launched more often than not from a position of marginality or low status in the discipline (Acker, 1981). However, because feminist sociologists addressed the problems that women were confronting daily as 'lived experience' in many educational contexts, whether as teachers or pupils, a strong dialectical relationship existed between their work and educational policy (Arnot *et al.*, 1999). Nowhere in feminist studies has the principle that feminism is not 'only about women, but for women', been more directly relevant.

In the early stages of the application of feminist theory to education, the charting of feminist perspectives seemed to many, at least on the face of it, to be relatively straightforward. (see Arnot, 1981: Connell, 1987; Middleton, 1987; Stone, 1994). Such heuristic simplicity, however, was soon criticized for failing to capture the range of different and conflicting approaches or to improve women's social positioning more generally (for example, Brah and Minhas, 1985; Ellsworth, 1989, 1998; Middleton, 1993). Many also argued that postwar versions of feminist academic research were entrenched in middle-class values and did not speak for (or about) women on the margins (for example, working-class and culturally oppressed women). In response, feminist debates moved beyond their traditional origins in Marxism and liberalism. Today, there are numerous 'feminism(s) in education' (Weiner, 1994) and theories of gender politics. Many of these 'new' positions derive from the expression of political, cultural and sexual identities in both society and the academy, and interdisciplinary and post-structural theoretical work in the social sciences. In contrast to second wave theorizing, these 'new' forms, which are often associated with late modernity, tend to emphasize change and fluidity (for example, shifting and performative notions of gender) over that of gender continuities and the stability of the gender order. The current research traditions within 'feminist' sociology of education thus are even harder to 'capture', drawing as they do upon divergent, yet sometimes overlapping, theoretical and empirical approaches to the study of gender and feminism in education.

Despite such difficulties, we believe that in order to understand the nature of current feminist sociological analyses of education, it is necessary to engage with the field as a whole rather than with particular examples of research. It is, therefore, still worth attempting to chart a rather informal (albeit retrospective) history of diverse feminist theoretical perspectives. We shall show that many of the key questions raised by early feminist studies, rather than being rejected, are still being addressed by feminist sociologists of education today.

A conceptual framework

Connell (1987), in *Gender and Power*, argues that positions on gender are more easily understood when examined in relation to broad epistemological, political and social questions. We have found Connell's distinction between *intrinsic* and *extrinsic* theories particularly useful in charting the trajectory of feminist sociology in education. Intrinsic theories are those which attempt to explain how strong conceptual and stable notions of gender (rather than shifting notions of gender) in society come into being. Such theoretical formulations are based largely on a kind of instrumental thinking which tends to focus on questions that concern 'individuals' and issues that are typically thought to be intrinsic to them (for example, self-esteem, sex differences). Extrinsic theories, on the other hand, tend to focus on the social and/or class-based nature of power relations in the polity. State structures, relations of production and the gendered nature of the public sphere all figure in the manner in which gender is understood in education from an extrinsic perspective.

In our view, both theoretical stances reside within what we identify as a *rationalistic* framework since they have either explained women's oppression on the basis of the authority of reason or on a corresponding theory of rationalism which ultimately reaffirms the gender binary (that is, male power over women) in educational thought. Rationalistic approaches either charted linear relationships between, on the one hand, individual behaviours (for example, gender roles, female characteristics) and women's oppression or, on the other hand, female marginality and what were often described as 'rationally' organized and deliberately controlled social structures (for example, state or the market).

Such theories stand in contrast to those which are *relational* (see Luke, 1989). These theoretical positions are most commonly, but not exclusively, accorded the terms postmodern or post-structural, yet they are not theories in the traditional sense. Rather, they are conceptual frameworks which serve to break down theoretical foundations and map a particular set of power relations which lead to 'local' understandings of gender in education. They also attempt to capture the fluid nature of gender as a temporality which is embedded in the power of language rather than merely charting universal laws about women's experience in the broadest sense.

These theoretical distinctions are discussed in the following sections. Below we attempt to capture both the diversity and creative tensions in the field as it developed, demonstrating that the central questions raised by feminism are still not only central to the development of sociology of education but also that the issues raised are still being returned to again and again, thus reflecting the continuity within the field.

Rationalistic theorizing: 'intrinsic' and extrinsic approaches

Liberal feminism

The historical roots of liberal feminism are well documented. Mary Wollstonecraft in *A Vindication of the Rights of Women* (first published 1792) set the tone when she argued that women, like men, are capable of reason and thus possess the right to be educated to their full capacities in similar, if not identical, forms of schooling. This notion of equal education formed the foundation of a liberal feminist philosophy of education including a vision of women as 'rational' beings (that is, honorable women) – hence educable – and a vision of society as equal, and as democratic (for a fuller description of this perspective, see Arnot and Dillabough, 1999).

Since the 1970s, respect for women's rights in a free and open educational system, individual autonomy, opportunity and choice in education, and gender equality (rather than political equality) in schools have been regarded as core female entitlements which can be achieved through female participation in various procedural forms of competition in an open school environment. The long-term goal of feminism here was to 'empower' women to take up their rightful place through the development of female autonomy. The key issue was the support of freedom, whether in relation to play, or subject and occupational choice; that is, the removal of barriers (such as discrimination or prejudice) as an individual right in a democratic society. Examples of sociological research which formed part of the liberal feminist imperative include, for example, the study of sex roles (Delamont, 1980) and sex differences (Maccoby & Jacklin, 1974), the relationship between teachers' expectations and girls' occupational choice, and the study of girls' self-esteem, and gender subject preferences (for example: Kelly, 1981). Noteworthy is that much of this research is still premised upon a male-centred rationality drawing upon, for example, formal quantitative methods such as self-esteem scales, student response checklists and questionnaires as tools for identifing gender inequality. Indeed many of these early conceptions have been adopted somewhat uncritically in much of the new literature on boys' underachievement (see Epstein *et al.*, 1998 for a discussion of this emerging perspective) ignoring the fact that feminist sociological research in this tradition has evolved with the passage of time, and that by the early 1990s, far more attention was being given to the particularity of context and the manner in which it shapes male and female identities and students' responses to their socialization (see Measor and Sikes, 1992). While much of this feminist work continues to endorse a focus on the modern liberal subject (rather than a feminist collective), it has exposed the many barriers to educational access for women and men in liberal democracies (Arnot and Dillabough, 1999 for a fuller discussion).

The critiques of such intrinsic theorizing set a new agenda for sociologists. They pointed to the failure to recognize feminism (rather than conventional gender attitudes shaping identity) as a social/political movement in its own right, and to understand the significance of community in the shaping of society. The gendered nature of hierarchical structures in schools tended to remain unexplored and society's role in the development of gender identities, relations and politics was substantially underestimated. For example, the political and economic structures and forms of power which constrain women's social and political agency in education, in the family and in the state remained uncharted territory. More significantly, little had been learned about the ways in which the opportunity structures in education suppress, for example, minority ethnic women and girls. Consequently, under liberal feminism, the significance of both identity-politics and difference was lost.

Feminist critiques of liberal theory (for example, Whelahan, 1995) also encouraged the development of a cluster of critical sociological theories of gender in education which explored concepts of state power and class relations as central to women's oppression in education. What varies among these perspectives, however, is the manner in which power is defined. Connell (1987) describes extrinsic theories as those which focus primarily on the following: (i) abstract forms of state power; (ii) collective notions of power as expressed in symbolic forms of the civil society (for example, Durkheimian/Marxist perspectives); or (iii) power which is thought to reside outside a women's control. Below we briefly distinguish between two seminal feminist traditions in the sociology of education which could be described as extrinsic: radical; maternal; and, socialist feminism.

Radical and maternal feminisms

Broadly speaking, radical feminist theorizing tried to address the problems represented by liberal feminism – that is, 'merely adding' women to a schooling agenda which was founded upon a historical trajectory of masculine thought. Drawing heavily upon the politics of popular feminism and feminist social movements in the 1970s and early 1980s, the goal of radical feminism was to expose the various forms of male domination in education. The 'conceptual device' drawn upon to challenge such male domination was 'patriarchy'. As Kate Millet (1977) maintains, patriarchal ideology resided at the very core of the state, amplifying the traditional divisions between the public (rationality, work, male centred) and private sphere (domesticity, nature, female-centered). A central concern, therefore, was to develop an understanding of the relationship between patriarchy and female sexuality and their complementary links to the subordination of women. Consequently, radical feminists addressed issues which sociologists traditionally had veered away from such as the study of symbolic forms of male power in school curriculum, texts and school subjects (Spender, 1980, 1987), the sexualized and gendered language of youth in schools (Lees, 1986), and the sexual dominance of boys in classrooms (Mahony, 1983, 1985). At the same time, radical feminists encouraged women to embrace the notion of liberation through a collective critique of male domination in education (Thompson, 1983). They emphasized the ways in which their voices were suppressed and women's knowledge devalued. On this basis, they constructed a politically functional category known as 'girl' with the implication that 'girls' in a real sense must rely upon radical politics within the feminist movement for their liberation.

Another strand of radical feminism known as *maternal feminism* (cf., Dietz, 1985) had a greater impact on education in America. The maternal feminist approach, influenced as it was by philosophy of education (for example, Roland Martin, 1982) was preoccupied with values (for example, caring) which were thought to be central to the mother–child bond. Thus while radical feminists argued for the elimination of conventionally conceived 'feminine values', maternal feminists argued for their celebration in public life (see Tong, 1989). This approach has been linked closely to the work of social psychologists and moral philosophers who have a particular interest in women and girls' development, particularly that of Chodorow (1979) and Gilligan (1982). Key to their versions of feminism is the importance of 'empowering' women in schools, drawing upon their personal knowledge and collective 'feminine' norms (for example, the ethics of care; connectedness) in creating a female-centered morality in the state (see Lyons, 1990; Noddings, 1988; Roland Martin, 1982). Therefore, the process of inclusion in education was understood not to be individual but to be collective, using 'women's ways of knowing' (Belenky *et al.* 1986) as the means by which such liberation could be encouraged. In this feminist model the category women not only remains intact, but is celebrated for its anti-elitist and less hierarchical forms of moral authority (for example, mother–child bond) (see Arnot and Dillabough, 1999 for a fuller discussion).

Radical feminist and maternal feminists had their critics. Early on, Wolpe (1988) took exception to the essentialism implied in the term patriarchy (that is, all men oppress – all women suffer), arguing that the formal categories of 'male' and 'female' merely reaffirmed crude gender divisions with little reference to the social complexity underlying the formation of ideas about 'masculinity' and 'femininity' in schools and the state. Both patriarchal relations and the concept of gender thus appeared as unchanging, decontextualized and ahistorical. Contradictions also emerged when examining the theoretical links between the sociological stance taken within radical feminism (that is, social constructivism) and the political line taken on issues surrounding male domination in schools (that is, the notion that all men dominate). Qualitative sociological research demonstrated that gender was a dynamic social construct which is reconstituted over time and space, and was shaped by complex social forces which cannot be solely restricted to male domination (see Connell, 1987;Walkerdine,1990).

Similarly while there can be little doubt that a concern with 'caring' should be central to education, problems were identified with the maternalist feminist approach. For example, the presumption that replacing male culture (in schools) with female culture will lead ultimately to a more just society is problematic largely in terms of its reproductive dimensions (that is, notion that all women are caregivers). Indeed, such a replacement strategy rarefies women's experience over that of men's – a strategy which does not do justice to women's diverse and complex views about gender and the elements of female identity (Dietz, 1985). There is also still concern about the erasure of alternative forms of gender identity, the misrepresentation of the constitutive experiences of the differently positioned women, and the failure to address the nuanced and contradictory ways that gender politics have challenged traditional thinking about the polity and women's values. These failures have led to concerns that a maternal feminist analysis only examines gender differences rather than social, cultural and ethnic differences *within* gender categories.

Socialist feminism

Differences within gender categories could also only be partially addressed by socialist feminists who attempted to reconcile theories of class and gender relations. Arguably, socialist feminists had an impact on sociology of education (Arnot and Dillabough, 1999) because they offered a feminist critique of liberal democratic theories (including their role in the shaping of educational institutions) which ran parallel to mainstream political economy of education. They recognized that in order to understand the social significance and impact of education, they would need to recognize the importance of the economic sphere and its effects on the institutional culture and structure of schooling. This led to an understanding of education as the site for the preparation (and reproduction) of a hierarchically stratified gendered work force, with women being prepared for lower status or marginalized positions in the 'secondary labour market' or the 'reserve army of labour'. The emphasis on the reproduction of the social and economic order led to a feminist version of *social reproduction* theory (MacDonald, 1980). Informed primarily by Bowles and Gintis (1976), feminist sociologists conceptualized education as an instrument of capitalism which reproduced the subordination of women, and in particular, the subordination of working-class girls (see Acker, 1989; Anyon, 1983). Social class, therefore, appeared with great regularity as the social formation which not only pre-figured, but determined, girls' educational experiences, identities and forms of consciousness. In this early version of gender reproduction theory, the study of school structures and their links to the economy was privileged over a notion of human agency as an explanatory theory of gender inequality.

Later versions of socialist feminism drew upon theories of class hegemony (Gramsci, 1971), cultural capital (Bourdieu and Passeron, 1977) and educational codes (Bernstein, 1977) which were used to describe and explain conflicts and contradictions in school life, and between school, culture and the economy. The structure of gender relations in schools ('gender codes' (Arnot, 1982) or 'gender regimes' (Connell, 1987)) was understood as constituting and thus reproducing particular versions of masculinity, femininity and family life (Gaskell, 1983), the dominant versions of which were associated with the upper middle classes. Such analyses focused attention on the simultaneous production of gendered and classed subjects and their contingent cultures of resistance (c.f., Anyon, 1983 on private/public accommodation and resistance). Of particular significance was the attention such analyses drew to the role of masculinity and femininity in shaping class relations: often disaffection in school was expressed as a celebration of particular masculinities (Willis, 1977) or a 'cult of femininity' (McRobbie, 1978). However, as we have argued elsewhere (Arnot and Dillabough, 1999), despite its ability to inspire what is now a 30-year debate about difference in education, socialist feminism tended to deny the significance of women's political agency and indeed of intra-class differences (such as ethnic and sexual identities). Although linking racial inequalities to capitalism and imperialism, the experiences of black women and girls in the educational system tended to be understood as deviations from the white working-class norms (Mirza, 1992). The primary focus of socialist feminism on the ideological nature of women's work in the public sphere and the political economy of girls' education was also weakened by a failure to understand the role of women's labour within the family, and within the educational system (David, West and Ribbens (1994); Dillabough, 1999). Such models of analysis were fundamentally constraining.

Rationalistic explanations of gender inequality and women's oppression were, therefore, challenged on a number of fronts, not least for the essentialism of their analysis of 'women' as a category, their somewhat behaviouristic models of socialization and identity formation and the failure to recognize and/or to account for cultural diversity and cultural oppression. At the same time, the parent discipline of sociology of education with its history of 'founding fathers' seemed to find such feminist research threatening. The analysis of gender relations was either treated as peripheral and hence diversionary, or as divisive. Despite feminists' early reliance on mainstream theory, critical male sociologists of education have been remarkably reluctant to assimilate feminist theoretical work perhaps on the grounds that they had over-emphasized the primacy of social class relations over and above other forms of social identification and the primacy of the economy over private, the domestic and familial relations (MacDonald, 1980; David, 1993) Yet despite such ambivalence, modernist explanations offered by feminist sociologists in the early 1980s raised key issues that were deeply relevant to men and women of all social classes. The analysis of the processes of identity formation, of the limits and possibilities of creating social change through educational reform (in which many feminist academics were engaged) and of the role of the state in regulating gender and social relations was to become central to the discipline in the next decade. Difference therefore emerged as central to feminist theories of education.

Relational epistemologies and the question of 'gender' in education

In some ways, the 'fragmentation' of the feminist movement in the early 1980s helped rather than hindered the development of feminist sociology of education, since it created the possibilities of working with other disciplinary traditions. The rising importance of black feminism, feminist social psychology and cultural studies, as we shall see, all enriched feminist sociology of education by introducing different 'knowledge claims' about gender relations into the study of gender and education. Modernist explanatory frameworks were increasingly challenged for their use of theoretical perspectives which were framed by and for men – what feminist postmodernists such as Lather (1991) described as the 'master narratives' of modernity.

Black feminists, in particular, took exception to the constraints of such rationalistic theorizing in education (Carby, 1982; Davis, 1983; hooks, 1989; Mirza, 1993) For example, much of the new sociological work analyzed the relationship of black families (Phoenix, 1987) and black women to capitalism and imperialism (Hill-Collins, 1990), and set an agenda for the study of black women's experience and gendered discourses of racism in schools (see, for example, Blair, 1995; Blair and Holland, 1995). The power and dominance of feminist sociological discourses on gender and education were thus exposed as Eurocentric, ethnocentric and colonialist in both form and content (Mirza, 1992). Black women were understood to inhabit 'other worlds'; their experiences of education and, indeed, of political struggle, were fundamentally structured around what Mirza and Reay (2000) recently described as the 'third space' – that of the community. Individual social mobility in this context was framed by a 'desire for inclusion that is strategic, subversive and ultimately far more transformative than subcultural reproduction suggests'.

Black women's political agency bears a fundamentally different relationship to structure than that accounted for in rationalistic models (see Brah and Minhas, 1985). Hence, black feminist sociologists ignited an interest in postcolonial accounts which were more relational in approach (Mirza, 1997). By the late 1980s, similar theoretical separations were made between mainstream feminist theorizing and, for example, lesbian, gay and transgendered feminism(s) (see for example, Epstein and Johnston, 1998). The variety of contemporary feminism(s), many of which now reside somewhat ambiguously in the postmodern or post-structural camp, to some extent represented the expression of emerging identity politics within the discipline. We focus next on one of the most important aspects of these new feminisms – the discursive shift to post-structuralism as an explanatory framework which could work with notions of culture, language and difference.

Post-structural feminism

Post-structural theorizing within education is now a vast terrain and laying out its distinctions within feminist theory is beyond the scope of this chapter. However, it should be said that what sets post-structuralism apart from rational forms of structuralism is its self-conscious and deliberate reflexivity, its link to deconstruction as political action, and its emphasis on the study of relational forms of power (often represented as a temporal manifestation of power in language) in education. Over the last 15 years, many post-structural feminists (for example, Davies, 1989; Ellsworth, 1989; Kenway, 1995 Walkerdine, 1990) have argued that social theorists should develop an anti-foundationalist approach to education in which false dichotomies (such as girls' versus boys' experience) should be understood as regulatory linguistic devices which concretize human experience and make them, therefore, difficult to contest. By contrast however, if gendered educational relations and experiences are read as complex representations of 'culture' and if men and women's lives could be read as 'text' (interpreted in diverse ways) then it is possible to de-stabilize the category 'woman' (Butler, 1990). This was a 'first' principle of feminist post-structural thinking.

The key terms drawn upon by post-structural feminists of 'identity', 'difference', 'deconstruction', 'performativity', 'discourse' and 'subjectivity' (cf., Scott, 1994) provide the conceptual tools for capturing the performative nature of gender and exposing the many gendered 'subject positions' within education and society. Broadly speaking, then, the theoretical task of a relational approach is to research schooling as a gendered process (rather than social institution), shaping and reconstituting identities in relation to time, place and space.

Foucault's analysis of modern society has had, and continues to have, particular relevance to such relational feminist theories. This is largely due to the seminal theoretical work of, for example, Valerie Walkerdine (1987, 1990) and Bronwyn Davies (1989) who applied a Foucauldian analysis to the study of infant and primary classrooms and pupils. In their analyses, classroom interactions (whether between teacher and pupil, or between pupil and text) are interpreted as regulating various social identities, only one of which is gender identity. Such regulatory mechanisms are configured discursively and subjectively, and are shown for example, to condition the everyday lives and understandings of teachers, pupils, staff and parents. The challenge for feminist post-structuralists is therefore to identify how such 'identities' are generated and regulated as 'truths' in schools, and how these regulative functions lead in turn to the reconstitution of gender hierarchies in schools and society. The strength of post-structural feminist accounts can be found in their analysis of the power of knowledge and language in shaping pupils' (teachers') multiple subjectivities (see Davies, 1989; Kenway, 1995) and, for example, the regulation of female bodies (Middleton, 1993, 1998). These accounts have demonstrated how such discourses are read and reproduced in the curriculum, and by pupils and teachers. In short, post-structural feminism challenged the simplicity of early reproduction theories and the totalizing effect of the capitalist–patriarchy relation.

More recent post-structural feminist theorizing has posed questions about the role of marketization, educational reform and what is now termed the 'new managerialism' in reconfiguring gender politics in diverse educational contexts (see Acker, 1994; Blackmore, 1996; Delhi, 1996; Kenway and Epstein, 1996). There is also increasing concern for the ways in which macro, cross-national global discourses shape questions about gender at a local, or indeed, micro-level of educational discourse (Blackmore, 1999; Brine, 1999; Kenway and Langmead, 2000). There has also been substantially more work on the role of parents in either challenging or reproducing gender hierarchies, through parental involvement in school choices and other related activities. For example, David, West and Ribben's (1994) work on mothers and school choice and Ball and Gerwirtz's (1997) study of parents' representations of single-sex girl schools points to the gendered nature of school choice and the reproduction, at least in part, of the traditional ideals and expectations attached to labels such as 'femininity' and 'motherhood' in schools. Some of this work is more of a critique of market theory than a commitment to post-structural influences.

However, despite advances made by feminist post-structuralists and post-structuralism more generally, there are remaining conceptual dilemmas. For example, many critics of feminist post-structuralism argue that in focusing almost entirely on the study of women's subjectivities, the feminist project and the notion of women as a political, yet heterogeneous, collective may have been collapsed into the realm of the unknown (see Young, 1995). After all, most research on gender equality in schools has identified 'girls' as the issue, their experience as the 'problem' and their needs as the purpose of educational reform. Educational critics of post-structuralism have, therefore, tended to argue that it is more difficult to understand, within such analyses, how feminist post-structuralism and other relational theories can address the 'real' problems of gender inequity in schools (see Kenway, 1996). What still remains problematic may be the desire by relational theorists to take the study of gendered subjectivities to an extreme, with less room for a more rigorous analysis of the role of the neo-liberal state and social change in women's lives. Nor indeed is it easy to see how other material realities (such as familial poverty) frame the discursive effects of schooling. As a consequence, the search for a necessary 'truth' about women's oppression can become all too provisional.

Another element of relational feminism still emphasized in feminist sociology is the importance of analyzing women's lived experience as a valid epistemological position. Such experiences are thought to represent a female standpoint, yet they should not necessarily be seen as shared experiential terrain. A good deal of this work bears the historical marks of modernism while still maintaining some semblance of postmodern thinking. In fact, some of these theoretical viewpoints have been quite explicit in their commitment to a particular strand of modernist feminist thinking, while venturing, ever so gently, into postmodern or Foucauldian terrain. As such, many of these new theoretical frames are not an abrupt break with the past but instead represent a kind of feminist dialectic which lead to the formal and informal synthesizing of new theoretical forms.

One such feminism in education is the brand of feminist materialism which has been articulated by a range of cultural theorists, especially those concerned with the impact of social change on youth. For example, Leslie Roman (1992) argues that knowledge about gender must be viewed as a dialectical construction which emerges as a consequence of the dynamic relation between women's subjectivity (that is, standpoint) and the particularity of women's material relations/conditions in society. Her interest in women's 'standpoint' reflects a concern with subjectivity as expressed through, for example, the discourse of youth cultures and the everyday experience of young women (see Roman, 1993). Related accounts point to the significance of subjectivity and women's standpoint as fundamental to a women-centered epistemology have also emerged. For example, the work of Foster (1993) and Luttrell (1997) draws upon women's discourse, everyday accounts and stories as epistemic tools for understanding how gender and social change are constructed in relation to educational practice. Much of this work draws on the voices (autobiographies, oral histories, narrative accounts) of women in education, or expressed by women about education). It has a distinctively 'relational' flavour, but like the work of Roman, it remains connected to the material conditions of women's lives.

Critical modernization theory

Feminist youth cultural studies have also focused upon the transformation and restructuring of gender relations in late modernity and its effects on young people today. Empirical research on young women's (and to a less extent young men's) identities engages with feminism in the historical sense. In these analyses, feminism itself becomes one of a range of contemporary discourses which defines and positions women and men in new sets of social expectations and in periods of social change. The goal of such work is to offer a finely detailed description of how young people negotiate and construct their various identities across diverse social contexts, such as new regimes of poverty, new family structures, new economic structures and demands, and school markets. The construction of new 'gender knowledge' itself can be an important element in the the shaping of gender identities. Epstein *et al.* (1998), for example, consider the discursive framing of the boys' education debate (the new moral panic about male underahcievement) in the media and government circles as one element in this process of regulation.

Feminist sociological studies of youth such as those conducted by Weis (1990), Bates (1993a and b), Chisholm and Du Bois Reymond (1993), Sharpe (1994), McLaren (1996), Skeggs (1997) and Volman and ten Dam (1998), among others, provide a wealth of information about the ways in which women's and girls' lives have been shaped by the forces of social change associated with late modernity. We have chosen to call this recent feminist research *critical modernization theory* since it addresses in a critical way current sociological theories of modernization. When analyzing the important transitions between education and the labour market, such youth researchers draw upon Beck's (1992) analysis of the nature of 'the risk society' and the pressures it places on individuals to engage in a process of 'reflexive individualization' when planning their lives. Beck has suggested that the forces of late modernity encourage youth to see the world as apolitical and the idea of solidarity as less significant. Rational modernizing forces, therefore, encourage youth to place themselves at the centre of their success, thereby choosing a life plan not on the basis of social meaning or virtue but on the premises of an instrumental notion of individual progress. According to Beck, what this means is that youth are able to detach themselves, to some extent, from traditional understandings of male and female. However, according to Beck, equality is not the likely outcome. He predicts instead that the differential impact on modernizing forces (rationality, self progress, risk) will lead to an increasingly divergent and unequal social order and 'people's awareness of inequality [will become] more conscious and less legitimated' (p.104). Such arguments already find support in the work of Volman and ten Dam (1998) who discovered in their study of 12–17-year-olds in the UK that 'the legitimacy of difference between gender groups that implies inequality is under pressure', but paradoxically 'equality, the sense of sameness' for boys and girls is also 'unthinkable'.

Sociologists, in general, have much to learn from the ways in which such new feminist research addresses the more traditional relationship between structure, agency and identity. What emerges from their highly sophisticated accounts of young people's transitions are the gendered processes of what Roberts *et al.* (1994, p.49) called 'structured individualization' whereby the processes of individualization (associated both with post-Fordism and the 'risk society') are mediated by the continuing effects of social reproduction (especially the reproduction of social class inequalities). Women's responses to such material and discursive complexity, as Skeggs (1997) argued, are 'always historically located, the product of positioning and partiality' (p.140). Women interpret global issues at a local level. Thus,

> their knowledge is produced from the unequal material relations in which they are inscribed. It is produced from the interpretations they make of their experience in relation to the frameworks which are available to them. Their positions inform their responses to feminism (p.140).

New feminist analyses of young women's lives point to the significance of the social transformations of female youth culture. In contrast there are few sociological accounts of male youth which capture empirically the complex discursive positionings and processes of identity formation of male youth. The work of, for example, Connell (1987, 1995), Mac an Ghaill (1994, 1996), Sewell (1997), Gilbert and Gilbert (1998), Kenway, Willis, Blackmore and Rennie (1998), Power *et al.* (1998), and Wright et al (1998) are exceptional attempts to interpret the difficult mediations of masculinity as a cultural identity in contemporary society.

Recognition of the general significance of gender research is only gradually being offered by mainstream sociology of education. When reviewing Hey's (1997) book *The Company She Keeps*, Mac an Ghail (1998) praized ethnographic work on girls' lives in schools for the ways in which it had successfully documented the effects of the struggle over identity politics and the politics of cultural difference since the 1980s. Such in-depth studies of girls' lives, he argued, successfuly integrated the analysis of political movements, social/economic change and individual identities. Yet despite such praise, many critical sociological analyses of the effects of post-Fordism on education fail to refer to relevant gender (or indeed race) research. As Carter (1997) argues, post-Fordist analysis failed to recognize that its own framework was built upon particular racialized and gendered patterns, and a particular linkage between public and private worlds. Consequently, he argues that contemporary sociological studies, which fail to incorporate the analysis of what he called 'non-class social divisions' into their analysis, run with 'an overly simplified and homogenized view of the social world' (p.50). This ommission blunts their 'theoretical integrity' and their 'applicatory edge'. They are therefore 'ill-placed and theoretically unarmed to explore important recent trends'.

Current research on the role of education in the lives of women offers rich data on the interface between material structures, identities and agency. Work is now focusing, on the one hand upon the relationship between government-led educational reforms and the processes of gender identification (see, for example, Dawtrey *et al.*, 1995; Epstein *et al.*, 1998; Weiner *et al.*, 1998), or, on the other hand, on the consequences of gender change on the patterns of educational performance (for example Moore 1996; Arnot *et al.*, 1998, 1999). The integration within new feminist theories, of economic and political structures and the discursive formations of individual and collective identities is already being successfully achieved. It is to be hoped that the consequences of such theoretical endeavours and specific educational policies both for women and men will in the future be brought into mainstream sociological discussions (cf., Power *et al.*, 1998; David, 1993).

Future considerations

What sociological history or narrative, if any, can be claimed in this account of feminist theories of education? Perhaps this exercise in theoretical narration has demonstrated that feminist theories cannot be understood merely on the basis of their institutional representation in sociology, or the functions they assume in education. Instead, this work must be seen historically as a diverse expression of perspectives that concern who or what may be responsible for women's oppression and how this took shape in education. It must also be seen as evidence of the strength and diversity of the feminist education project and its ability to struggle with 'history, structure and biography' within the educational sphere.

What then is the future of a feminist sociology of education? The emerging critical tradition of research on the processes of modernization, described above, demonstrates the potential for mapping social change and its gendered manifestations in contemporary educational institutions. It also gives us a purchase on the ways in which social change impinges on gender identities and consequent gender relations between male and female youth. Such attempts to grapple again with the relationship between structure and agency from a gender perspective could lead to a greater understanding of the role of micro and macro social forces in identity-formation and to a greater, albeit still limited, understanding of the sustained ontological and structural links between the gendered 'self' and gender politics in society.

The development of theories which resuscitate the importance of theorizing about contemporary gender politics and relations, the gendered nature of political communities, institutions, states and nationhood seem most promising. While feminist sociology of education has drawn upon psychoanalytic traditions, post-structuralism, cultural theory, political economy and anthropology to sustain and develop its concerns, there has only been limited connection until recently with the wealth of feminist political theory. There is now a growing body of feminist sociological work on citizenship in education which draws upon female political theorists such as Pateman (1988; 1992), Young (1995) and Yuval-Davis (1997) to address questions about gender as a *political* rather than simply a social identity. Such theorizing has the potential to challenge, at a more fundamental level, the construction and taken-for-grantedness of the knowledge categories (for example, the sexual/social contract, public/private distinctions) underlying liberal democratic social orders, and their impact on the concepts of the worker and the learner citizen promoted by schools (see Dillabough, 1999; Gordon *et al.*, 2000; Arnot and Dillabough, 2000). Feminist educational research is, as a result, delving into new and more complex political terrain. Such work maintains a sociological stance, but has developed a stronger political analysis of gender relations based on its reliance on feminist political theory.

Our consideration of feminist theories of education has been limited. Such considerations do not, in themselves, explain every aspect of feminist sociology of education. Indeed, such storytelling can accommodate only a reconstruction of the past and, in many cases, much of the story is lost. However, at the same time, such mapping at the very minimum signals the diversity and momentum of the current feminist theoretical project. We hope we have identified the creative potential and momentum of such feminist theorizing and the key role it still plays in sociology of education today.

Acknowledgement

A version of this chapter will be published in D. Levinson, A. Sadovnik, and J. Cookson, (eds) *Education and Sociology: An Encyclopedia.* New York: Routledge Falmer.

3
Rethinking Social Justice: A Conceptual Analysis

Sharon Gewirtz

Given the centrality of issues of social justice to so much policy–sociology research in education, surprisingly little attention has been devoted to exploring precisely what we mean, or ought to mean, when we talk about social justice. This chapter represents an attempt to begin to remedy this situation. It is in three parts. In the first part, I argue for an extension of the boundaries of what is usually thought of as social justice, suggesting that it should include a *relational* as well as a *distributional* dimension. I then go on to provide a critical review of four approaches to social justice – the *liberal distributive* approach, *communitarian mutuality*, *postmodernist mutuality* and the *freedom from oppressive relations* model propounded by the socialist feminist theorist, Iris Marion Young. In the final part, I draw on insights derived from the earlier discussion to briefly sketch out a research agenda that education policy–sociologists concerned about issues of social justice might pursue.

Rethinking the boundaries of social justice

Social justice has traditionally been understood as referring to the way in which goods are distributed in society. I want to suggest that social justice is more usefully understood in an expanded sense to refer to a family of concerns *about how everyone should be treated in a society we believe to be good*. Broadly conceived in this way, social justice can be said to encompass two major dimensions – a *distributional* and a *relational* dimension.

The distributional dimension is concerned with the principles by which goods are distributed in society. This is the conventional conception of social justice, classically defined by Rawls (1972: 7) as follows:

the subject matter of justice is the basic structure of society, or more exactly, the way in which the major social institutions...distribute fundamental rights and duties and determine the distribution of advantages from social co-operation.

For Rawls, the concept of justice refers to 'a proper balance between competing claims'. How goods are distributed is clearly a vital component of how we treat each other. A society perceived to be good clearly can not exist without a fair distribution of resources, both material and non-material. Therefore, it is important for researchers concerned about social justice to be clear about the principles which govern the distribution of goods in society. However, to 'read' social justice as being *exclusively* about distribution is severely limiting and it is important that we conceptualize social justice in a broader way.

The relational dimension refers to the nature of the relationships which structure society. A focus on this second dimension helps us to theorize about issues of power and how we treat each other, both in the sense of micro face-to-face interactions and in the sense of macro social and economic relations which are mediated by institutions like the state and the market. For Rawls, justice is about the distribution of rights, duties, and the social and economic goods accruing from social co-operation. It does not appear to be about the *form* of social co-operation itself. It is the form of social co-operation – that is the political/relational system within which the distribution of social and economic goods, rights and responsibilities takes place – which is the concern of the relational dimension. In one sense this can be conceived of as another dimension of distributive justice in that in part it refers to the way in which relations of power are distributed in society. But it is not just about the *distribution* of power relations, nor is it just about the *procedures* by which goods are distributed in society (commonly referred to as *procedural* justice). Relational justice might *include* procedural justice, but it is about more than this. It is about the *nature* and *ordering* of social relations, the formal and informal rules which govern how members of society treat each other both on a macro-level and at a micro interpersonal level. Thus it refers to the practices and procedures which govern the organization of political systems, economic and social institutions, families and one-to-one social relationships. These things cannot, unproblematically, be conceptually reduced to matters of distribution.

One way of distinguishing between the distributional and relational dimensions is by thinking of them as rooted within two contrasting ontological perspectives. The distributional dimension is essentially individualistic and atomistic, in that it refers to how goods are distributed to individuals in society. In Miller's well-known formulation it means 'ensuring everyone receives their due' (Miller 1976: 20). By contrast, the relational dimension is holistic and non-atomistic, being essentially concerned with the nature of interconnections between individuals in society, rather than with how much individuals get.

It could be argued that in separating out social justice into these two dimensions I am creating a false distinction. Such an argument would go something along these lines:

> Social justice is about the distribution of goods. Whilst goods are more usually narrowly conceived as referring to material things, the definition of goods can and has been extended, as it was by Rawls, to include non-tangible things, for example particular forms of relationships. If relationships are goods, then the distinction disintegrates.

While this argument might be logical, I would nevertheless argue that it is extremely worthwhile thinking about the two dimensions as separate, albeit strongly connected. If we were to prioritize matters of distribution and treat relationships as merely goods to be distributed, then we may neglect proper consideration of the nature of those relational goods to be distributed. As Young has argued, the 'logic of redistribution' leads us to focus upon 'what individual persons have, how much they have, and how that amount compares to what other persons have' rather than on 'what people are doing, according to what institutionalized rules, how their doings and havings are structured by institutionalized relations that constitute their positions, and how the combined effect of their doings has recursive effects on their lives' (Young, 1990: 25).

Concepts like power, opportunity and self-respect are misrepresented if subsumed into the distributional paradigm because they are more about 'doing' than 'having'. To illustrate this point, Young takes the example of opportunities. Within the distributional paradigm, opportunities are made to sound like discrete goods that we can be allocated more or less of. In contrast, Young argues that 'opportunity is a concept of enablement rather than possession' (p.26). As a result, it is wrong to think of opportunities as things which are *distributed*. We have opportunities if we are not constrained from doing things or if the conditions within which we live enable us to do them. Therefore, the extent to which we have opportunities depends upon the enabling possibilities generated by the rules and practices of the society within which we operate, and by the ways in which people treat each other in that society. So making a judgement about the extent of opportunities we have involves 'evaluating not a distributive outcome but the social structures that enable or constrain the individuals in relevant situations' (p.26).

In short, by isolating relational justice as a separate dimension, we are forced to think in greater depth about the nature of the relationships which structure society and which structure what we do, what we have and the effects of what we do and have on our lives.

Four approaches to justice

I now want to go on to examine some of the most prominent ways in which social justice – in both its distributional and relational senses – has been understood within contemporary debates around social theory and social welfare. I want first to look at dominant conceptions of distributive justice and their shortcomings before going on to examine two contrasting relational approaches. Finally, in this section of the paper I want to consider a conceptualization of social justice that manages – in my view successfully – to fuse the distributional and relational dimensions. I will then go on in the final part of the paper to use this discussion as a basis for outlining an agenda for research on education policy and social justice.

Distributive justice

Dominant notions of distributive justice have tended to fall within two categories. There is the traditional 'weak' liberal definition of justice as *equality of opportunity* and the more radical 'strong' liberal version of justice as *equality of outcome*. The equality of opportunity conceptualization is neatly summarized by Kathleen Lynch (1995: 11) as follows: 'Unequal results are justified if everyone has an equal opportunity to succeed.' There are competing conceptions within the liberal tradition of the precise conditions which need to be met for equality of opportunity to exist. But usually equality of opportunity is viewed as being dependent upon the existence of equal formal rights, equality of access and equality of participation. Equality of outcome differs from equality of opportunity in that it seeks to ensure equal rates of success for different groups in society through direct intervention to prevent disadvantage, for example via positive discrimination or affirmative action programmes.

Both of these liberal conceptions of social justice are limited, however, to the extent that they do not confront what Lynch (1995: 24) refers to as 'the fundamental problems of hierarchies of power, wealth and other privileges':

The fact remains that in a highly unequal society, someone has to occupy the subordinate positions even if the identity of those occupying them may change from white to black, from citizens to migrant workers etc.

(Lynch 1995: 12)

It is in response to the limitations of liberal conceptualizations of equality that Lynch proposes a further 'equality objective' which she refers to as *equality of condition*:

If equality of condition were adopted as an objective, it would involve the development of an egalitarian society which would be committed to equality in the living conditions of all members of society (both citizens and non-citizens) taking due account of their heterogeneity be it arising from gender, ethnicity, disability, religion, age, sexual orientation or any other attribute. It would not simply be concerned with equalizing the position (access, participation and outcome) of marginalized groups at each level within the hierarchies of wealth, power and privilege. Rather, it would involve the equalization of wealth, power and privilege. It would mean having substantial equality in working conditions, job satisfaction and income across different occupations; an educational system devoted to developing equally the potentials of every member of society; a radically democratic politics which aimed at the equal participation and influence of all citizens; and a restructuring of family and personal life for the sake of enriching the personal relationships of every individual.

One of the attractions of Lynch's 'equality of condition objective' is that it encompasses both distributional and relational dimensions of social justice and therefore offers a more holistic conceptualization than the narrower more atomistic liberal conceptions. It is a conceptualization which is complemented and extended by Young's formulation – *justice as freedom from oppressive relations* – which I discuss below. But first, I want to discuss two conceptualizations which are more firmly rooted within the relational dimension.

Communitarian mutuality

Currently, extremely influential in mainstream social policy discourse is the American sociologist Amitai Etzioni's notion of communitarianism, the idea that a good society is one in which there is an ethic of mutuality in which citizens are bound together through a system of duties and obligations. For Etzioni (1996) communitarianism is concerned with achieving a balance between centrifugal forces drawing individuals towards autonomy with centripetal forces drawing them towards the collectivity. Etzioni argues that a lack of equilibrium between the two forces will either threaten the common good, through too much emphasis on the individual, or threaten autonomy, through too much emphasis on social duties. Communitarianism, according to Etzioni, operates at the midpoint between the anarchy of excessive individualism and the authoritarianism of excessive order.

Etzioni-inspired communitarianism carries a powerful normative agenda which has led some commentators to refer to it as moral communitarianism. (This label is also used to distinguish Etzioni's communitarianism from the communitarianism espoused by 'radical left pluralists' – see Hughes and Mooney, 1998.) In particular, Etzioni's communitarianism is based on a diagnosis of the contemporary United States as having experienced a degeneration of moral and social values and a breakdown of families and communities as a consequence of the liberal commitment to rights which separate people from each other. Its core argument is that people need the stability provided by agreed modes of behaviour bolstered by shared moral values.

Strongly linked to ideas of communitarianism are discourses of citizenship, stakeholding, inclusivity and social capital. I do not have the space here to discuss all of these narratives of mutuality. Instead, in order to provide a sense of communitarian conceptions of mutuality, I will focus on some of the recommendations of the Commission on Social Justice (CSJ) which was set up by the late leader of the UK Labour Party, John Smith, with a brief to develop a 'practical vision of social and economic reform for the next century'. The CSJ's report (CSJ 1994) drew heavily on a selection of communitarian narratives. For example, Putnam's (1993b) notion of social capital was taken on board by the CSJ and summarized as follows:

> Social capital consists of the institutions and relationships of a thriving civil society – from networks of neighbourhoods to extended families, community groups to religious organizations, local businesses to local public services, youth clubs to parent–teacher associations, playgroups to police on the beat. Where you live, who else lives there and how they live their lives – cooperatively or selfishly, responsibly or destructively – can be as important as personal resources in determining life chances.... The moral and social reconstruction of our society depends on our willingness to invest in social capital.

We badly need to mend a social fabric that is so obviously torn apart.

(CSJ 1994: 308–9)

For the CSJ, investment in social capital was partly about a redistribution of resources to ensure, for example, that children do not grow up in poverty. It was also about a redistribution of responsibilities, obligations or duties around, for example, childrearing. But it was not just about redistribution. It was also about shifts in the nature of participation and about a restructuring of power relations in society.

Communitarian ideas were manifested in a range of policy proposals put forward by the CSJ. For example, the commission advocated the setting up of a 'Citizens' Service':

> a new voluntary community service scheme reflects our ambition to create a 'something for something' society, rich in civic wealth and social capital, where rights are matched by responsibilities, where mutual respect and individual fulfilment proceed side by side, where independence and mutuality are not opposed but can be combined.
>
> (CSJ 1994: 362)

The aim was to give young people 'a stake in the system – some power, responsibility, opportunity'. This proposal and the notion of a 'something for something society' owes much to Etzioni's belief that there is a moral deficit in society arising from an imbalance between rights and responsibilities. For Etzioni, provisions are needed which will enable individuals to accept greater responsibility towards themselves and others as a way of recompensing the community for any excess of rights received. Similar thinking underpins New Labour's Welfare-to-Work scheme, within which the right of unemployed people to state benefits is counterbalanced by a duty to take up one of the offers provided by the state.

These versions of mutuality are essentially neo-Fabian and reformist. They differ from traditional Fabianism in some respects in that they embody a degree of scepticism towards the paternalism of old-style Beveridgean welfare bureaucracies (CSJ 1994: 104–6). However, the discourses of inclusion and accountability are Fabian in the sense that they are about reimporting a social conscience into capitalism and curbing its worst excesses, but the social relations of capitalism are not in themselves problematized.

Let me now turn, to a somewhat different approach to the concept of social justice as mutuality – that adopted within certain variants of postmodernist thought.

Postmodernist mutuality

From a Foucauldian position, it is neither possible nor desirable to develop universal principles from which we can determine the validity or desirability of particular social or political programmes of reform. The suggestion is that universal notions like justice are dangerous and oppressive (Foucault, 1974; Rabinow, 1986). As a result, there is seen to be no value in attempting to identify one set of principles which is applicable to the specific situations of all social groups in all kinds of society. For Foucault, political struggle involves each social group speaking for themselves and reacting to the particular power structures within which they are enmeshed, rather than being spoken for by others (Macey, 1993). From this perspective, one of the dangers of universalizing theories of justice is that they can marginalize or oppress particular social groups. David Harvey captures the essence of this critique as follows:

> too many colonial people have suffered at the hands of Western imperialism's particular justice, too many African-Americans have suffered at the hands of white man's justice, too many women from the justice imposed by a patriarchal order and too many workers from the justice imposed by capitalists, to make the concept anything other than problematic.
>
> (1993: 95)

Postmodernist versions of mutuality arise from attempts by what Ebert (1991) has called resistance postmodernists to avoid the extreme relativism of the Foucauldian position in order to develop principles of justice which can form the basis of a postmodern politics. The challenge is how to balance two apparently oppositional moral obligations – to recognize different cultural identities and experiences and to create forms of solidarity – in order to construct a politics:

> which works with and through difference, which is able to build those forms of solidarity and identification which make common struggle and resistance possible but without suppressing the real heterogeneity of interests and identities...
>
> (Hall, 1988: 28)

A postmodernist ethic of mutuality represents an attempt to resolve this tension between the heterogeneity of interests and identities, on the one hand, and solidarity and common struggle, on the other. I want to explicate this approach by drawing on the work of Peter Leonard (1997) who discusses what a postmodern ethic of mutuality might mean in the context of welfare practice.

Leonard attempts to resolve the tension between solidarity and difference by arguing that whilst it is vital to recognize difference it is important also to recognize that there is a degree of *sameness* in people's experiences:

> exclusive emphasis on individual biography fragments resistance and leads to a focus on an assertion of individual pathology which is innocent of the structural forces which constitute the determining context of people's health and well-being. An alternative practice is one which, while recognizing individual difference and cultural diversity, engages in a discourse on the similarities between subjects confronting problems of health, personal identity or material survival, similarities which may be embedded in common experiences of class, gender and race.
>
> (1997: 165)

For Leonard, this practice, with its emphasis on commonality and solidarity may enable subjects to participate in collective resistance in pursuit of claims for welfare. Leonard sees feminist practice in psychiatry, psychology, social work, counselling and therapy 'as the exemplar of the possibilities of an approach to solidarity in the context of diversity which could be further widely developed within the welfare field' (1997: 166). His solution is '*a discourse on interdependence*' that is opposed both to the atomism implicit in the extreme relativism of sceptical postmodernism and the atomism explicit in neo-liberal discourses:

> Human needs might be seen as the expression of the mutual interdependency of human subjects, an interdependence which dominant discourses attempt to mask in their opposition to a politics of collectivity which ultimately rests on the mutual dependency of subjects upon each other. It is, perhaps, a recognition of this mutual interdependence which would be at the root of a reinvented idea of welfare, an idea which is alien to the ideological commitments of those who would diminish it in the interests of a Hobbesian and

neo-Darwinist conception of welfare as, at most, a grudging, residual function of the state.... A concept of mutually interdependent subjects, then, is crucial to a politics of collective resistance and, in particular, community action. The point is to extend the actual experience and realization of interdependence beyond the boundaries of a politics of particular identities, 'imagined communities' or single-issue social movements. Only by such an extension to include, at least potentially, all the communities and social identities that experience the present social order as domination, is postmodern particularist politics likely to have any possibility of rectifying its present weakness – its inability to challenge the politics, economic priorities and mass culture of late capitalism.

(1997: 158–9)

Postmodern conceptions of mutuality also rest upon what Fraser (1997a), drawing on the work of the political theorists Axel Honneth (1992) and Charles Taylor (1992), has called a *politics of recognition*:

we owe our integrity... to the receipt of approval or recognition from other persons. [Negative concepts such as 'insult' or 'degradation'] are related to forms of disrespect, to the denial of recognition. [They] are used to characterize a form of behavior that does not represent an injustice solely because it constrains the subjects in their freedom for action or does them harm. Rather, such behavior is injurious because it impairs those persons in their positive understanding of self – an understanding acquired by intersubjective means.

(Honneth 1992: 188–9; cited in Fraser 1997a: 14)

A politics of recognition demands a commitment to respond to others in a way which does not injure their positive conceptions of themselves, and to avoid practising the power of surveillance, control and discipline upon others. Drawing on a Foucauldian critique of power as exercised by professional experts, it attempts to identify an alternative stance that welfare professionals can take up which is resistant to surveilling and disciplining others. Practically, according to Leonard, this entails listening before we act, and he gives the example of the response of white people to the plight of Aboriginal peoples:

When we face the enormity of the cultural losses experienced by many Aboriginal peoples at the hands of the state health, welfare and education services, we may feel compelled to act, to put things right again in their interests. But we are told to listen first, to glimpse the overwhelming pain which cultural loss brings and to remember that it was the modern responsibility to act which led to the cultural losses in the first place. We may act if the Other wishes us to, and on their terms, but only after reflection, trying to relax the imperative to organize and classify with our plans and projects.

(Leonard 1997: 152–3)

A politics of recognition is valuable because it can inform more socially just micro practices of welfare. Rather than the welfare professional surveilling, controlling and disciplining their clients, what is proposed – and practized by some feminist counsellors and therapists – is the

co-authorship of a joint narrative about problems, needs and claims. Because every narrative (of the professional as well as the client) is open to interpretation, we are speaking here of efforts to establish a dialogue of the interpretations of narratives where recognition of the diversity of subjects is established as a priority.

(Leonard 1997: 164)

However, what postmodernist versions of relational justice fail to do is to specify in any developed sense the *particular* conceptions of social justice which need to inform collective resistance to the dominations experienced by various groups of marginalized others. Leonard identifies some potential targets of that resistance, namely the disciplinary power of professionals, the commodification of culture and the manufacture of desire and the economic discourse of global market necessity. But he does not identify precisely what conceptions of social justice underpin his choice of targets. I now want to turn to a conceptualization of social justice which builds on postmodern insights around mutuality and recognition but which, I would suggest, can more usefully inform anti-oppressive political and social activities.

Iris Young's conception of justice as 'freedom from oppressive relations'

In this chapter I have argued that conventional distributive conceptualizations of social justice are limited because they fail to address the forms of social co-operation – for example, the hierarchies of power and privilege – within which distribution takes place. I have also pointed to some of the weaknesses in the communitarian and postmodernist relational versions of justice. One of the key limitations of communitarian mutuality – apart from its heavy moral authoritarian overtones – is that, by attempting to promote a coincidence of interests between capitalists and other citizens, it ignores the injustice of exploitation which is inherent within capitalism. Postmodernist mutuality also fails to properly address capitalist structures of oppression. This is, at least in part, because it tends to focus on the level of 'unmediated face-to-face relations'. Harvey explains why this is a problem:

> In modern mass urban society, the multiple mediated relations which constitute that society across time and space are just as important and as 'authentic' as unmediated face-to-face relations. It is just as important for a politically responsible person to know about and respond politically to all those people who daily put breakfast on our table, even though market exchange hides from us the conditions of life of the producers.... Relationships between individuals get mediated through market functions and state powers, and we have to define conceptions of social justice capable of operating across and through these multiple mediations. But this is a realm of politics which postmodernism typically avoids.
>
> (Harvey 1993: 106)

A discourse of interdependence and a politics of recognition are important, insofar as they provide an ethical and practical basis for relationships marked by mutuality and a celebration and respect of difference. Ideas of interdependence and recognition are also valuable politically to the extent that they may help produce a sense of collective resistance to domination of various kinds. They are however also *limited* politically because they are not conceptions of social justice which can usefully inform the *direction* and *content* of collective action. A more useful conceptualization in this sense is provided by Young who identifies 'five faces of oppression':

> *exploitation* (the transfer of the fruits of the labour from one group to another, as, for example, in the cases of workers giving up surplus value to capitalists or women in the domestic sphere transferring the fruits of their labour to men), *marginalization* (the expulsion of people from useful participation in social life so that they are 'potentially subjected to severe material deprivation and even extermination'), *powerlessness* (the lack of that 'authority, status, and sense of self'

which would permit a person to be listened to with respect), *cultural imperialism* (stereotyping in behaviours as well as in various forms of cultural expression such that 'the oppressed group's own experience and interpretation of social life finds little expression that touches the dominant culture, while that same culture imposes on the oppressed group its experience and interpretation of social life'); and *violence* (the fear and actuality of random, unprovoked attacks, which have 'no motive except to damage, humiliate, or destroy the person').

(Harvey 1993: 106–7, citing Young 1990)

Young's multi-dimensional conception, I would suggest, represents a rich and holistic fusion of distributional and relational approaches to social justice that is sensitive to the inextricable linkages between the two dimensions. Thus exploitation, marginalization and powerlessness are all viewed as emanating from forms of structural and institutional relationship that limit the material resources of subordinated groups and deny them concrete opportunities to develop and exercise their capacities (Young 1990: 58). Young also usefully incorporates post-modernist conceptions of mutuality and recognition into her frame-work, partly through the identification of cultural imperialism as a mode of oppression that is produced and sustained by dominant groups managing to establish their own perspectives and experiences as uni-versal or neutral. The experiences of those who are culturally oppressed are thereby rendered invisible or defined as deviant or 'other' (1990: 60). But Young's conceptualization also addresses the limitations of post-modern conceptualizations. It seems to me, that because it is rooted in a political–economic analysis of social life, it constitutes a more useful underpinning to political action than the other conceptions I have identified. It focuses on the 'multiple mediated relations' of mass urban society as well as upon unmediated face-to-face relations and thereby specifically can help inform identification of the necessary targets of any collective political action, while not losing sight of the importance of mutuality and recognition. As Harvey notes, it is also useful because it

emphasizes the heterogeneity of experience of injustice – someone unjustly treated in the workplace can act oppressively in the domes-tic sphere and the victim of that may, in turn, resort to cultural imperialism against others.

(Harvey 1993: 107)

Young's attempt to integrate the distributional and relational dimensions of justice is not however universally acclaimed. In particular it has been challenged by Nancy Fraser (1997a and b) for failing to recognize the tensions between a politics of redistribution and a politics of recognition. However, as I have argued elsewhere (Gewirtz 1998), while valid in certain respects, Fraser's exposition of what she calls 'the redistribution–recognition dilemma' is flawed in some senses and leaves Young's conceptualization largely intact. A more compelling and politically useful aspect of Fraser's contribution to the debate, as I see it, is her 'critical theory of recognition', which distinguishes between four contrasting attitudes towards 'difference'. The first sees differences as artefacts of oppression. Fraser argues that the proper political response to such differences, like the stunting of skills and capacities, is to abolish them. The second sees differences as manifestations of the cultural superiority of the oppressed over their oppressors. These differences, like 'feminine nurturance', Fraser suggests, should not be celebrated as differences but should be extended to those who manifest inferior traits like competitiveness and instrumentalism. The third views differences as simply variations which should neither be abolished nor extended but affirmed and valued. The fourth attitude, and the one advocated by Fraser, is that there are different types of difference:

> Some differences are of type 1 and should be eliminated; others are of type 2 and should be universalized; still others are of type 3 and should be enjoyed. This position .... militates against any politics of difference that is wholesale and undifferentiated. It entails a more differentiated politics of difference.
>
> (Fraser 1997a: 204)

It is clearly vital that we do not uncritically affirm and celebrate *all* expressions of difference. This is not simply because some expressions of difference are antagonistic to a politics of redistribution, but because some are oppressive in themselves (for example neo-Nazism). However, the critical theory of recognition does not undermine Young's freedom from oppressive relations conceptualization of social justice, since that conceptualization is perfectly capable of accommodating a 'a differentiated politics of difference'. I would want to elaborate Young's framework in only one respect in response to Fraser's objections. That is, in thinking about the third face of oppression, cultural imperialism and how we oppose it, we need to adopt Fraser's more differentiated theory of difference. In other words we need to consider which aspects of difference ought to be abolished (either because they are themselves oppressive or because they interfere with redistribution), which should be affirmed and which universalized.

Conclusion: a social justice agenda for education policy sociology

The breadth and richness of Young's conceptualization of social justice, I want to suggest, makes it a useful framework for thinking about an agenda for social justice research in relation to education policy. I have argued that it incorporates what is good in postmodern conceptualizations of social justice, but overcomes their limitations as well as those of the more traditional liberal distributive conceptions. Modified to take account of Fraser's concerns – about the need to avoid a 'politics of difference that is wholesale and undifferentiated' (Fraser 1997a: 204) – Young's framework provides us with a wide-ranging set of questions which need to be – and indeed in some quarters are being – addressed by the education policy sociology community. These questions might be formulated as follows:

How, to what extent and why do education policies support, interrupt or subvert:

1. exploitative relationships (capitalist, patriarchal, racist, heterosexist, disablist and so on) within and beyond educational institutions?
2. processes of marginalization and inclusion within and beyond the education system?
3. the promotion of relationships based on recognition, respect, care and mutuality or produce powerlessness (for education workers and students)?
4. violent practices within and beyond the education system?
5. practices of cultural imperialism within and beyond the education system? Finally, which cultural differences should be affirmed, which should be universalized and which rejected?

Clearly this framework is broad and needs further clarification and explication, and further questions need to be asked. For example, if we agree that Young's conceptualization is a useful starting point, does the agenda I have set out ask the right questions in the right way or are there other questions we need to ask? We then need to think about how successfully our own research to date has contributed to a social justice agenda of whatever type we identify as being appropriate. What have been the strengths and the limitations and what work still needs to be done?

Acknowledgements

I am very grateful to Alan Cribb and Carol Vincent for their very useful comments on an earlier version of this chapter which appeared in the *Journal of Education Policy* (Gewirtz 1998).

4
The New IQism: Intelligence, 'Ability' and the Rationing of Education

David Gillborn and Deborah Youdell

Bad blood, feeble-mindedness, genetic inferiority, eugenics . . . these terms are associated with another age: they are the discredited and disgraced language of a pseudo- scientific tradition that wrought incredible injustice during the 20th century and are widely viewed with contempt. Such terms are no longer used but, we will argue, the same underlying approaches continue to exert a powerful influence on the policy and practice of contemporary education. This is the *new* IQism where talk of '*ability*' replaces (and encodes) previous talk of *intelligence*.

In this chapter we explore the school-based processes that might explain why, at a time of rising overall achievement, there has also been a consistent increase in relative inequalities of attainment, especially in relation to social class and ethnic origin. In a chapter of this length we cannot address all the complexities involved, and elsewhere we have considered some of these questions in considerably more detail (see Gillborn and Youdell 2000). Our purpose here is to focus on one particular aspect of the processes, namely, the role of 'ability' in the dominant discourses. We argue that 'ability' has come to be understood (by policymakers and practitioners alike) as a proxy for common sense notions of 'intelligence'. These views, long discredited by science and history alike, offer an apparently fair and just means for the rationing of education. In fact, 'ability' is constituted in ways that provide for the systematic disadvantaging of particular socially defined groups, especially children of working-class and Black/African-Caribbean heritage. In this way the discredited and abhorrent ideologies of hereditarian IQism have come to exercise a powerful influence on the realities of contemporary education. In this new IQism, talk of 'ability' serves the same purpose and creates the same consequences as earlier, more explicit notions of 'intelligence' and 'IQ'.

Our chapter begins by outlining the scale of the inequalities associated with the period of English education reform that started in the late 1980s. A brief introduction to our qualitative research project then leads into a discussion of the '*A-to-C economy*'; our term for the competitive and increasingly fraught realities of secondary schooling in a system dominated by annually published league tables of performance. We then consider how 'ability' is constituted in teacher discourse, looking at how teachers' talk and act in relation to a particular view of what 'ability' is and who has it. We explore the links between this discourse and hereditarian understandings of 'intelligence' and IQ. The parallels are much closer than most policymakers and teachers might suppose and, in particular, echo the hereditarian view that working-class and Black children do not share equally in the distribution of 'ability'. Finally we show how these beliefs are institutionalized through the rationing of education that schools adopt as a means of surviving the A–to–C economy. In this form of educational triage the needs of some pupils are sacrificed to the more important goal of raising attainment in the league table statistics. The decisions are justified by recourse to differences in 'ability' and, in this way, the systematic failing of disproportionate numbers of working-class and Black children is legitimized.

Reform and equity

The Education Reform Act (1988) heralded the beginning of a period of education reform in the UK that has been more extensive, and divisive, than anything undertaken since the post-war period of the late 1940s and 1950s. Whereas the movement toward 'comprehensive' education in the 1960s was widely supported within the teaching profession and moved ahead locally at different paces (not least depending on the views of Local Education Authorities), for example, the reforms of the late 1980s and 1990s have been pushed through by successive governments often in the face of opposition from the teaching profession and/or LEAs.

The reforms in Britain,[1] like those promoted in many other capitalist societies during this period, have sought to create an education marketplace where education is reconceptualized as a 'product' and where pupils and parents become 'consumers', free (within limits) to exercise choice. In this way, so the theory runs, 'standards' will be driven up in a market where poor producers will simply go out of business.[2] In many-ways the English reforms go beyond those enacted elsewhere and anticipate measures advocated by some reformers in the US (Chubb and Moe

1992). The reforms included the creation of new types of school (Grant Maintained schools and City Technology Colleges) that were centrally funded and independent of LEA control (and often funded more generously than comparable LEA schools). Additionally, a National Curriculum was introduced, dictating the broad content of the curriculum for children aged 5–16 (the years of compulsory schooling), and enforced first, through an increasingly punitive inspections service (with the power to declare schools as 'failing'),[3] and second, by a system of national tests (Standard Assessment Tasks – SATs) administered at particular 'key stages'. Another innovation was the publication of national 'performance tables', which list each school in the country and give a range of information about their size and the test grades attained by their pupils. Tables of secondary school performance were first published in 1992 and were immediately seized upon by the press as '*league tables*' that could indicate the 'best/worst' schools in every LEA and, indeed, nationally (more on this below). Subsequently, in 1997, similar tables were produced listing all primary schools.

The reforms have been associated with some dramatic changes in the outcomes of compulsory schooling. In the decade following the 1988 Education Reform Act, the proportion of pupils attaining five or more higher grade passes rose significantly, so that half as many again now achieve what used to be considered an elite measure (see Figure 4.1). This is an important change but it does not necessarily spell good news for everyone. In fact, behind the headline figure of year-on-year improvements lies a pattern of growing inequality.

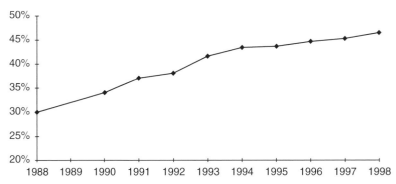

Figure 4.1 Pupils attaining five or more 'higher grade' GCSE passes (A*–C), England 1988–98

Source: adapted from data published in Payne (1995) and the Department for Education & Employment

The area of attainment inequality[4] that has generated most concern among media and policy commentators in recent years concerns gender or, to be more precise, the attainment of *boys*. There has been a good deal of critical discussion about these issues and it is clear that talk of a crisis of boy's under-achievement is over-blown (David and Weiner 1997; Epstein *et al.* 1998). Nevertheless, it is true that, particularly at age 16, there is a now a clear and growing inequality of attainment between boys and girls (Arnot *et al.* 1998; Murphy and Elwood 1998). This trend is clearly visible in Figure 4.2. Such a stark comparison between the sexes should always carry a strong health warning: there are considerable complexities that are hidden in such bold figures, not least differences in curricular specialization. Yet even this apparently stark difference pales somewhat when compared with inequalities related to ethnic origin and social class.

Patterns of attainment related to ethnic origin are increasingly complex. Contemporary research is better able to deal with some of the subtleties of ethnic identification and new approaches reveal divisions and differences that were often obscured in previous work (cf. Gillborn and Gipps 1996; Modood *et al.* 1997; Richardson and Wood 1999). Nevertheless, it remains the case that several minority ethnic groups experience significant and consistent inequalities of attainment, especially pupils of Bangladeshi, Pakistani and African-Caribbean heritage (Ofsted 1999). As yet unpublished research, by scholars working at

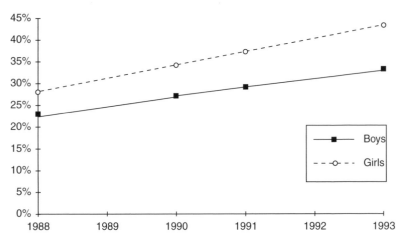

Figure 4.2   Five or more 'higher grade' GCSE passes (A*–C) by gender, 1988–93
Source: Demack *et al.* (1998)

Sheffield Hallam University, indicates clearly that young people in these minority groups have not shared equally in the overall improvement in attainment.[5] Although Bangladeshi, Pakistani and African-Caribbean pupils now achieve higher average scores than at any time in the past, their pattern of improvement has not been as consistent or as high as that of their white peers. *Consequently the relative inequality of attainment has actually worsened.* This is shown most clearly in Figure 4.3, which compares the attainments of white and African-Caribbean pupils between the mid-1980s and 1990s. White pupils have drawn most benefit from the improved levels of attainment associated with the reforms: despite doing better than ever before, African-Caribbean pupils now face a Black/White gap that has grown by more than half as much again since the mid 1980s.

Social class, like 'race' and ethnicity, was systematically removed from the policy agenda under the 18 years of Conservative rule that began in 1979. The realities of an economically stratified society were denied by the ideology of individualism and market economics that sought to present everyone simply as self-sufficient consumers. Margaret Thatcher's (in)famous statement that there is 'no such thing as society' perfectly encapsulated an ideological drive that reduced everything to individualized relationships between providers and consumers, and understood inequality variously as a sign of personal/community deficit or part of the necessary spur to achievement in a meritocracy:

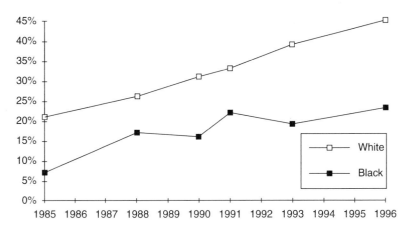

Figure 4.3   The Black/White gap (1985–96): five or more 'higher grade' GCSE passes (A*–C) by ethnic origin, both sexes

Source: adapted from YCS data published previously in Commission for Racial Equality (1998: 2), Drew (1995: 76) and Demack *et al.* (1998).

If irresponsible behaviour does not involve penalty of some kind, irresponsibility will for a large number of people become the norm. More important still, the attitudes may be passed on to their children, setting them off in the wrong direction.

(Thatcher 1993: 626–7)

Not surprisingly, in the face of such a policy stance, the Tories' education reforms did nothing to address existing class inequalities. Indeed, as was the case with 'race' issues, the refusal to address present inequalities left the way clear for even greater divisions to emerge. As Figure 4.4 demonstrates, the national data again show a pattern of growing inequalities. The inequalities are even greater than those associated with ethnic origin and it is interesting to note the pronounced differences in attainment between the various non-manual groups (often lumped together in previous analyses).

Quantitative evidence charts a clear association between the education reforms and a dual pattern of first, rising levels of overall achievement, and second, growing inequalities between different social groups. This pattern is true for gender but most pronounced in terms of ethnic origin and social class. This provides the context for the qualitative research reported in the remainder of our paper: it is a context of continual reform, pronounced teacher uncertainty and heightened surveillance and control. Building on two-years ethnographic research, we will outline an analysis of increased selection and segregation which, we believe, sheds light on the wider processes by which a concern with 'standards' and 'accountability' has led to increasing inequality of educational opportunity.

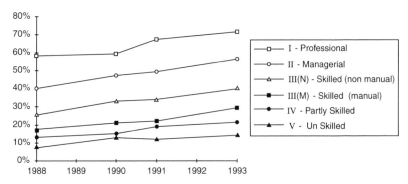

Figure 4.4   Five or more 'higher grade' GCSE passes (A*–C) by social class, both sexes, 1988–93

Source: Demack *et al.* (1998)

The research

This chapter draws on qualitative research conducted in two London secondary schools, which we call *Taylor Comprehensive* and *Clough Grant Maintained*.[6] Between 1995 and 1997 we conducted interviews and observations with teachers and pupils in both schools, focusing in particular on two year groups. First, a group of pupils in year 9 (aged 13 and 14), who we followed through the subject 'option' process. This is a key point in the pupils' secondary schooling where their aspirations can clash with the school's judgement of their past and likely future academic performance. Second, we worked with a group of year 11 pupils (aged 15 and 16) who we followed through to the end of their compulsory schooling, including the completion of their examination courses. In both cases we used mixed ability form groups as the basis for our sample.[7]

The schools provide a fascinating combination of similarities and differences (summarized in Figure 4.5). Both are located in outer London boroughs and serve a pupil population where around one-in-three are in receipt of free school meals (FSM) – a common proxy measure to indicate family poverty. Both schools are multi-ethnic and co-educational. In other respects they differ considerably: Taylor enjoys a consistently full roll and compares favourably in the local GCSE 'league table'. In contrast, Clough GM has a relatively poor reputation locally and is under-subscribed. Perhaps the most important difference between the schools lies in their ethos. Many teachers in Taylor describe it as 'the last comprehensive'. They are proud of its tradition of drawing from across a wide range of class backgrounds and strongly support the headteachers' commitment to mixed ability teaching. Teachers in Clough GM often complain that the school is 'not a proper comprehensive', by which they mean that it does not attract a 'balanced' intake. A striking feature of the school is how frequently staff emphasize the 'bottom heavy' nature of the intake, what one teacher refers to as its 'long tail' of low attaining pupils. The school has adopted a policy of increased selection 'by ability'. One of the spurs for leaving LEA control and adopting Grant Maintained (GM) status was to take advantage of the possibilities for selection on entry that Conservative governments had extended to GM schools. Additionally, the school's headteacher promotes the use of selection internally, including the use of 'setting' by ability in separate subject areas.

Clough GM and Taylor Comprehensive, therefore, adopt markedly different policies toward the use of selection: the former has embraced

TAYLOR COMPREHENSIVE
'the last comprehensive'

Composition
- co-educational (roughly balanced)
- multi-ethnic:
    principal groups: White (75%) & African-Caribbean (10%)
- around one-third pupils receive free school meals
- attracts some middle class pupils

Profile
- consistently full roll
- 6th form (80% of leavers return)

Achievement
- exceeds national average for five-plus A*–to–C passes
- highest achieving maintained co-educational comprehensive in its borough

---

CLOUGH GRANT MAINTAINED
'not a proper comprehensive'

Composition
- co-educational (60% boys)
- multi-ethnic:
    principal groups: White (57%), African-Caribbean (16%) & South Asian (20%)
- around one-third pupils receive free school meals
- overwhelmingly working class

Profile
- under-subscribed
- no 6th form

Achievement
- below national average for five-plus A*–to–C passes
- poor reputation; low in LEA league table
- seeking to extend selection (at entry and throughout years 7–11)

Figure 4.5   Taylor Comprehensive & Clough Grant Maintained

selection while the latter continues to champion mixed ability grouping. Despite these differences in policy, our data suggest that *both* schools are increasingly rationing the time and effort they expend on different groups of pupils. This similarity reflects the crucial importance that both schools accord to the level of examination success that is recorded in the officially published performance tables.

The A–to–C economy

A school now lives or dies on its results.
(Pastoral Head of Year, Taylor Comprehensive)
the staff here now are under pressure to get As–to–Cs. I mean considerable pressure like, you know, that's never existed before.
(Head of Department with more than 15 years teaching experience, Clough GM)

The annually published school performance tables have attained a position of enormous influence. Since their inception, in 1992, there has been considerable debate about the unfairness of publishing raw data on examination performance in the absence of contextualizing information on the pupil cohorts concerned. For example, LEA-maintained comprehensive schools, that operate no selection at entry, are listed alongside private schools that select up to 100 per cent of their pupil intake. The tables are published by the Department for Education and Employment (DfEE) in alphabetical order within each LEA district but they are frequently turned into 'league tables' by national and local newspapers keen to attach 'best' and 'worst' labels to individual institutions. Whenever this occurs one measure dominates as a basis for the ranking; the proportion of final year pupils attaining five or more higher grade passes in their GCSE (General Certificate of Secondary Education) exams. 'Higher grade' passes include grades from A* (the so-called 'starred A'), through A, B and C grades. The remaining pass grades (D through F) are not generally considered to carry weight with employers or institutions of further and higher education.[8] New measures have been added to the secondary school tables each year but the dominant criterion remains the same. Despite the caveats surrounding the interpretation of such material, whenever schools are called upon to describe their attainments, whenever the media (including the educational press) describe a school, and whenever the government talks of 'standards', the first statistic to be quoted is most likely the proportion of pupils attaining at least five higher grade passes.

Both our case study schools recognize the importance attached to this measure of performance and have prioritized it within their own discussions and policy decisions. Teachers, from the headteachers through to the most junior member of staff, feel under scrutiny according to this measure and, with varying degrees of reluctance, most have come to view it as the dominant measure of their own success as educators. Our interview data project a strong and consistent picture of teachers feeling trapped within a wider system that not only judges them according to an unfair criterion but demands year-on-year improvements. In this sense schools and teachers are in competition with themselves, as well as others, because a stable performance rating can be interpreted as showing a lack of progress:

> I don't think we're getting much understanding from senior manage-ment over that sort of thing but, you know, they've got targets to hit 'cause they're set targets by the governors. So they then put the pressure on us (...) the whole thing's motivated by league tables now isn't it? That's what's motivated everybody.
>
> *(Head of Faculty, Clough GM)*

We describe this situation as *'the A–to–C economy'*.[9] The economic metaphor encapsulates how participants, both teachers and pupils, experience the current situation (as competition); how they talk about it (where grades are the 'currency' of education); and how high are the stakes (survival for the school/access to education and labour markets for young people). The notion of an A–to–C *economy* also captures something of the de-personalized nature of the processes within which teachers and pupils feel caught. There is a very real sense in which participants on both sides of the school desk feel trapped within a system where the rules are made by others and where external forces, much bigger than any individual school, teacher or pupil, are setting the pace that all must follow.

In both our case study schools the A–to–C economy has been largely accepted as a fact of life (though not necessarily welcomed) by most members of staff. In particular, the headteachers and other members of the schools' senior management teams (SMTs) have played a crucial role in translating the national reforms into a particular agenda for their institution. In Taylor Comprehensive, for example, in an internally circulated document to staff the headteacher identifies the school's main task as to:

> prepare pupils for the demands of the GCSE. All else at KS4 [Key Stage 4] is subordinate to this supreme and unavoidable constraint.
>
> *(Headteacher, memorandum to staff, Taylor Comprehensive)*

The identification of the GCSE as a 'constraint' might be taken to suggest that the headteacher does not wholly subscribe to its 'supremacy'.

However, its presentation as 'unavoidable' confirms the status accorded GCSE grades and, in the headteachers' eyes, this criterion is so powerful that pupils' interests are now assumed to be *synonymous* with the terms of the A–to–C economy:

> the best thing that we can do for our pupils is to strive to get the greatest possible proportion achieving that five high-grade benchmark.
>
> *(Headteacher, memorandum to staff, Taylor Comprehensive)*

The headteacher in Clough GM adopts the same position. He is certain that higher grade passes are the only hard currency in this economy:

> we do emphasize the fact that if at all possible you should attempt to achieve a grade C. They're not really, I mean not necessarily because of league tables but because the *fact* of the matter is that Cs and above have some currency in the world out there, whereas Ds and below are still viewed by most people as failures. (...) the *hard facts* are that Cs are worth very much more than anything below a C.
>
> *(Headteacher, Clough GM)*

Elsewhere we have examined in detail how the case study schools have responded to the A–to–C economy (Gillborn and Youdell 2000). In this chapter we wish to focus on the view of 'ability' that informs their actions. Our argument is that 'ability' has come to act as a respectable and officially sanctioned proxy for the more highly contested notion of intelligence. We conclude that a *'new IQism'* is emerging, where the beliefs and prejudices familiar as a facet of eugenicist IQism[10] are operationalized (usually without debate nor critical reflection) as part of a 'common-sense' solution to the problems posed by the A–to–C economy.

Constructing 'ability'

In seeking to respond to, and survive, the A–to–C economy both schools have come to rely on a particular understanding of 'ability'. This understanding is vitally important because it informs the schools' decisions about how best they can raise performance in relation to the A–to–C criterion and, most significantly, it shapes their views about which pupils can and cannot be expected to enhance the league table scores.

Before examining how certain groups are positioned as 'less-able' it is useful, therefore, to clarify the dominant view of 'ability' that circulates within the schools.

Talk of 'ability' is extremely common in contemporary education discourse but the meaning of the term (let alone its consequences) are rarely discussed. For example, teachers daily talk of differences in 'ability' between pupils and Government policy takes for granted a common sense view of 'ability' as unevenly distributed between individuals. In 1997 the incoming Labour government made education the focus of its first detailed policy statements and asserted that:

> The demands for equality and increased opportunity in the 1950s and 1960s led to the introduction of comprehensive schools. All-in secondary schooling rightly became the normal pattern, but the search for equality of opportunity in some cases became a tendency to uniformity. *The idea that all children had the same rights to develop their abilities led too easily to the doctrine that all had the same ability.* The pursuit of excellence was too often equated with elitism.
>
> (DfEE 1997: 11, emphasis added)

This further reinforced a position outlined in the Labour Party's election manifesto which confidently asserted:

> *Children are not all of the same ability, nor do they learn at the same speed.* That means 'setting' children in classes to maximize progress, for the benefit of high fliers and slower learners alike.
>
> (Labour Party 1997: 7, emphasis added)

In this way the Government has not only asserted that ability exists as an apparently measurable trait but also that it is unevenly distributed and that the best way of teaching is to separate pupils accordingly.[11] Although Taylor Comprehensive largely resists the push towards formal selection into 'set' teaching groups, both our case study schools evidence the same common sense understanding of ability. It is an understanding which is largely assumed, and rarely discussed in any reflective or detailed way. The following interview transcript is unusual, therefore, in that the nature of 'ability' is thrown into the spotlight. This happened partly by chance as, during an interview with the headteacher at Clough GM, a deputy head overheard him state that pupils cannot 'over-achieve':

Head:	You can't *give* someone ability can you? (. . .) You can't achieve more than you're capable of can you? Can you? There are kids who *surprise* you but I'm not sure that's quite the same thing.
Deputy:	If you can *under*-achieve why can't you *over*-achieve?
Head:	What does over-achieve mean? That you've done more than you're capable of doing? You can't do more than you're capable of. You can do less than you're capable of, as most of us do most of the time. Don't we? (. . .) if I sat and did that test I'm sure I'd do less well than I *should* do because I frankly couldn't be bothered to do it because I don't like doing them, I find it tedious, so I really wouldn't give it much attention. But I couldn't do better on it. Not absolutely. I might *by freak* do better than I should do but that wouldn't be over-achievement, that would just be a flaw of the test that it allowed me to randomly achieve better than I'm really capable of. Statistically it would be possible for me to guess every answer in that test and come up with 100 per cent. It's a small percentage possibility but it is possible. So, but that wouldn't mean I'd over-achieved, it'd mean that the test is sort of, well the test isn't flawed but statistically it's a possibility. But I can't do better than I can do. Can I?' (. . .)
Deputy:	It's semantics. If you guess and you do better than you should have done you *have* over-achieved, whether it's by guessing, depends how you get there.
Head:	But I haven't achieved anything really.
Deputy:	You've achieved a result in the test.

It is significant that although the deputy challenges the head's refusal to accept 'over-achievement' as a concept, the deputy does not challenge the view of ability which the head marshals in support of his claim. The headteachers' perspective, stated with unusual clarity in this extract, is in fact shared widely among teachers in both schools. It is a view of ability that has certain vitally important features, each of which is echoed in government policy. First, *ability is seen as relatively fixed*. There is an assumption that those with more or less 'ability' will be similarly distinguished throughout their education. This assumption is evident in the Government's support for grouping by ability which separates pupils according to the 'speed' at which they learn. The view is starkly summarized by the head teacher (above) in his assertion that 'You can't *give* someone ability...'.

Second, in addition to being relatively fixed, it is widely assumed that 'ability' can be *measured*. Judgements about pupils' ability are made constantly throughout their school careers, often on the basis of formal tests and examinations. This process has been taken a stage further in Clough GM where all pupils entering the school in year 7 are given a paper and pencil test of 'cognitive ability'. This is the test to which the headteacher refers in the extract quoted above. It is a test purchased from, and analyzed by, an external agency. Such tests only relate to a finite range of tasks but within Clough they are seen as accurate measures of 'ability' that can predict likely success and failure in the future:

> we have found them [the tests] helpful as indicators of GCSE performance, and in that there is some correlation between the standard tests and the GCSE outcomes.(...) So for a significant proportion you can be confident that the thing *is* a good predictor of their GCSE results. (...) there will always be a number for whom the correlation doesn't work, a percentage. But what you don't know is who the individuals are. That's the nature of the statistical analysis. So for a significant proportion you can be confident that the thing *is* a good predictor of their GCSE results. But some kids will score, on a standardized basis, 80 and get good results which they shouldn't, and some kids will score 110 and not get good results and that will happen.

It is important to pay attention here to the role of the headteacher's warning that 'some kids will score, on a standardized basis, 80 and get good results which they shouldn't'. This harks back to the point he makes in the longer extract (in discussion with the deputy) where he asserts 'Statistically it would be possible for me to guess every answer in that test and come up with 100 per cent. It's a small percentage possibility but it is possible.' He makes it clear that this is no reason to junk the test, or alter his belief in its predictive power: 'the test isn't flawed but statistically it's a possibility.' This is vitally important because it provides a defence against evidence that challenges the predictive power of the tests and, more fundamentally, the view of 'ability' that underlies their use in Clough GM. Where pupils do not perform in line with their measured 'ability' this can be written off as an anomaly, leaving the test's wider validity and the concept of 'ability' intact: 'for a significant proportion you can be confident that the thing *is* a good predictor of their GCSE results'.

Ability is seen, therefore, as both fixed and measurable. Finally, it is frequently seen in terms of a *generalized academic potential*. This can be seen in the following statements; first, from the Clough headteacher, and second, from one of his Faculty heads. The latter is especially interesting because it shows the routine and common sense way in which this view of 'ability' influences teachers' decisions. In this case pushing teachers to re assess their own verdict on individual pupils if there are discrepancies with teachers in other parts of the curriculum:

> There's a standard test that kids do when they, we give every kid in year 7 a standard test. (...) And they're *indicators* of ability, whatever that means. And obviously indicators of some sort of *general* ability rather than just sort of subject specific ability. (...) These kind of tests wouldn't necessarily tell you that someone's really good at art. So you might get a good result in art. And you might have a particular *talent* in those areas where it's that kind of thing. But, you know, even that, I have to say, is fairly infrequent.
>
> *(Head, Clough GM)*
>
> when you do your estimated grades you do it isolated. So once you can get an overall picture of how a kid's performing elsewhere, you may look at a pupil and think, well he's only ever going to achieve a level D but then by looking at his other grades and maybe he's picking up As and Bs in history and English, that can then raise teacher expectations of the kid. 'Cause we're all only human.
>
> *(Head of Faculty, Clough GM)*

Teachers in both our case study schools shared the same basic understanding of 'ability' as a fixed, measurable and generalized academic potential. It is an understanding that is supported by 'common sense' notions of intelligence and enshrined in contemporary education policy. It is also an understanding that provides a basis for systematic (though often unwitting) discrimination, especially on the basis of social class and ethnic origin.

Ability, intelligence and IQism

> ...the IQ test has served as an instrument of oppression against the poor – dressed in the trappings of science, rather than politics. The

message of science is heard respectfully, particularly when the tidings it carries are soothing to the public conscience. There are few more soothing messages than those historically delivered by the IQ testers. The poor, the foreign-born, and racial minorities were shown to be stupid. They were shown to have been born that way. The under-privileged are today demonstrated to be ineducable, a message as soothing to the public purse as to the public conscience.

(Kamin 1974, p.15–16)

Leon Kamin's criticism of the historical misuse of 'intelligence' tests is as valid today as it was when first published more than 25 years ago. Indeed, the intervening years have seen the periodic fall and rise of popular IQism in the media, never more dramatically than in the furore that surrounded Richard Herrnstein and Charles Murray's *The Bell Curve* (1994); a monumental tome of some 800–plus pages, which made *The New York Times* best-seller list with its claim that *'success and failure in the American economy, and all that goes with it, are increasingly a matter of the genes that people inherit'* (Herrnstein and Murray 1994: 91: original emphasis). The book generated enormous controversy. On both sides of the Atlantic it was seized upon by right-wing politicians, columnists and academics keen to claim a scientific basis for their prejudices (see, for example, Eysenck 1994; Johnson 1994; Tooley 1995a and b). The book was soundly and comprehensively de- bunked by numerous critics who pointed to the pseudo-scientific nature of its claims (Gould 1995), their inadequate (at times fabricated) evidential basis (Kamin 1999), their faulty statistics (Drew *et al.* 1995) and their eugenicist roots (Lane 1999). Even within psychometrics itself, among some who use and analyze IQ tests, there is clear refutation of the belief that they measure any kind of innate potential. The Cleary Committee, appointed in the 1970s by the American Psychological Association's Board of Scientific Affairs, stated that:

A distinction is drawn traditionally between intelligence and achievement tests. A naive statement of the difference is that the intelligence test measures *capacity to learn* and the achievement test measures *what has been learned.* But items in *all* psychological and educational tests measure *acquired* behaviour...

(quoted in Kamin 1981: 94 emphasis added)

This statement's central proposition, that there is no qualitative dif-ference between 'IQ' tests, tests of 'cognitive ability' and *any* other test,

has been repeated many times since, most recently by Robert J. Sternberg, the IBM Professor of Psychology at Yale, in an article entitled
'*Abilities are forms of developing expertize*':

> tests of abilities are no different from conventional tests of achieve-
> ment, teacher-made tests administered in school, or assessments of
> job performance. Although tests of abilities are used as predictors of
> these other kinds of performance, the temporal priority of their
> administration should not be confused with some kind of psycholo-
> gical priority.... There is no qualitative distinction among the vari-
> ous kinds of measures. (...) The fact that Billy and Jimmy have
> different IQs tells us something about differences in what they now
> do. It does not tell us anything fixed about what ultimately they will
> be able to do.
>
> (Sternberg 1998: 11 and 18)

Sternberg's warning is highly significant. First, it makes explicit the
connection between talk of 'ability', IQ tests and intelligence. Although
'ability' features heavily in teachertalk and education policy, the term
'intelligence' does not: undoubtedly this is because of the past controversies about the vacuous and dangerous nature of most claims made in
the name of IQ testing.[12]

This is not to suggest that everyone who uses the word 'ability' is
consciously substituting it for a more controversial alternative. We
believe that most teachers, certainly a majority of those we have worked
with, would reject the excesses of the IQ lobby and would distance
themselves from works such as *The Bell Curve*. The greatest danger in
current uses of the word 'ability' is that it acts as an *unrecognized* version
of 'intelligence' and 'IQ'. If we were to substitute 'IQ' for 'ability' many
alarm bells would ring which currently remain silent because 'ability' acts
as an untainted yet powerful reconstitution of all the beliefs previously
wrapped up in terms such as 'intelligence', 'IQ' and, in earlier decades
of the twentieth century, 'superior/inferior blood', 'feeblemindedness'
and 'normal/abnormal' (see Selden 1999).

This leads to a second reason why Sternberg's intervention is so
timely. Not only does it make explicit the connection between talk of
'ability' and intelligence, but it firmly places all tests of such qualities in
the same category: as measures of learnt skills. Sternberg emphasizes
that whatever term is used and however the test is constructed, *all* such
tests measure acquired behaviour – they are tests of what has been learnt
so far, not an indicator of what can be learnt in the future. These are vital

points because they challenge key fictions at the heart of contemporary discourses about 'ability'. Whether the term is used by politicians, academics, teachers or pupils we should beware of the hidden slippage of meaning that usually occurs. To say that a pupil is 'more' or 'less' able *should* only be taken as a verdict on their past performance; that such a statement often labels individuals as somehow inherently destined for relatively high or low achievement reveals the extent to which the pseudo- scientific IQism of Jensen, Herrnstein and company has penetrated 'common sense'.

The dangers involved in this common sense notion of 'ability' should now be clear. Talk of 'ability' repackages the old and discredited IQism. Sadly, the consequences of this situation have been predictably negative for those social groups that have typically borne the brunt of past inequalities, especially those marked by social class and minority ethnic heritage.[13]

'Race', class and ability

During our two years of fieldwork in Taylor and Clough we were struck by how teachers' notions of 'ability' seemed to reflect judgements about the nature of particular social groups. We began to feel that working class pupils and those of African- Caribbean heritage (often regardless of their social class background) face a particular hurdle in convincing teachers that they have 'ability'. Only rarely do teachers draw a direct connection between 'ability' and a pupil's class or ethnicity, but such a connection seems to be operating tacitly in the ways that certain pupils are perceived as lacking in effort or the necessary skills to achieve.

We have already noted that 'ability' itself is rarely interrogated or challenged; 'ability' is something that teachers infer from a range of markers or cues. Some of these are quantitative (such as test scores) but it is also clear that social class and ethnicity can also act as powerful markers of 'ability'. In Clough GM, for example, many teachers complain that the school's 'unbalanced' intake means that they are disadvantaged in the school league tables. This lack of 'balance' is not simply related to tests of prior attainment but also to the social class composition of the school. The fact that the school's intake is overwhelming working class is interpreted by some teachers as necessarily skewing its achievement to the low end. As the headteacher explains:

> it's no coincidence that year-after-year certain schools are at the top of the table and certain schools are at the bottom. It's purely down,

not *purely* but it's largely, *principally* due to the nature of the intake. So year-after-year [particular local schools] are at the top of the table, [other local schools] are at the bottom (...) we're just above the bottom.

(Headteacher, Clough GM)

The class specific nature of these beliefs is made explicit in the following comments from a Head of Faculty:

Our main intake, you know, (...) feeder schools are on the [local council] estate and we are looking at lots of kids who are coming from families where the parents have never worked, you know, there are no wage earners in the family, they're on Social Security. They do not have the expectations for their kids from education that your 'middle class' or your upwardly mobile working class parents are going to have for their kids, you know. (...) We are weighted down the lower end, unfortunately, because we are a working class school.

(Acting head of Faculty, Clough GM)

In this way the social class composition of the school is seen as causally, and inevitably, linked to the level of achievement that can be attained. 'Ability' here takes on additional dimensions, including parental expectations and pupil motivation, but the relatively fixed and generalized nature of the problem is clear: it's 'because we are a working class school'.

Pupils in both Taylor Comprehensive and Clough GM complain that certain peers are favoured over others. The issues that are most frequently cited in relation to teacher treatment are 'ability', 'attitude/behaviour' and 'race'. The first two categories are suffused with notions of social class although the links are not always made directly. For example, many pupils say that 'clever', middle class and favoured pupils receive much lighter punishments than themselves (or even no punishment at all) for minor disciplinary issues such as lateness, forgotten equipment or chewing gum. Furthermore, it is felt that these favoured pupils are allowed to speak to teachers in a way that is not tolerated from other pupils: 'they're rather cheeky but in a posh way, cheeky to the tutor but in a posh way, and their work's good.' *(Lisa, Taylor Comprehensive, year 9)*

Similarly, pupils' complain that 'race' has a negative impact on teachers' expectations but find it hard to point to conclusive evidence or blatant acts of discrimination: 'It's not blatantly there. I mean, you can't, you wouldn't be able to just walk in the school and say 'Oh the school's racist'. You have to take time before you knew that.' *(Marcella, an African-Caribbean pupil in Taylor Comprehensive, year 9)* In talking about racism in their schools, many pupils (especially those of African-Caribbean and dual heritage) were convinced that minority ethnic pupils were not given fair treatment. To substantiate these feelings they pointed to numerous individual acts, especially concerning teachers' differential punishment of certain individuals. They found it harder to make a concrete connection to how this would impact on their studies but they were certain of its negative influence:

Jason (African-Caribbean):	Some of the classes are sexist or racist.
Researcher:	How do they show that?
Kofi (African-Caribbean):	How they don't pick you [to answer in class], they pick on, like, particular people. Like you can put your hand up and they'll always pick the person next to you, the person on the side, the opposite side, they never pick you. *(Clough GM, year 9)*
Marcella (African-Caribbean):	I mean sometimes Molly [white member of the friendship group] is so rude to her [the teacher], I mean. This is another thing with racism, and *I* wouldn't be able to do that because she'd just like refer me [sending the pupil to another room] or.... Yeah, or give me to [a senior teacher] (...)
Researcher:	Does any of this kind of translate into the classroom when you are learning, or supposed to be learning?
Marcella:	Sometimes I suppose, not all the time.
Juliette (mixed race):	If you're being picked on by a teacher then you'll suffer, your work will suffer.
Marcella:	Mr (...) is the worst, he's always picking on me and Jasmine. (...) I had this teacher called Hatchett and he didn't like me. And one time I went home and I told my mum and she said,

'Could you ever think that he would put down your grades because he doesn't like you?' I said, 'This man seriously doesn't like me'.

(Taylor Comprehensive, year 9)

We observed many occasions when Black pupils seemed to be dealt with more harshly or to face lower expectations than their peers of other ethnic backgrounds: a finding in common with almost all previous ethnographies of multi-ethnic schools (see Bhatti 1999; Connolly 1998; Gillborn 1990; Green 1983; Mac an Ghaill 1988; Mirza 1992; Nehaul 1996; Sewell 1997; Wright 1986, 1992). Only rarely, however, did teachers' make explicit reference to ethnicity and ability in the same context. When this did occur the incidents supported the view that teachers' judgements of 'ability' were indeed linked with negative expectations about certain groups, especially African-Caribbean young people:

I found that quite strange that the kids had their estimated grades because they then came back at you and gave you earache, you know, would challenge you in the corridor and so you were under threat. You know, 'why have you only given me that grade', you know? Because kids, you know, have different perceptions of themselves, they have no understanding, you know, and some of them live in cloud cuckoo land. I mean we've got, we had a whole period where we had Afro-Caribbean kids running around with gold rimmed glasses on with plain glass in them because they thought it made them look more intelligent, you know, they really had highly inflated opinions of themselves as far as academic achievement, and this is fact. I mean there were a whole group of kids that put on glasses and wandered round the corridors with gold rimmed glasses on because they really felt that they were sort of A/B . . .

(a Faculty head, Clough GM)

On the basis of this teacher's account it is clearly impossible to discern whether Black pupils were wearing non-prescription glasses and, if they where, what their motivations for doing so might have been. Nor is this quotation irrefutable evidence that this or any other teacher was actively or unwittingly making poorer predictions for Black pupils than for their peers from other ethnic groups. Nevertheless, this account does give a worrying insight into several relevant issues. It shows quite clearly, for example, that this teacher recognizes that the predicted grades are important to pupils but that he is dismissive of their protests that the estimates are too low: 'kids, you know, have different perceptions of themselves, they have no understanding.' The quotation seems especially dismissive of protests by Black pupils: 'they really had highly inflated opinions of themselves as far as academic achievement'. Furthermore, it is noticeable that the pupils' concerns (which *could* have been interpreted as a sign of motivation, a thirst for achievement and success) are experienced negatively as 'challenge' and 'threat'. There is a strong echo with previous research that has suggested teachers' readiness to impute a challenge into the actions of Black pupils (cf. Gillborn 1990; Gillborn and Gipps 1996; Sewell 1997, 1998; Wright 1992).

Ability, selection and the rationing of education

In the previous sections we have identified several key factors in the ways that 'ability' is currently conceptualized. First, we have seen that 'ability' is commonly viewed as a relatively fixed, measurable and generalized academic potential. This echoes the most crude and regressive notions of 'intelligence' but reconstitutes them in a more acceptable discursive package. Second, we have shown that there is evidence, from our own study and in previous work, to suggest that teachers sometimes view ability as unevenly distributed between social groups. Furthermore, these beliefs operate to the distinct disadvantage of working-class and Black young people. A final element in this potentially devastating equation is supplied by the increased use of selection within secondary schools: this provides a mechanism by which numerous, often ill-defined and even unrecognized differences in teacher expectations can be given concrete existence through their institutionalization within the organization of teaching groups and, in some cases, the placing of literally impenetrable limits on the exam grades that are available.

Although there are no definitive statistics on the picture nationally it is widely believed that selection 'by ability' in general, and in particular the use of setting, has become more widespread since the major education reforms began in the late 1980s. Research consistently indicates that selection into separate teaching groups does *not* deliver a net improvement in attainment but does lead to disenchantment among pupils in lower groups and acts to reinforce social and minority ethnic disadvantage (for reviews see Gillborn 1997; Hatcher 1997; Hallam and Toutounji 1996; Sukhnandan and Lee 1998). Nevertheless, many teachers believe that selection will enhance the performance of some pupils and, as we have already seen, the policy has been explicitly supported by the Labour government. Inspection reports by the Office for Standards in Education (Ofsted) indicate an increase in the use of setting in secondary schools in the late 1990s (Budge 1998) and recent research suggests that primary schools are increasingly adopting setting, especially in mathematics and English (Hallam 1999).

Both Taylor Comprehensive and Clough GM have increasingly turned to the use of internal selection in a bid to raise their profile in the school performance tables. We noted earlier that the schools have a markedly different ethos in relation to selection: Clough GM views selection (on entry and internally) as a key improvement strategy, while Taylor Comprehensive is committed to retaining mixed ability teaching. Nevertheless, both schools have increasingly adopted setting, especially in Key Stage 4. Additionally, both schools use the subject options process in year 9 as a form of hidden selection and they have developed a range of what might be termed '*D–to–C conversion strategies*'; that is special initiatives that identify supposedly 'borderline' pupils and offer them additional support and teacher time. In Clough, where the ethos strongly supports selection, setting and other forms of ability grouping are used from year 7 onwards and strategies in Key Stage 4 even include the use of a pupil league table – publicly ranking pupils according to their predicted GCSE performance (see Gillborn and Youdell 2000).

Finally, in a piece of selection that receives little academic attention and almost no media coverage, all secondary schools are now required to select pupils to '*tiered*' examinations in a majority of GCSE subjects. The late 1990s saw a change in many GCSE examination courses which require teachers to decide the 'appropriate' level of entry for each pupil. The decisions are viewed with trepidation by many teachers and are vitally important for pupils because they can place an impenetrable ceiling on the grades that they can attain. Figure 4.6 illustrates the tiering models currently in operation. Pupils are entered in a particular tier and can only attain the grades associated with that level. In the two-tier model, for example, pupils in the Higher Tier can attain grades A* through D: a pupil performing below the level required for a grade D will usually be given a U (Ungraded) result. Tiering means that a pupil placed in the Foundation Tier *cannot* attain the highest grades (A*–B). Worse still, in mathematics (where a three-tier model applies) Foundation pupils cannot attain a C grade – taken as the basic requirement by many and given a crucial weight in job and education marketplaces.

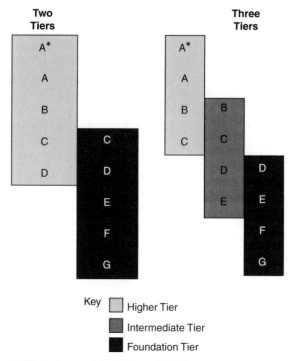

Figure 4.6   GCSE tiering models (1998 and 1999)

The increasing use of selection lends institutional weight to differential teacher expectations about the 'ability' of various pupils. It is our contention that these processes are effectively leading to the rationing of educational opportunity.

Education as *triage*

> triage, n. of action f. *trier* to pick, cull...1. The action of assorting according to quality...2. The assignment of degrees of urgency to wounds or illness in order to decide the order of suitability of treatment.
>
> (*Oxford English Dictionary*)

In a medical crisis *triage* is the name used to describe attempts to direct attention to those people who might survive *if* their needs are given immediate attention. Other categories of patient are required to wait: some patients will have less pressing needs and can safely be left; other less hopeful cases have needs so great that they are judged unlikely to survive even if prioritized. A similar approach is being adopted in Taylor Comprehensive and Clough GM. Teachers are engaged in a series of activities that seek to identify 'borderline' pupils, that is those expected to only narrowly miss the five A–to–C barrier. By emphasizing the needs of such pupils, it is reasoned, the greatest impact can be made on the schools' league table position. Consequently the needs of other pupils, be they 'safe' or 'without hope', are given less attention. In this way *educational triage is acting systematically to neglect certain pupils while directing additional resources to those deemed most likely to benefit* (in terms of the externally judged standards). These strategies seek to maximize the effectiveness of scarce resources but their effect, in practice, is to privilege particular groups of pupils. The process is represented schematically in Figure 4.7.

Schools are responding to the A–to–C economy by emphasizing the needs of particular groups of pupils over others. 'Able' students are generally placed in higher sets with greater resources and the most experienced teachers. Those deemed to have 'ability' but not attaining the predicted levels are identified and subject to a range of 'D–to–C conversion strategies', including mentoring by senior teachers and the possibility of additional lessons. These developments are not uniformly welcomed by teachers, and there is some resistance, but in the main

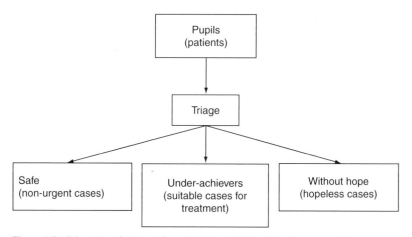

Figure 4.7   Educational triage: the rationing of educational opportunity

they are seen as unavoidably pragmatic moves in the face of the league table requirement to deliver year-on-year improvements in the proportion of pupils attaining five or more higher grade passes.[14] In all of this the discourse is framed in terms of 'ability'; hence the differential distribution of resources (such as teacher time, support and effort) is presented as socially just in meritocratic terms. In practice, however, the processes are exclusionary and embody assumptions that further entrench and extend 'race' and class inequalities.

In both Taylor Comprehensive and Clough GM working-class pupils (especially those in receipt of free school meals) and their peers of African-Caribbean heritage (regardless of social class) are less likely to be viewed as 'able'. In contrast, these pupils are much more likely to be viewed as disruptive, as lacking in motivation and as the product of a home and/or community culture that does not support education. For example, in both schools, Black pupils and their white peers in receipt of free school meals (FSM) are significantly more likely to be placed in Foundation Tier examinations and less likely to be placed in the Higher Tier. This is just part of a wider process of labelling and the rationing of opportunity that works through the routine operation of stereotypes at the classroom level. In isolation such beliefs and practices can seem trivial or of limited importance. As we noted earlier, for example, many pupils are convinced that racism is at work in their schools but it is not easily identified in crude acts; in Marcella's words, 'it's not blatant'. It is only when viewed cumulatively, at the end of the pupils' secondary education, that the devastating effects of these processes come clearly into focus.

Overall levels of GCSE attainment are higher in Taylor Comprehensive (despite the schools' commitment to mixed ability teaching which the government views as less desirable at this stage). However, the patterns of achievement between different social groups – the educational winners and losers – are largely the same in both schools (see Figures 4.8 and 4.9). In relation to pupils who attained at least five higher grade GCSE passes (the defining criterion of the A–to–C economy), in both schools the patterns of achievement reflect inequalities by gender, social class and ethnicity. Boys are less likely to attain the five A–to–C benchmark than girls, but the scale of the attainment inequality in relation to gender is significantly less pronounced than the inequalities by 'race' and class. In both case study schools white pupils are around twice as likely to attain the benchmark than their African-Caribbean peers. In Taylor the attainment inequality between FSM and non-FSM pupils is a little less pronounced but in Clough GM, where selection is

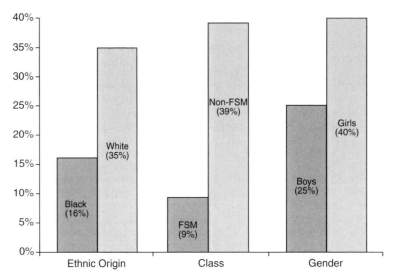

Figure 4.8 Five or more 'higher grade' GCSE passes by gender, class and ethnic origin (Clough GM)

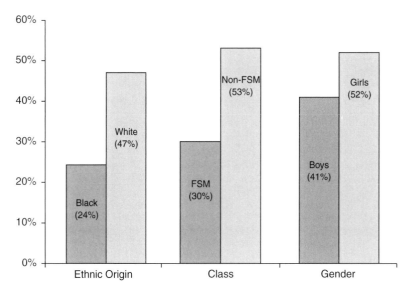

Figure 4.9 Five or more 'higher grade' GCSE passes by gender, class and ethnic origin (Taylor Comprehensive)

most intensive, the class inequality is the greatest of all: here non-FSM pupils are four times more likely to attain the benchmark than their peers in receipt of free meals.[15]

These inequalities in attainment are highly significant. However, an even more distressing picture is revealed if we interrogate the statistics further. Not all GCSE subjects carry equal status in the eyes of potential employers and in terms of college and university admissions. It is not possible to grade all subjects by their relative status but a simple (yet meaningful) criterion is whether pupils attain higher grade passes in each of the three 'core' subjects in the National Curriculum (mathematics, science and English). Since the National Curriculum was first introduced these subjects have enjoyed special status, including guaranteed curriculum time. Furthermore it is known that many employers (and some HE institutions) view higher grades in some or all of these subjects as a prerequisite – functioning as a further selection device that limits the number of applicants they have to consider. As can be seen in Figures 4.10 and 4.11, the attainment inequalities become even more pronounced in relation to this measure.

Once again, although the gender inequalities are in the predicted direction they are not as great as those associated with 'race' and social class. In Clough GM *no* pupil in receipt of free meals attained five or

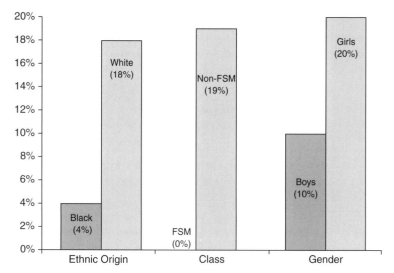

Figure 4.10   Pupils attaining at least five 'higher grade' GCSE passes that include maths, science and English Language (Clough GM)

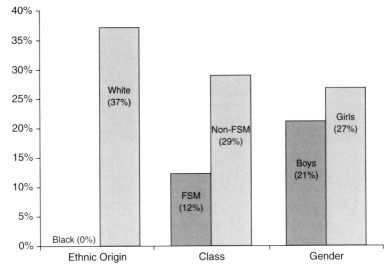

Figure 4.11 Pupils attaining at least five 'higher grade' GCSE passes that include maths, science and English Language (Taylor Comprehensive)

more higher grade passes including the core subjects: around one in five non-FSM pupils attained this level. The situation is a little better in Taylor Comprehensive but here too the inequality is clear: non-FSM pupils in Taylor are twice as likely to attain five higher grades including the core subjects. In Clough white pupils are about four times more likely to achieve five higher grades including the core subjects; in Taylor not a single African-Caribbean pupil attained this level of success compared with almost four-in-ten of their White counterparts.

Conclusions

After two-years research in Clough GM and Taylor Comprehensive one of our most striking findings is just how few people (teachers and pupils) seem to be comfortable with the present state of the schooling. Teachers, from the most experienced and senior members of staff through to the most junior newcomers, feel pressured to perform in relation to targets and surveillant systems that are beyond their control. Their discomfort, however, is as nothing compared to the costs borne by some of their pupils. All of them, teachers and pupils, experience a schooling process that is increasingly dictated by external performance measures; in trying to survive that process, familiar social divisions (especially by 'race' and class) are being reworked and further entrenched through a discourse that stresses individual 'ability' but seems actually to revolve around group identities and stereotypes.

The A–to–C economy has touched every aspect of schooling in Taylor and Clough; it is an economy that sprung from the Conservative education reforms begun under Margaret Thatcher and it continues even more powerfully under Tony Blair's 'new' Labour administration. This is not to deny that Labour have made significant changes. Blair has made 'social inclusion' a key part of the Government's stated agenda and equal opportunity (for so long derided under Conservative governments) is once again viewed as a legitimate policy aim. Unfortunately, these changes have traded on a narrow and superficial understanding of social justice and have not provided a springboard for genuinely egalitarian policy (see Demaine 1999; Gillborn 1999; Hatcher 1998; Whitty 1998). Labour's interpretation of 'standards' has been no more sophisticated than the Tories' and the publication of school league tables is a taken-for-granted part of national policy.

We began this paper by examining the patterns of growing educational inequality that characterize the period of reform that started in the late 1980s; we have used our qualitative data on life in Taylor Comprehensive and Clough GM to get behind the statistics in an effort to understand the processes that are producing these inequalities. Despite their many differences, Taylor and Clough share a perception of the 'A–to–C economy' and their role within it. As a direct result of these perceptions *both* schools have moved to select pupils earlier, more intensively and with greater finality than at any time in their recent history. Clough GM seizes the opportunity, viewing selection (internally and at the point of entry) as a major improvement strategy; Taylor seeks to maintain its commitment to mixed ability teaching but nevertheless sets 'by ability' in some subjects and increasingly segregates children as they move into their GCSE courses. Partly this is a consequence of the GCSE exams themselves, which force schools to *tier* children – closing down opportunities and lending institutional weight to differential teacher expectations. In both schools there is a rationing of educational opportunity, never clearer than in the D–to–C conversion strategies adopted as a final desperate attempt to lever up 'success' in the league tables at the cost of judging some pupils (disproportionately Black and working-class young people) as without hope. The schools do not set out deliberately to fail particular groups but, in the face of the A–to–C economy, they must find some way of deciding where best to focus their limited resources. This is educational *triage* and the decisions are based on judgements of 'ability'. But 'ability' is a loaded, fallacious and highly dangerous concept. 'Ability' offers a supposedly fair means for condemning some children to second class educations: it is a discourse that characterizes national educational policy, draws on common sense prejudices and misconceptions, and acts to legitimate the systematic failing of Black and working-class young people. This is the constellation of forces we describe as '*the new IQism*'.

We have noted the periodic fall and rise of debates about supposedly inevitable hereditary differences in educability. The most recent episode, sparked by Herrnstein and Murray's *The Bell Curve* (1994), was typical in the pseudo-scientific guise that the IQist lobby sought to construct around a familiar conservative anti-welfare and elitist message. The book provided an opportunity (on both sides of the Atlantic) for 'experts' and other commentators to re-assert the inevitability, and indeed the justice, of inequality. Arguing simply that people are in poverty because of their own intellectual (genetically-based) shortcomings, the book became part of a wider discourse that attacks any liberal compensatory programme as futile and anti-democratic. It is an approach that is anti-working class, disablist, sexist, and racist:

> *A man's IQ predicted whether he described himself as disabled better than the kinds of job he had held. We do not know why intelligence and physical problems are so closely related, but one possibility is that less intelligent people are more accident prone.*

> > (Herrnstein and Murray 1994: 155, original emphasis)

> *At lower educational levels, a woman's intelligence best predicts whether she will bear an illegitimate child.*

> > (ibid. 167, original emphasis)

> *ethnic differences in cognitive ability are neither surprising nor in doubt. . . . the average white person tests higher than about 84 percent of the population of blacks . . .*

> > (ibid. 269, original emphasis)

These kinds of perspective are repugnant to many people. Teachers, although not versed in the detail of the 'nature versus nurture' debates over IQ and heredity, *are* often aware of past controversies where testing has been found to discriminate against particular groups. Additionally, many working in the British system remember (having experienced it as pupils and/or professionals) the selective tripartite system that dominated after the Second World War; a system based on the hereditarian perspectives of Sir Cyril Burt[16] and ultimately abandoned in most LEAs

because of its obvious inequities. Finally, of course, anyone even re-
motely aware of 20th century history needs little reminding of the
atrocities carried out in the name of genetic superiority.[17] These events
are part of the reason for the furore that justifiably surrounds public
interventions by those in the hereditarian camp. And yet our data
suggest that, in one sense at least, the hereditarians have already won.
*Without any genuine debate the British education system is increasingly
returning to policy and practice that takes for granted the assumptions proposed by IQists like Herrnstein and Murray.*

The hereditarian view of intelligence as 'a matter of the genes that
people inherit' (Herrnstein and Murray 1994: 91) is certainly *not* proposed as an explicit element in most policy discourse and, boldly stated
(as above), we imagine that many (most?) teachers would reject such a
perspective as abhorrent. However, exactly the same principles that
underlie the IQist position *are* embraced and enacted within the detail
of contemporary education policy and practice in Britain. We are not
arguing that policymakers and teachers consciously accept the hereditarian position but that they *behave* as if they do. This is the *new* IQism, a
situation where *hereditarian assumptions (and all the concomitant inequalities of opportunity that they produce and legitimate) are coded and enacted
through the discourse of 'ability'.*

Hence, education policy asserts that 'Children are not all of the same
ability, nor do they learn at the same speed' and uses this as the rationale
for an extension in the use of 'setting by ability', so as to 'maximize
progress, for the benefit of high fliers and slower learners alike' (Labour
Party Manifesto 1997: 7)(see above). We have shown that both Clough
GM and Taylor Comprehensive work with a view of 'ability' as a fixed
and generalized intellectual potential: echoing the IQists' notion of
'intelligence' (cf. Herrnstein and Murray 1994: 19–24). We have shown
also that this view of ability underlies multiple and complex selections
that separate out the 'able' and the 'less-able' within the schools: some
decisions are explicit (such as the creation of separate 'sets'); some are
camouflaged as advice on 'appropriate' courses (for example during
'options' processes and tiering decisions); others are a mixture of public
and private (including various D–to–C conversion strategies). Regardless
of the form taken, however, these decisions have a clear and discrimin-
atory effect. Our data show that Black pupils and their peers in receipt of
free school meals are considerably more likely to be judged as lacking
'ability' and, therefore, find themselves in the lower sets, entered for the
lowest tier of examination, and judged least worthy of additional support through the rationing of education in the A–to–C economy.

The new IQism informs, and is in turn strengthened by, contemporary policy and practice. *The view of 'ability' that currently dominates education, from the heart of government through to individual classrooms, represents a victory for the hereditarian position without debate and without conscience.* At the school level this IQist notion of ability provides an opportunity for teachers (and especially senior management) to identify the winners and losers at the earliest possible stage, allowing continual checks to insure that those predicted success 'fulfil' their potential. This perspective, and the decisions it supports, are serviced by a testing industry only too happy to sell schools what they want to hear.[18]

Gross inequalities of attainment and opportunity currently characterize the British education system. These inequalities have grown as the A–to–C economy provides the impetus for schools to pursue increasingly frequent and final forms of internal selection. The notions of 'ability', that inform such decisions, are powerful and dangerous. Unless policymakers and practitioners (at all levels) challenge these common sense fictions about intelligence and ability, the future is likely to hold even greater inequalities.

Notes

1. The reforms were enacted by British governments but do not always include each member state of the United Kingdom; the most far reaching changes have been felt in England and, since that is where our qualitative data were collected, in this chapter we focus mainly on the English case.
2. The term 'quasi-market' has been preferred by some (see Whitty 1997) because, despite the many reforms, the situation is still some way from the model proposed in a purely 'free market'. For example, parents are free only to express a 'preference' for a certain school (they have no guarantee of access) and the state remains both a major provider and regulator of education.
3. Schools identified as 'failing' face a series of requirements and re-inspection that can lead, ultimately, to closure.
4. We prefer the term 'attainment inequality' to the more common notion of 'under-achievement' because of problems of labelling and misinterpretation associated with the latter term. For a discussion of these problems see Gillborn and Gipps (1996) and Mirza (1992).
5. Our thanks to Sean Demack, David Drew and Mike Grimsley for generously granting permission to reproduce their findings.
6. We gratefully acknowledge the funding made available for this project by the Nuffield Foundation.
7. For more detail on the schools, the pupil sample and the research techniques, see Gillborn and Youdell (2000).
8. The special significance of *five* higher grades reflects their past use in England as a means of selection to the professions and Higher Education, where five

higher grades has traditionally operated as a basic cut-off point below which candidates are not considered (see Drew *et al.* 1992; Goacher 1984).

9. In everyday language, in school and the media, people commonly refer to higher grades as 'A-to-C', adopting a shorthand that ignores the starred A grade (A*). We mirror this in describing the situation as the 'A-to-C economy' although, of course, A* grades are included in all relevant calculations.

10. In relation to the controversy surrounding Jensen's hereditarian claims in late 1960s and early 1970s (see Jensen 1969), Samuel Bowles and Herbert Gintis (1976) use the phase 'IQism' to describe the theory of social inequality that locates the causes for poverty in the genetic and, particularly, the intellectual make-up of people (both individually and as a group).

11. For a more detailed critique of Labour's approach to issues of selection and equity see Gillborn (1998a), Hatcher (1998) and Whitty (1999).

12. Significantly, Herrnstein and Murray themselves use a variety of terms in addition to intelligence (especially 'cognitive ability') because 'the word *intelligence* carries with it undue affect and political baggage' (Herrnstein and Murray 1994: 22. original emphasis).

13. Interestingly, gender dynamics have not worked out so predictably. The widespread panic about 'boy's under- achievement' has actually worked to raise teachers' expectations about 'girls' ability'. However, this has not meant that girls uniformly benefit from teachers' expectations – indeed, we found considerable evidence of negative stereotyping (see Gillborn and Youdell 2000).

14. See Gillborn and Youdell (2000) for detailed accounts of the various perspectives adopted by teachers in the two case study schools and a critique of the role of *pragmatism* in the discourses and processes.

15. Because of the relatively small numbers involved it is not sensible to carry out numerous cross-tabulations, such as controlling for class and ethnicity together. However, it should be noted that the proportion of FSM pupils was not significantly different between the ethnic groups in the study and so the Black/White attainment inequality should not be dismissed as an artefact of social class.

16. Cyril Burt was the leading British hereditarian psychologist, knighted for his services to education, whose ideas exercised considerable influence over the shape of the selective post war education system. In the early 1970s Leon Kamin raised serious doubt over the authenticity of Burt's work, noting that in view of his published sample descriptions, the statistical correlations claimed by Burt were literally incredible (Kamin 1974). The issue made front page headlines (after Burt's death) when Oliver Gillie, of the *Sunday Times*, discovered that two 'research associates' who had supposedly gathered the data for some of Burt's most famous work had, in all likelihood, never existed. Initially the charge of fraud was vehemently defended by Burt's supporters, such as Hans Eysenck, who complained of 'character assassination'. Later, however, Burt's authorized biographer (Leslie Hearnshaw) unearthed further evidence and Burt's supporters began to accept publicly that he had behaved 'in a dishonest manner' (for an account see Kamin 1981: 98–105). The late 1980s, however, witnessed an attempt to rehabilitate Burt's reputation (Joynson 1989) every bit as flawed and selective in its evidence as was Burt himself (cf. Hearnshaw 1990). Nevertheless, the attempt to

reconstruct Burt as victim rather than fraud was partially successful. Reviewing the Joynson book for the *Guardian* newspaper, for example, Clare Burstall (then director of the National Foundation for Educational Research) declared 'Burt stands exonerated'. A conclusion that she reached with obvious relief, 'I found it impossible to accept anyone who could write as Burt did, and who had for so long, and with such obvious justification, been held in such high esteem by so many of his contemporaries, could possibly be the confidence-trickster, liar and fraud that he was now being made out to be'.

17. Eugenic ideology was by no means limited to Nazi Germany. In Britain and the United States many prominent politicians viewed unchecked 'breeding' with alarm. For a revealing history of Eugenics in the US see Selden (1999).

18. The National Foundation for Educational Research (NFER), for example, currently markets a test on the basis that GCSE outcomes can be reliably predicted across the range of pupil backgrounds as early as year 7. See Gillborn and Youdell (2000) chapter 3, for a detailed critique of these claims and the assumptions they embody.

5

New Teachers and the Question of Ethnicity

Bruce Carrington, Alastair Bonnett, Anoop Nayak, Geoff Short, Christine Skelton, Fay Smith, Richard Tomlin and Jack Demaine

During the 20 years since the publication of the Rampton Report (1981) concern has been voiced about the under representation of minority ethnic groups in teaching in England and Wales, and their relative lack of opportunities for career advancement. The Commission for Racial Equality (CRE) has lobbied for policy interventions to address the issue and in the mid 1980s carried out a survey of staffing in eight local authorities that had 'higher than average' minority populations. This revealed that less than three per cent of teachers came from minority ethnic backgrounds and also showed that such teachers were disproportionately concentrated on lower pay scales (CRE 1986, 1988). By 1992 the CRE was urging the Conservative government to take appropriate steps 'to ensure that people from the ethnic minorities will be recruited for teacher training without unlawful discrimination' (cited in Osler 1997, p.47). Subsequently, the Higher Education Funding Council responded by funding 17 projects to widen ethnic minority participation in initial teacher training between 1993 and 1994 (HEFC 1995).

In October 1997 the Teacher Training Agency (TTA) and the CRE launched a series of regional conferences addressing the theme 'Teaching in Multi-ethnic Britain'. This initiative to boost minority recruitment was compatible with the newly-elected Labour government's commitment to the principle of social inclusion, articulated three months earlier in the White Paper, *Excellence in Schools* (Department for Education and Employment 1997). The subsequent Green Paper, *Teachers: Meeting the Challenge of Change* (DfEE 1998) declared that 'Teaching must attract recruits from every section of society, bring strengths and qualities which ensure that teaching is a vibrant and diverse profession.' The paper went on to announce that the TTA would be asking all training providers 'to set targets for the number of ethnic minority trainees to whom they offer places' (DfEE 1998, p.46).

Osler (1997), Jones, Maguire and Watson (1997) and Siraj-Blatchford (1991) provide invaluable insights into the careers of minority ethnic teachers and their experiences during training. But relatively little has been written about teacher trainers and the issue of ethnicity, or about the strategies deployed in the recruitment and retention of minority ethnic student teachers. The research reported in this chapter is one strand of an ongoing investigation (begun in 1998) into the motivations and experiences of minority ethnic students from the start of their initial teacher training on Postgraduate Certificate in Education (PGCE) courses through to their first teaching posts. The research invest-igates the practices of a group of teacher training institutions that have been particularly successful in recruiting minority ethnic students.

Briefly, the first stage of the project involved a postal survey of all those identifying their origins in ethnic minority groups on their Graduate Teacher Training Registry (GTTR) application forms for the PGCE. The second strand of the project, which is the one reported in this chapter, involved interviews with admissions tutors, course directors and other senior staff at teacher training institutions. A third strand involved inter-viewing students about their experiences towards the end of their train-ing course. Finally, a postal survey and follow-up interviews were carried out during the first year of full-time teaching. Of course, the authors of this chapter have long been aware of the methodological difficulties associated with this kind of research and with the use of conventional ethnic group categorization (see for example, Demaine 1989, Mason 1990 and Bird 1996). In order to proceed in these early stages of the research we had to make use of 'official' categories. On balance, we consider the research worthwhile despite the limitations.

The scope of the research

The role of 'gatekeepers' is regarded as significant to recruitment to many occupations, and teaching is no exception, although it must be borne in mind that there are strict requirements laid down by the TTA which admissions tutors in teacher training institutions are not at lib-erty to ignore. Rather than concerning ourselves with these more or less 'fixed' requirements, our research focused on 'positive' features that admissions tutors might regard as 'good practice' in encouraging recruit-ment. We followed this line of enquiry in the hope of making a positive contribution to minority ethnic recruitment to teaching. To this end, a series of interviews (with individuals and groups) was undertaken with admissions tutors, course directors and other teacher training staff in 15 English universities and an institution providing School Centred Initial Teacher Training (SCITT).

We provided written details of the scope and purposes of our research prior to the interviews and we gave formal assurances that appropriate steps would be taken to maintain both individual and institutional anonymity. A list of questions, providing a basis for discussion, was sent in advance of the interviews. The following questions were explored: what do you perceive to be the major constraints upon ethnic minority recruitment to, and completion of, PGCEs?; to what extent do your admissions and selection procedures take account of ethnicity?; what special steps, if any, does your institution take to attract ethnic minority teacher-trainees?; to what extent do issues relating to ethnicity feature in your staff training schemes and mentor development programmes?; what strategies do you employ to support ethnic minority students during training?; how are the data supplied by the GTTR utilized by your institution? The interviews were conducted between July and December 1998.

A coding frame was devised on the basis of participants' responses to the core questions in the interview schedule described above. This allowed us to compare and contrast institutional differences across the former 'binary divide' (that is between pre- and post-1992 universities) and also to explore the impact of geographical variations on policy and practice. The results were then compared with independent assessments made by other members of the research team. In adopting this strategy we were cognizant of criticisms that have been made about the reliability of qualitative work (Tooley and Darby 1998; Foster, Gomm and Hammersley 1996). The use of multiple research methods (quantitative and qualitative) enabled us to provide a more comprehensive analysis. Course documentation, prospectuses and other promotional materials, together with evidence from other strands in the research (for example from our student survey), were utilized for purposes of triangulation.

In addition to the SCITT, our research focused on seven 'old' universities and eight 'new'; the later having been polytechnics prior to the abolition of the binary divide in Britain in 1992. The significance, for our study, of the distinction between the old and the new lies in the observations made in the Dearing Report (1997) and other commentators (Modood and Shiner 1994) that the new universities often have better track-records in widening participation and promoting access.

Because of our concern to identify good practice, the investigation focused on institutions with relatively high levels of minority ethnic recruitment. Indeed, over 50 per cent of the minority ethnic trainees accepted for the PGCE in 1996 (GTTR 1997) were located in the institutions in our study. We were aware of the geographical variations in minority ethnic participation in initial teacher training, and in particular the regional concentration in London and southeast England, the Midlands and certain parts of northern England. Two of the institutions in our study were located in northern England, three in the Midlands, four in southeast England and seven in the London area.

The evidence of the gatekeepers

The interviews revealed differences between institutions in the measure taken to attract ethnic minority students. While seven of the universities in our research (which it should be remembered had been drawn specifically from institutions that had been successful, historically, in recruiting ethnic minorities) took no special steps to attract ethnic minority trainees, five institutions used targeted advertising in specialist minority press and other media. The use of 'taster' courses was more common among the new universities.

The variation in recruitment practice was consistent with the long-standing difference between the new and old sectors noted by Coffield and Vignoles (1997). In their paper on access, prepared for the Dearing Inquiry, the post-1992 universities have tended to promote equal opportunities in their public image and they pursue strategies directed towards specific groups. While the institutions in our sample did not experience difficulty in attracting applications from minority ethnic students, there was geographical variation as well as variation between the ethic groups attracted to particular institutions.

Admissions tutors said that their location, closeness to concentrations of minority ethnic populations, and their reputation were the main factors accounting for their relative success. The PGCE course director at one old university said, 'I think ethnic minority students are attracted to this institution in many ways. Not only by the university and the campus and the kind of reputation that the university has got but also by the range of (teaching practice) schools that we work with that have a multi-ethnic, multi-cultural backgrounds. Many students come to us because they feel that their experience of teacher training will be enriched by working in the kind of schools that we work with.' The course director at another old university made a similar point. 'We are definitely not a local provider, I mean it's less than thirty percent of our students who go on into local schools, but people do choose to come here because of the multi-cultural nature of the area.'

Our earlier postal survey had indicated that proximity to place of residence is often a critical factor for many minority ethnic student teachers, particularly mature students with family commitments, and this was confirmed by the interviews. The following response from a tutor at the SCITT makes the point. 'We have older people – not as old as me! – but older people with families, married ladies with families for whom the distance is an accessible distance. The schools are near their homes, this (SCITT) operates near their homes, so that's one of the attractive things. We have got quite a few married ladies (who) need to think about home life and accessibility. And perhaps, if the course was somewhere else, they may not have been as easily accessible.'

An emphasis on establishing and maintaining links with the local community was a common feature in the approach to recruitment taken by most of the institutions in our study. This community orienta-tion was not directed only at ethnic minorities but was part of a broader recruitment strategy. Location in a large, multi-ethnic conurbation was generally regarded as a 'selling point'. The new universities in our study tended to project themselves as local providers with a commitment to equal opportunities and multiculturalism. One new university head of department told us that 'the whole University is very strongly focused on its local community, its regional identity and it's well renowned for its commitment to increasing access to higher education. It was one of the first institutions to start Access courses in order to try and increase the representation of groups historically under-represented in higher education – and that certainly included ethnic minority groups. The School of Education, here, has really taken on the University vision and applied it in the context of teacher education and professional develop-ment. And so our commitment is to serving the educational needs of the local community. It doesn't mean we're introspective. We have interna-tional and national links as well, but we're very keen to work effectively in this urban context and we are keen to recruit students from within the community'. And it is worth re-emphasising, here, that this sense of commitment to the locality did not result in a parochial outlook. Indeed, the same institution also targeted international language students (a fact readily apparent in its course publicity materials) and attracted a significant number of students from abroad.

While the new universities had a more explicit emphasis on local recruitment, this is not to say that the issue was unimportant to the old universities in our sample. Explaining buoyant levels of minority ethnic enrolment, one admissions tutor at an old university told us that 'the most common reason is the content of our course – the vast majority of them said it was the form and structure of our course that attracted them. The second reason was to be near home. But thirdly, because they wanted to be in this city. Over half of them were recommended by a friend.'

Institutions on both sides of the former binary divide and the SCITT in our study deployed a wide variety of recruitment strategies to attract applications from minority ethnic communities. Examples included targeted advertising in the minority ethnic press (for example, *The Voice*, *The Asian Times* and other similar local publications); liaising with community organizations; and offering taster courses for minority ethnic students and other under-represented groups (males, for example). Other approaches included advertising on the world-wide web and the use of local 'black' music stations to promote courses. In their various advertisements, brochures and prospectuses many institutions featured multicultural representations and emphasized their commitment to minority ethnic recruitment. One of our respondents, a tutor at a new university, reported that 'we started a programme that involves support from the TTA for taster courses for people from ethnic minority backgrounds. These are TTA funded in conjunction with two LEAs. We have two programmes this year specifically for ethnic minorities.' The Secondary course director at our SCITT reported that 'we run what are called taster courses funded by the TTA and these are specifically designed – in most cases – to attract ethnic minority candidates. They have been successful in the sense that we've been oversubscribed. These are two-day courses, where they go into schools and they have an opportunity to discuss what it means to be a teacher with other teachers, both here and in the school.' The Primary course director added, 'I think because we have had ethnic minority students in the past there is a grapevine. There are quite a few that come to us because ethnic minority students have had a successful time and have got jobs, I think that's one thing.'

Other respondents also stressed the significance of the 'grapevine' and personal recommendation in minority ethnic recruitment. For example, the course director at one of our new universities accounted for her own institution's success in attracting applicants saying that 'word is out in the community that we run a very successful course with a high percentage of ethnic minorities working in schools with ethnic minority children. Because somebody has actually been here and has family or extended family at university, the word seems to get around. I think, that's why we've been successful.' The Secondary course director at an old university concurred with this view, saying that although her institution had made some use of targeted advertising, it was likely that personal recommendation was a more important influence upon its relatively high levels of minority enrolment. 'We advertise – when we've got the money – in ethnic minority newspapers. But the impact of that must be pretty marginal. I assume it must be word of mouth.'

Perceived constraints on recruitment

A recruitment drive, which has included a television, cinema and poster campaign using the theme that 'No One Forgets a Good Teacher' was running concurrently with our research. We did not seek admissions tutors' views on the campaign but it was raised by them on several occasions in response to our more general question, 'Is there anything you would like us to pass on to the TTA about how they could improve ethnic minority recruitment into teaching?'. The admissions tutor at one of the new universities said, 'I genuinely couldn't because we've been striving for many years to maximize the numbers. But I don't think very much of the TTA's current series of advertisements – "No One Forgets a Good Teacher". That garbage would not attract me into the teaching profession'. And the Secondary course director at an old university said that 'with teacher recruitment generally, there is conflict between the image of the advertising campaign and the other messages from officialdom. For example, the constant derision, and complaints about the standard of teaching – it needs to be more consistent. Don't have Chris Woodhead (from 1994 to 2000 Chief Inspector of Schools) shooting his mouth off. Students are very conscious of the adverse, negative stuff – not the advertising campaign. It needs to focus on the image; teaching needs to be seen as a more professional occupation.'

Our earlier postal survey had indicated that admissions tutors' attitude during early contacts, and at the interview, were influential in students' eventual decisions about training at a particular institutions. The first direct experience that an applicant had of the institution was very important. Twelve institutions reported that they took 'no special steps' to vary their admissions or selection procedures to take account of ethnicity and were often at pains to emphasize that every case was treated on its merits. In those institutions where tutors said they did take special measures when interviewing minority ethnic applicants there was, nevertheless, a reluctance to deploy overtly different criteria, or to vary procedures. Respondents were often guarded and sometimes gave ambivalent accounts of their practices.

One course director in an institution that endeavoured to interview all minority ethnic applicants insisted that there was 'no dilution of quality' as a result of what was described abstractly as 'affirmative action measures'. A tutor at another old university alluded to the controversy surrounding such measures: 'positive discrimination within the existing rules? I think that positive discrimination is an issue, and I think that it's a difficult issue to discuss as a staff.' At the same time, the Primary course director at a new university said, 'We actively seek to offer interviews to any ethnic minority students who apply, and to any men. We offer them the opportunity of an interview but do not lower the standards that they have got to achieve.' Another institution offered advisory interviews for all prospective minority ethnic applicants. They said that potential trainees with 'lower degree classifications would be welcomed' on the basis that, in the words of a Primary course director at an old university, 'the class of degree actually bears no resemblance to what that person is going to end up like as a teacher'. However, the extent to which institutions can continue to operate this kind of flexibility is circumscribed by the stringent course entry requirements laid down by the DfEE and TTA, now reinforced by the publication of institutional Performance Profiles (see TTA 1998). Our respondents said that they thought that the cumulative effect of externally imposed requirements was to leave institutions with very little latitude. The concern for standards, which is shared by all, appears to be increasingly translated into a uniformity of practice that might deny opportunities to respond specifically to cultural and ethnic diversity.

The admissions tutors at many of the institutions in our study said that they wanted to offer all minority ethnic applicants an interview but that this was not straightforward because the GTTR does not provide the institutions with advance information about a candidate's ethnicity. A Primary course admissions tutor at a new university, clearly frustrated by the lack of information, remarked 'we can't actually identify them (minority applicants) because the GTTR takes the ethnic monitoring bit off the form before we get it. But as I said to you earlier, you can guess possibly by looking at their names or place of birth. Whilst we can't lower the standards for the candidates we choose even for interview, we would look favourably at any ethnic minority students, and any men.' Details of candidates' ethnicity are withheld on the grounds that decisions could be negatively influenced by such information. At the time of writing, this data is sent to institutions only after the students have started their courses.

Some institutions have their own databases and monitoring systems in place; these institutions were among the most critical of the data provided (and withheld) by GTTR. A question about use of GTTR data elicited the following response: ' "Used" might be putting it a bit strongly! It's kept a careful eye on. We keep an eye on the proportions of applicants interviewed, given places, etc. It's hard to keep track using the GTTR data because it's retrospective.' One new university head of department said, 'We make very little use of GTTR data. We generate our own data, which is at least as sophisticated and more detailed.'

Despite the reported shortcomings of the GTTR data, five institutions made use of them for *post hoc* monitoring of their intakes on a year-by-year basis, and also as an aid to tracking students' progress during training. One old university tutor reported using these data as one of a series of indicators in its annual quality assurance review. But we found a small number of institutions where the senior staff were unaware even of the existence of the data, and others where no use at all was made of them. An admissions tutor in a new university when asked how GTTR data were used said, 'I don't know who gets it in the institution, or even if anybody even looks at it. No I can't answer that question; I don't know who would be able to answer that one.'

Our postal survey had revealed concern about morale within the teaching profession, the pay and conditions of teachers and the high political profile of education. Admissions tutors articulated similar concerns when discussing their perceptions of the constraints on minority ethnic recruitment to PGCE courses but our respondents suggested that this factor had salience for all candidates irrespective of background. However, one tutor said that she thought that 'students from ethnic minority backgrounds who have higher degrees go elsewhere, they don't go into teaching, that's the problem'. And another tutor said, 'this may be slightly anecdotal evidence but I've heard from certain students that within the Asian and the African Caribbean community, images of teaching may be slightly negative'. Another admissions tutor said, 'the Asian community are often looking for their young people who do well at school – to become doctors, lawyers, accountants – all things with high status and good money; and teaching is not seen as having high status or good money. Young people of Asian origin, and students actually on our course have told me that.'

On several occasions, admissions tutors indicated that they thought that course entry requirements for the PGCE served to prevent some ethnic minority applicants from gaining a place. As we have already seen, some course providers felt that the current entry requirements are inflexible and allowed few opportunities for discretion. In particular, non-UK qualifications were not always recognized. This is a problem where students start their education in one country and continue it in another. Our earlier survey showed that graduates with non-UK qualifications represent an important source of minority ethnic recruitment to PGCE courses. Several institutions reported that a more flexible policy would have enabled them to increase their minority ethnic recruitment. The introduction of Performance Profiles, which include quantitative data on students' prior academic attainments both at school and degree levels, could make admissions tutors reluctant to admit students whose qualifications cannot readily be mapped onto the specifications for the Profiles. Crucially, any degree obtained from an institution outside the UK is recorded in the Profiles as a 'Pass' degree, regardless of the actual achievement of the student concerned (TTA 1998).

Assessment of the impact of Performance Profiles was outside the immediate scope of our study, but admissions tutors' concerns about meeting prescribed entry standards was evident during our interviewing; this was not confined to recruitment of international students. The following comment, from a senior member of staff at a new university is characteristic. 'Now that we have Performance Profiles ... they will demonstrate publicly that institutions such as ours have amongst the lowest 'A' level entry grades and also have the highest proportion of minority ethnic students. The association in the public mind, unfortunately, is not going to be very positive. The pressure, indirectly perhaps, will be to change our admission procedures to try to recruit students who have better 'A' level points.' This suggests a possible limiting factor to the TTA's efforts to increase minority ethnic recruitment into the teaching profession. There is a body of evidence that shows that the overall attainment levels of pupils from African Caribbean and Bangladeshi backgrounds, for example, tend to be lower than those of other ethnic groups (Gillborn and Gipps 1996). The TTA policy of driving up the average 'A' level entry score could press institutions to exclude the very same groups of students from disadvantaged backgrounds that the Higher Education Funding Council is encouraging universities to accept through its Widening Access Initiative (HEFCE 1999).

The issue of qualifications is a greater barrier to recruitment of minority ethnic students to the old universities, which are more likely to be over-subscribed, by well-qualified students, especially in the arts and humanities. The older universities are often able to use high level of entry qualification as a simple and transparent means of selection. As one Secondary course director in an old university put it rather succinctly: 'We are traditional in as much as we say, "You come to us with your degree and we'll decide whether we want to take you or not".' A tutor in another old university said: 'we don't discriminate in any nice or bad sense as far as we know against any particular group of students. The arguments or discussions we have (between ourselves) at the end of our selection interviews are about whether students would be able to survive in an inner-city classroom. We look carefully at those who have been very quiet at interview; who haven't been able to express themselves and don't seem to be very sure of themselves. We certainly don't operate any positive discrimination in any overt way.' An admissions tutor in a new university said that any such measures, if adopted, 'could be a breach of the university's equal opportunities policy and possibly also be in violation of anti-discrimination legislation.' At one of the new universities that is successful in attracting students from Asian backgrounds to its Maths PGCE course, the Secondary course leader noted that, 'our Maths PGCE recruits a large number of male Asian students. However, we are not taking note of ethnicity when selecting for interview or when we interview. We are just simply noting general qualities, you know, communication skills and all that sort of thing.'

Staying on the course or dropping out

Admissions tutors were divided over their assessment of the factors affecting the retention of ethnic minority trainees on the course. Given the proportion of mature trainees among the ethnic minority entrants to PGCE courses, the issue of financial hardship and domestic responsibilities were of particular significance. This had already been apparent from responses to our earlier postal questionnaire. Financial hardship impacts in at least two ways. Some students find that they are unable to complete their course because of lack of funds, while others prejudice their chances of successful completion by taking on part-time jobs to supplement their income. A tutor in an old university said, 'I'm doing some exit interviews at the moment with those who successfully completed the course and I've discovered that a large numbers of them were, in fact, working throughout. They will only tell me now, of course, because they were not supposed to be working.'

Our postal survey had highlighted concerns about students encountering racism in schools. In particular, respondents said they were concerned that they might experience isolation in staff rooms, be 'cold-shouldered' by teaching staff and be confronted by racist attitudes among some pupils. Such concerns have been noted in earlier studies including those by Osler (1997), Jones, Maguire and Watson (1997) and Siraj-Blatchford (1991). Osler's interviews with sixth-form students revealed that Black and Asian teachers were perceived as being given 'a harder time' than their white counterparts. The ethnic minority trainee teachers in her study expressed anxieties about placements in schools in areas with racist activity. The kinds of question raised included whether 'a white tutor could understand their experiences' of racism (Osler 1997, p.179). Osler's study suggests that ethnic minority trainees may be subjected to a variety of additional pressures during their teaching practice. Jones, Maguire and Watson (1997) echo this finding and it suggests that pressure may be less pronounced in multi-ethnic schools where staff tend to be more sensitive to the needs and concerns of minority ethnic trainees.

Although PGCE staff in only a handful of institutions saw explicit racism as a major constraint upon minority ethnic retention they certainly did not convey the impression that they were blasé about the issue. As one Secondary course director at a new university said, 'it's much easier to be a white, freewheeling male of twenty-one. That's the easiest thing to be.' An admissions tutor at another new university said that 'in some of the schools where there aren't any black teachers there is an undercurrent of racism in the staff-room and from the parents.' Another tutor referred to a student who had 'walked into the classroom and the children had said, "Oh, here comes a Paki teacher". But the student didn't tell me about that until she left the school.'

Supporting ethnic minority students

The staff in university departments of education expressed concern about placing trainees in environments where the level of racist activity was perceived to be high. But they were also anxious not to appear to be 'labelling' particular schools or appearing to treat minority ethnic trainees differently from their white peers. An admissions tutor at a new university said, 'there are schools where I wouldn't place certain students from ethnic minority backgrounds because of the pressures they might be subjected to. I'm able to skirt around that to some extent.

Certainly, there are racist tensions in some areas.' The course director at another new university recalled that 'about five or six years ago in a particular part of the city where there was evidence of high activity amongst right wing racist groups, and I remember an Asian student saying, "Hang on, I'm sorry I don't think it's a good idea for me to go there".' Another tutor said that 'we think very carefully before we put black or Asian students in...we do de-select, that's to say we take students out, put some in, it's a really delicate issue.'

There was a broad consensus among those tutors we interviewed that school placement is a sensitive issue which ideally should not be unduly influenced by concerns arising from trainees' ethnicity. Most institutions encouraged their students to gain a broad range of experience in a variety of contexts. They wanted to be supportive while not being overprotective. They were concerned to provide trainees the opportunity to learn from experiences (both positive and negative) while not exposing them to undue risk or pressure. One institution sought to reconcile these competing demands by giving the trainees themselves a large say in their choice of school placement. A tutor in an old university described her approach saying that 'we give a clear indication of the kind of background of the school, its size, what kind of age-groups would be taught, and then we have a "post-it" label system so they can stick their names down and they can elect where to go.' If several trainees wanted to attend a particular school and there were not enough places, they would be encouraged to discuss it among themselves and come to a collective decision. A similar practice was described by the course director at another old university, who said, 'the principle is quite clear. The students select the school they wish to go to based on the information that the schools have provided. They just go through this with their friends. When they go along for their interview that school has been chosen by them, so there is a sort of psychological bonding almost before they get to the school. It hasn't been imposed upon them.'

Many of the tutors we interviewed referred to the significance of peer group networking and student support groups. Some of these were formally constituted within the university education department while others were *ad hoc* 'self- help' groups organized by the students themselves. A tutor in an old university said that 'once they go onto teaching placements we suggest to every cohort of students that there are opportunities for a ethnic minority support group to be set up, if they want it. Most years, there will be some such group set up, a smallish group. That group has the right to talk to me and to the

PGCE sub-committee if there are any issues to bring forward'. A tutor in another old university said 'we make an arrangement – very early in the course – to meet students and talk to them about providing some kind of support forum. We've called it all sorts of things: 'support group', 'discussion group', 'support forum'. We've had lots of words for it. If students want to be part, they are part but if they don't, they needn't be. In fact the majority want to be and they appreciate the opportunities to talk to other people during the year.' The course director at the SCITT said 'there is a high population of ethnic minority trainees on the course who group together, and there is a self-support group. You know, I think that's a very positive thing, it provides affirmation, self-esteem, those kind of things.'

As well as encouraging ethnic minority trainees to develop their own peer networks, many teacher trainers recognized that course modules on multicultural and anti-racist education offer an additional means of support. In one of the new universities trainees were provided with the opportunity to explore 'issues of identity and ethnicity' during the PGCE course induction week. The merits of this particular initiative were described by the Primary course director who said that 'almost everyone who's done that course has said what a difference it made to their feeling of being valued. And all kinds of aspects of their experience being, not only talked about, but seen as something valuable and interesting to discuss.' Despite the potential benefits of such initiatives (for all trainees irrespective of ethnicity) there would appear to be relatively few opportunities for work of this kind in the PGCE. Because of the intensive nature of the course, the current priorities of educational policymakers and the numerous competing demands upon staff time, such work has been largely relegated to the periphery. According to the Primary course director at one of the new universities 'people are feeling greater and greater pressure with numeracy, literacy and science becoming the big areas. There is lots of pressure and students' own subject competence is becoming a big issue.'

Several respondents described the strategies employed in their institutions to offer specialist support to speakers of English as an Additional Language. However, in one old university which had taken particular steps to monitor the progress of trainees experiencing difficulties in English, the staff reported that such trainees were sometimes reluctant to take up offers of extra tutorial help with their written work. In another old university the Secondary course director pointed to the resource implications of such provision, particularly in institutions which recruited internationally. 'We can provide support for written language skills because the institution as a whole has an English Language Unit to service all the overseas students. But they can't provide support in terms of oral and communicative, interactive skills, which really is where the need lies. Some sort of resourcing which would enable us to put courses on either prior to, or towards the beginning of, the PGCE year, together with ongoing support to develop communicative skills. There are resource implications though.'

As we have already seen, tutors often went to considerable lengths to ensure that ethnic minority trainees were adequately supported both in their placement schools and on campus. Some teacher training tutors said that specific account was taken of religious and cultural difference in the allocation of placement schools. For example, a senior member of staff at an old university stressed that every effort was made 'to accommodate student preferences in terms of religious beliefs, dress codes, and other cultural factors'. Despite the efforts of institutions to meet the religious and cultural needs of individual trainees during placement, there could be no guarantee that staff in partnership schools would show the same sensitivity to difference. A senior tutor at an old university said, 'I was just talking with a young Muslim PGCE science student. She says, "There is a problem as soon as I walk into a school. They look at me and they know I'm different, and I'm immediately treated differently". And I didn't know how to respond to her. She feels there's something – perhaps she's just sensitive to the way she's dressed differently to the majority of the people in the school. There was another story, also (involving) a young Muslim. She was allocated to a school in .... She walked into the school and the deputy head, in the middle of the staff room, walked across and said "welcome". And she said, "Sorry, I don't shake hands with men", and he went white. He was so angry (that) he phoned me up. Now this indicates the mentor training that we still need to do. He was an experienced deputy head, had lived in this area twenty years, and he made this elementary cultural mistake.'

At this stage of our research we are unable to say how frequently minority trainees experienced similar incidents during their school placement but a secondary course director at an old university said that in surveys carried out in his institution, reported incidents were 'very, very small indeed'. The same respondent also stated that where such incidents were brought to the attention of university staff, they were dealt with in a prompt manner. For instance, when a student had complained about racist graffiti in one of the lavatories on campus it was 'dealt with within a week. It was taken off the wall, it was painted over, and to me that was an adequate response to an issue that he or she had raised.' While it is a relatively straightforward task to respond robustly to blatant racism, arguably, other more insidious manifestations, such as the 'elementary cultural mistake' referred to above, may be far harder to monitor and challenge. The implications for staff training and mentor development would seem to be self-evident.

Equal opportunities issues, including those relating to ethnicity, did not appear to figure prominently in mentor training and staff development programmes at the institutions in our study. Nevertheless, our respondents did not present themselves as at all blasé about equal opportunities matters. On the contrary, many had a longstanding and active commitment to multiculturalism and anti-racism. However, a number took the view that 'curriculum overload' on the PGCE and the changing priorities of educational policymakers had led to the marginalization of such issues. As one Secondary course director said 'we had a staff development session that focused on equal opportunities and, as a consequence of that, we've got a departmental working party. We used to do more, but everyone is now running to keep up with ICT (and) the English, Maths and Science curriculum. The TTA agenda has crowded out at lot of other issues.' Mentor training programmes were similarly circumscribed according to the head of department at a new university who said that these 'sessions tend to be tightly focused and "instrumental" in their concerns.' But despite the constraints, staff in several universities reported that they had taken steps to ensure that equal opportunities were addressed in their mentor training programmes.

Conclusion

In this chapter we have reported some of the findings from our research at 16 English initial teacher training institutions. This work builds on our earlier postal survey of ethnic minority entrants to the PGCE in 1997–98 (see Carrington *et al.*, 1999a). The chapter has focused on the work of admissions tutors and other key staff at institutions with a relatively buoyant level of minority ethnic recruitment across different parts of the country. The institutions in our research were all located in urban areas with substantial minority ethnic populations. In addition to recruitment practices, we have described some of the strategies employed to support postgraduates during their teacher training courses.

A variety of strategies were employed by teacher training institutions to attract minority ethnic trainees. Their prospectuses, brochures and other promotional materials were found to underline their commitment to cultural pluralism and social inclusion. While some institutions made use of targeted advertising in the ethnic minority press, others sought to promote their teacher training courses via the world-wide web, local black music stations or community organizations. A number of institutions offered prospective minority applicants 'taster' courses or advisory interviews, or were proactive in cultivating links with their local communities. Although the significance of the 'grapevine' and personal recommendations in ethnic minority recruitment was recognized by institutions on both sides of the former binary divide, the 'new' universities and the SCITT seemed to place greater emphasis on local recruitment than the old universities. Although seven of the universities in our study (four old and three new) took no 'special steps' to attract ethnic minority trainees, admissions tutors and other staff did not convey the impression that they were complacent about ethnic minority recruitment.

The staff interviewed recognized that the location of an institution and its academic status were important reasons for success in recruiting ethnic minority trainees. This corresponded with the findings of our earlier postal survey. Although some institutions took special measures in relation to the interviewing of ethnic minority applicants, in general terms, admissions tutors were reluctant to take explicitly 'affirmative action' that might be construed as leading to 'a dilution of quality'. Nonetheless, admissions tutors recognized the need to achieve a better balance in their intakes but complained that the data supplied by the GTTR were, at best, of limited value for this purpose.

A number of admissions tutors said that they felt that the current entry requirements for the PGCE allowed few opportunities for discretion, either in relation to UK applicants or applicants from overseas. In particular, they would have welcomed a more flexible institutional policy with regard to non-UK qualifications. In addition, some interviewees thought that the TTA requirements relating to proficiency in spoken English could serve to deter some international students from applying to the PGCE. Although admissions tutors were divided in their views about the constraints upon ethnic minority recruitment, a number voiced concern about the public image of teaching that was seen to have an adverse impact on all potential entrants to the PGCE, irrespective of ethnicity. With the relatively large proportion of mature trainees among the ethnic minority entrants to PGCE, financial hardship during training was also seen as an additional constraint on ethnic minority recruitment. This factor was also perceived to be a barrier to retention.

While racism in schools was not perceived as a particular barrier to ethnic minority recruitment or retention, tutors were concerned to avoid placing black and Asian trainees in schools where levels of racial harassment were known to be high. Teacher training staff faced a number of dilemmas when allocating ethnic minority trainees to their placement schools. They were concerned to be supportive but not to cosset. They were conscious of the dangers of labelling schools, and they were concerned to be seen by all trainees as acting in a fair and even-handed manner. In some cases tutors reconcile these competing demands by involving the trainees themselves in decisions relating to the allocation of school placements.

A variety of strategies were employed by universities to support ethnic minority trainees both on campus and during school placement. Amongst other things, some staff underlined the important role played by trainee self-support groups and they drew attention to the provision of multicultural and anti-racist education, and to extra-curricular provision of English as an Additional Language. The question of financial support for mature entrants to the PGCE was a matter for concern. Staff said that unless specific measures were adopted to meet their specific needs, the current drive to increase ethnic minority recruitment could founder. Many Black and Asian prospective teachers are 'career changers', who may well balk at the prospect of a significant drop in income during teacher training. In view of the evident tendency for ethnic minority entrants to opt for PGCE places in institutions close to their homes, admissions tutors said that initiatives to extend access in multi-ethnic localities should be encouraged. An expansion of PGCE provision in these areas may be required, coupled with enhanced support for teacher training providers to take a more proactive stance in local recruitment.

As we have indicated in our formal reports to the TTA (Carrington *et al.*, 1999a,b,c and 2000) the existing system of ethnic monitoring needs overhauling. If teacher training institutions are to be encouraged to recruit more ethnic minority trainees, the withholding of GTTR data on the ethnicity of applicants is no longer appropriate. Our research indicates a need for much clearer guidelines for admissions tutors on the issues surrounding the question of 'positive action' and particularly their legal position in this respect.

Acknowledgements

We would like to thank the students and staff whose views we have sought during this research, and the Teacher Training Agency for financial support of the research. In particular, thanks to Jane Benham who was head of teacher supply and recruitment at the TTA at the time of this research. The views and interpretations in this chapter are ours and are not those of the TTA or any other agency.

6
Manufacturing the Global Locality, Customizing the School and Designing Young Workers

Jane Kenway, Peter Kelly and Sue Willis

At the end of the 20th century young people's 'transitions' (Sweet, 1995) from school to work unfold in places which are marked by intensifying globalizing processes. These processes have different implications for different places, schools and identities and they provoke a variety of responses as localities, schools and young people seek to position themselves favorably in relation to other places, institutions and people. Their positioning practices are becoming more and more rationalized and sophisticated. In globalizing economies, localities, schools and young people are threatened with 'permanent disadvantage' (Beck 1992). They are thus almost compelled to manufacture and market an identity.

In this chapter we identify some key logics of globalization and their consequences for the manufacturing of place, school and youthful identities. We tell of the ways in which a remote rural region in the south west of Western Australia harnessed some of the key features of contemporary times to manufacture itself as an archetypal global locality. This chapter also explains how a Vocational Education and Training (VET) programme in a local secondary college in this region was manufactured to fit this location – also drawing on some key logics of contemporary times. We examine the manufacturing of youthful identities, ideal and deficit, by certain class segments of the locality. In so doing we point to the ways in which the 'regional entrepreneurs' in both the school and the locality 'customize' the VET programme in order to 'design' young workers.

Researching VET in globalizing circumstances

Over recent years sponsoring VET programmes in Australian post-secondary schooling has become central to government education policy (see Freeland, 1996; Kenway, Tregenza and Watkins, 1997; Probert, 1995). The emergence of VET has largely been driven by powerful narratives of globalization – about the need for certain skills in competitive global markets. VET policies, purposes and practices are then reduced to and read off from such a view. VET has thus come to be understood mainly in technical and instrumental terms – as both a function of the global economy and as serving a training function for Australian industry in the global economy (Kenway, 1999).

Research into VET in schools has largely adopted this technicist and instrumental mentality and as a consequence it is most often geared towards describing the 'take up' of policy, counting human and other 'inputs and outputs' and identifying 'best practice' models which can be emulated across the field. Such research is often blind to the social and the cultural. Thus these dimensions of local economies, labour markets and communities and the various institutions involved in delivering and supporting VET programmes are largely absent from analysis. Equally, such research is also often blind to the biographies and identities of the diverse range of students who participate in VET programmes.

In contrast, our three-year empirical study[1] is considering VET in schools in changing economic, technological, institutional and cultural contexts in Australia. Through an examination of various aspects of localities (for example, local labour markets, local government policies, local information and communication networks), the project is studying the schools' and the local workplaces' reconstruction of themselves as suppliers of various forms of VET. It is being conducted in 12 schools in two states of Australia and in several different types of locality. However, all the localities have been reconstituted in one way or another as a result of changes in global markets, transnational business practices, the globalization of the market metanarrative and the privatization and downsizing of the provision of state services (Kenway and Kelly, 2000). Through a series of interviews with students, teachers, local business people and community education and training workers, this study is identifying different adults' methods of remaking students and different students' reconstructions of themselves as worker/citizens in the uncertain labour markets of globalizing economies. The male and female students involved come from different socio/cultural backgrounds. All have been anonymized here where we offer a case study of the way in which one locality and one school manufacture, and market, a globally competitive identity.

Global economies of signs and spaces

How are we to understand the processes of globalization? What are their implications for localities, the VET agenda in schools and the identities of young men and women? Scott Lash and John Urry (1994) provide a framework that is useful in this context. They have identified several key features of contemporary times. These include intensified transnational flows, burgeoning aesthetic reflexivity, the increased power of information and communication networks, and the manner in which place is reinforced even as many spatial boundaries are breaking down.

They focus on globalizing 'economies of signs and space' in which objects and subjects are 'amazingly mobile'. They understand this mobility, in terms of 'flows' and point to the vast expansion in transnational 'flows' of 'capital, money, goods, services, people, information, technologies, policies, ideas, images and regulations' (1994, 280). The causes, processes and consequences of different kinds of mobility are key foci for their analysis. Of course, as they say, embodied subjects such as workers and tourists are far less mobile and thus less powerful than digital information flows and the ideas, signs and symbols associated with them (1994, 12).

Overall they observe that such flows are both 'structured and structuring' (p.3). They are 'relatively independent' of individual nation states (p.280) but not entirely free or unregulated. The forms of regulation that they highlight are associated with the continual monitoring and adjusting of these flows by expert systems. Here they refer not only to the rise in importance of particular sorts of expertize associated with developments in industry, science, technology, but also to those associated with new capitalist processes of production, circulation, consumption and accumulation. Accompanying this rise in the activity and influence of abstract and expert knowledge, is a reflexive modality (Beck, Giddens and Lash, 1994; Lash, 1994).

They have developed the notion of aesthetic reflexivity. They believe this is a characteristic of current sign saturated global economies. Such reflexivity is manifest in the rise of what some call 'promotional culture' and others have called 'the aestheticization of everyday life' Here they point to the 'ever-growing centrality of design intensive' production and to the 'increased sign value or image embodied in material objects'. They also observe that with regard to the consumption of goods and services, the expressive components is now seen as the best value to add.

Expert systems and the various reflexivities associated with them are strongly intertwined with what Lash and Urry (1994) call information and communication (I&C) structures. These I&C structures consist of 'the networked channels in which information flows' and the 'spaces in which the acquisition of information-processing capacities take place' (p.121). The construction of these networks and the reflexive monitoring of them have become the domain of various forms of expertize. Production and production relations are still important here, but are 'subordinated' to the information flows and networks (Lash 1994, p.129). Lash (1994) suggests that 'winning' or 'losing' in this context is influenced by 'access to productive capital or production structures', but, additionally and most importantly, by 'access to and place in the new information and communication structures' (p.121).

The sociology of place in globalizing contexts is a key concern of Urry (1995). He explores the ways in which place and its dynamic articulations with wider global forces, fashions the ways local people live and change their lives. His work points to the sociological, cultural and spatial issues associated with the localization of the global through the restructuring of local economies and public services. He is concerned with the rapidly changing 'economic base of place' and draws particular attention to 'economies of signs' via the tourism, holiday and leisure culture industries that have become increasingly important in the regeneration of certain regional economies. A major aspect of Urry's work is the consumption of place. He identifies four aspects and notes that there are contradictions and ambiguities between them. First, he shows how places have become centres for consumption – 'the context in which goods and services are compared, evaluated, purchased and used' (1995, 1). Second, he observes that places are consumed by those who utilize them and that services are provided to enable this, for example, to assist the 'tourist gaze'. Third, he notes that places can be literally consumed in such a way as to deplete their resources. Finally, he says that places can 'consume one's identity'. They can produce 'multiple local enthusiasms, social and political movements, preservation societies, repeat travel patterns, the pleasures of strolling around and so on' (1995, 2). Let us now turn to the locality under scrutiny.

Manufacturing place in global economies

Margaret River is a town (population 3000) and a region in the south west of Western Australia. This locality has positioned itself favourably within the new spaces opened up by the cultural and economic logics of globalizing economies. In this it has not only taken on many features of contemporary economic and cultural forms, it has also attempted to secure some sort of economic and cultural security. In the process, the location has been similtaneously eroded and intensified.

In the early 1970s this was a traditional agricultural (wheat, cows) area in trouble as global processes began to transform the commodity-dependent Australian economy. However, in the 1970s and early 80s there was an inward migration of alternative life-stylers ('hippies'), often disaffected young middle-class professionals who brought with them both intellectual and cultural capital. Over the subsequent two decades, these 'hippies' and the well-heeled 'yuppies' who followed them with investment money and business expertize, led an economic recovery. This eventually involved new primary production in the form of viticulture and the detraditionalization (Giddens 1994a) of older forms of primary production – eg 'gourmet beef'. The region's wineries now produce very fashionable, internationally acclaimed, table wines.

The new arrivals were also instrumental in generating new non-rural industries, drawing on the cultural capital they brought with them, with regard to the visual Arts. Tradition and nature became further commodified. So the region witnessed the emergence of various art and craft 'cottage industries', for example, glass and pottery, hand crafted furniture and 'new antiques'. Equally, leisure, tourism and holidays industries flourished as people came from inland, from the city and eventually from around the world. Surfing became a major attraction, as have other nature-based enterprises such as sightseeing in the caves and bush walking in forests. Here nature has been appropriated, not for production, but for leisure and pleasure. Offering people enhanced opportunities for visually and sensually consuming the environment has become an accepted part of Margaret River's promotional culture.

Many secondary industries have grown up around all the above. They make much of their international connections and sponsorships. These industries include wine tasting at the various vineyards, restaurants, surf shops (surfboards and surfing clothing); *Wet Dreams Surf Accessories* exports all over the world. The area now also holds various festivals and sporting and cultural spectacles – the Coca-Cola Surf Classic, for instance. It has a reputation for its connections to the culture industries. The following gives some flavour (excuse the pun) of the processes reshaping this locality.

.... Leeuwin Estate wines have received outstanding accolades from the international wine press and are exported to 25 countries. Open daily for public tours, comprehensive wine tastings and cellar sales. The award winning restaurant specializes in local produce and is available for private functions. Leeuwin Estate holds a number of concerts in summer, culminating in the famous Leeuwin Concert which features the world's leading musical superstars. WINE FESTIVAL Open all weekend 10am – 4.30pm . . . . .
LUNCH, DINNER, CRAYFISH & CHARDONNAY The restaurant will feature a special lunchtime menu showcasing new season crayfish and Leeuwin Estate chardonnay or enjoy the four course set menu Festival Dinner, accompanied by Leeuwin Estate's fine wines at $90 a head. Crayfish rolls will also be available on the lawns. Be inspired by the talents of master painter, Robert Juniper, who will be completing a work in progress from the verandahs during the Festival weekend.   (http://www.margaret-river-online.com.au/cape/towns/ margarets.htm)

During the Margaret River Food and Wine Festival, thousands of people attend the Leeuwin outdoor concert. Companies from far and wide bus down important international and Australian guests here to enjoy a gourmet picnic and concert at dusk. This high culture/popular culture hybrid involves symphony orchestras, in full dinner dress, and also such international superstars as Elton John, Cleo Laine and Dianna Ross.

Margaret River is not experiencing the rural decline that besets many rural towns in Australia. It cleverly anticipated the rise of the tourist and culture industries – a rise that is a major international trend. Indeed, tourism is one of the largest industries in the world in terms of employment and trade (Urry 1995, p.173). The region has been very successful in attracting investment, people and reputation by promoting itself as a centre for the consumption of both nature and culture. The town's up-to-date, well structured, multilayered, colourful and image-rich website testifies to the ways in which Margaret River deploys digital information flows, and their associated ideas and images, to assist the tourist gaze and encourage people to consume what it produces. This website provides an example of the manufacturing processes – the discourses that are mobilized – to position the local in global economies of signs and spaces.

The website page for Margaret River town says that 'Margaret River is a small town with a mighty reputation'. It was once a service town for the dairy and timber industry. But, the success of the wineries changed all that. The town rubbed the sleep out of its eyes and while the rest of Australia was having a recession, Margaret River and its surrounding district was booming.

The website then identifies the town's assets, which include what might normally be expected in any county town. In addition they include, a 'big tourist bureau', a 'host of specialty shops', 'several superb restaurants and cafes', art galleries, weekend markets and 'a superb Cultural Centre'. Much is made of the growth story and the astounding rise of the cost of land.

> Twenty years ago you could not sell a block in the main street. Now you need several hundred thousand dollars in your hand before you even start looking, and there's not much available.

But the website text makes it clear that too much tourist consumption may, in effect, deplete the very resources and atmosphere which attract tourists in the first place – the 'away from it all' rustic, countryside/sea side allure. So it makes the following assertions pointing both to its 'fierce' insistence on maintaining this feeling factor and its success in so doing.

> These days, the Cape has lost little of the charm it had in the early days of its tourism industry. But that's only because its residents fiercely battle to keep it that way. Thousands of tourists visit . . . every year, and many of them choose to either stay or come back to live. That puts a tremendous amount of pressure on the district's planners to retain its charm while allowing for growth.

Retaining the unspoiled aesthetic while still attracting large numbers of visitors is a highly reflexive process – addressed in part in Margaret River township by a 'low key' tourism development philosophy.

> The local authority in its wisdom set a policy of low-scale tourism development and the community applauded and started to build. Rather than create high-rise resorts the community built a range of accommodation from so called chalets on farms to bed and breakfast in suburban homes, beach side apartments, rural lodges and motels.

Place managers and marketeers form a mutually beneficial alliance. This is common in the selling of places as Kearns and Philo (1993) demonstrate. Furthermore, as the following comment from a local person indicates, the manufacturing of this locality's exclusive and desirable identity has shrewdly identified the particular logics that energize global economies of signs and spaces.

> It's been very cleverly marketed by the real estate agents. We have, for a small town, a huge number of real estate agents. The two storey buildings are the real estate agents. For a little town we have people from Singapore, Germany buying land. Now you name a little town of 3 to 4000 people that you know in Germany. You haven't got a clue. But Margaret River would appear once a week in the paper or an ad. Supplement. So it's very, very cleverly marketed for such a small town, and that has led to huge, silly prices in real estate. Absolutely unbelievable.

The more the local real estate agents produce what Duncan (1992) calls 'elite landscapes' the more they ensure their own status as reflexivity winners.

This website is an example of place advertising. Advertising is a complex form of communication. It is selective and strategic; it advocates and seeks to persuade. It is about *face value* and *best face*. Advertising's 'art of social influence' involves an expert understanding, not only of the utility role of goods and services in the lives of consumers, but also the social and cultural value of goods and services to the consumer (sign value). As Lee (1993) argues, goods and services are used as a form of cultural expression by the consumer. Advertisements also 'produce dream-scapes, collective fantasies and facades' (Zukin 1991, p.219). Through their advertisements, places construct lifestyle dreams – they tap into a whole range of fantasies including, in this case, those of escape.

Place myths

Marketing place results in the development of 'place myths' (Urry, 195, 29). They conceal that which detracts from 'best face'. Such myths usually hide the ways in which place is divided, stratified and conflictual. The following is one view of the divisions which exist in Margaret River.

> There are almost three layers. There are the new comers, people who have come out of the mining towns with quite a bit of money buying into vineyards or local businesses . . . . There are the hippies who went

down there in the 70s, a lot of drug use, big, big drug use. And then there are the farmers, the original families who are quite different again. They're the original settlers who had a country town sort of view.

There is a suggestion that newer populations have displaced old. When the hippies came to town in the 1970s and early 80s (an artefact of history overlooked on the website), there was much local consternation and policing of the boundaries with regard to who was and was not entitled to live in the region and claim it as home. The 'hippies' were seen as invaders, disrupting others' sense of self and their identification with their place. Since then other displacements have occurred.

> You can't be a hippy in Margaret River it's too expensive. Our cheapest house to rent in Margaret River is $150 a week. There may be people who in the past had some ideas of conservation and that sort of thing, recycling whatever, but the hippies have gone. Margaret River is a yuppie town now.

There are, then, some who believe that Margaret River is a middle-class community and playground and others that it is still something of a 'hippy retreat'. But of course it is not that simple. Definitions of 'hippies' vary and hippies change. They are variously associated with drugs, with environmental movements, and with alternative and protest lifestyles. All may apply in the Margaret River region as a whole but one thing is clear, many of the alternative lifestylers of the 1970s have cashed-in their intellectual and cultural capital to become the successful artisans and small business people of the 1990s. Along with the yuppies many are also reflexivity winners. But, there are also outsiders within. For example, some escape fantasies have not been realized.

> Somewhere along the line we ended up with a lot of little urban areas that are quite expensive to live in. A lot of people had come down with a dream from Perth to live the healthy, country life style and hadn't counted on it being economically expensive. Of course you got the situation where mum and dad both had to work to pay the mortgage and the kids are at home unsupervised etc, etc. You were getting these almost ghetto pockets in the town and we were starting to get things for the first time like vandalism, and young people hanging on streets with nothing to do.

New 'landscapes of exlusion' (Sibley, 1992) are emerging.

The manufacturing and marketing of Margaret River itself has also caused division.

> The town itself with tourism and the rest had changed from a sleepy little hollow to a big up market town. A lot of people hadn't coped with that transitional stage and there had been a lot of divides created in the community over different development issues.

Again, this is not the website's tale for tourists, which claims that 'the community applauded low-scale tourist development'. Neither is what follows for the consumption of tourists.

> They don't like tourists in Margaret River. Locals call them terrorists. They rely on the income but they don't like them, they don't want them there. No they only want the money, they want the income but they don't like them. They're a necessary evil. Even the kids don't want them there.

The 'packaging and selling' (Sadler, 1992, 178) of this place then is partly about 'willing away difference' (Carter *et al.*, 1993, p.xiii). It represses those who feel 'displaced', 'dislocated' and 'fragmented' as a result of place making. As Keith and Pile, (1993) show such feelings are not uncommon given that place and identity intersect. But it is also about the identification of difference, where this differentiation marks the place as unique. In the latter instance it is about manufacturing an identity which attempts to connect to new class urban myths of a rural idyll in which caffe latte, chardonnay, the artefacts of artisans, preserved forests and beaches dominate over traditional Australian rural stories of toil, uncertainty and natural calamity. This transformed local identity produces, as we will see, new imperatives for particular types of youthful identities.

Manufacturing enterprising young people

One aspect of the manufacturing of this locality has been a reflexive attempt to structure VET programmes that connect strongly to these transformed economies. Overwhelmingly these VET programmes take as their object the attitudes and behaviours necessary to make young people 'job ready' and 'enterprising'. As a member of the Enterprise Business Centre says '[We need] to help young people see self employment as a viable career option . . . . [M]any people in Australia will be self employed, they will have to buy themselves a job to do. The enterprising, job ready young person is both an ideal and a deficit identity that shapes many of the discourses that circulate in relation to the locality's young people.

Much of Margaret River's new tourist work is casual and seasonal, the demand for local jobs exceeds the supply and full-time jobs are few and far between.

> It's nothing for people to have four and five jobs. Those who have got work, not that many people have got full time work. I mean your accountants and your doctors and your lawyers and those sorts of people do have. But if you haven't got a lot of marketable skills you are going to have to pick up lots of bits and pieces.

For the 'bits and pieces' of work that do exist outside the trades and the services there are just too many people. For the more specialized work on some of the vineyards, employers 'can employ people from all round the world and they're going to take the best'. The casualization of work and the deterioration of working conditions can be understood as a consequence of globalizing economies in which differently energized, invigorate flows of goods and services and wilful bodies (as consumers and workers) intersect in novel ways to restructure work places and work practices. Of singular importance in these new spaces is attitude. The work ethic is a marketable work 'skill' in emerging global economies where, as Urry (1995, p.23) observes, there is 'increasing competition between places to present themselves as attractive to potential investors, employers, tourists, and so on, to promote themselves, to sell themselves as service and skill-rich places.'

In the early 1990s it emerged that the business sector of the town (including Rotary and the Chamber of Commerce – both powerful business networks) was concerned about local young people. They did not seem to be getting the available jobs and their skill base was seen as inadequate to the particular skill needs of this global locality. So was their attitude. There was a belief that their homes had not instilled 'the work ethic'. Some employers even indicated that local young people were not welcome in their shops as either workers or customers. Interestingly, the relaxed lifestyle that was appropriate for hippies and tourists was not seen to be producing the next generation of workers. For Margaret River to continue to sell itself as a 'service and skill rich place' there was a view that young people's attitudes needed to be redesigned. This is evident in the following quote from a community youth worker.

> There was a really negative perception of youth in the district too, that they were undisciplined, they were unreliable, they were all into drugs. It was just this really negative cloud hanging over the youth of the district and people had no tolerance for them whatsoever.

The concerns about un-enterprising youth led to various successful applications for government funding. These processes mobilized the expertise of survey researchers and enterprise consultants to assess the needs of youth in the area and also to find out employers' training needs. When the local Business Enterprise Centre, a branch of a state-wide network, surveyed employers about their training needs, they found considerable dissatisfaction among employers with local young people, many of whom, it appeared, had bought the 'laid back' lifestyle message rather too well. 'Well, if the surf is up, I'm surfing, so you can keep the job'. Employers said,

> the training needs in my business are that I need young employees who know how to smile at people; look them in the eye; have a work ethic that means that if the shop opens at 9.00 you are here at 10 minutes to, not 30 minutes past or sort of lounging in whenever you feel like it; and that you pay attention to the work that you do.

One outcome of these moves was the development of various schemes designed to create enterprising young people. A Youth Council, youth café, skateboard park and 'school shop' were some examples.

An associated community concern in the early 1990s was the fact that Margaret River had no senior high school and that after Year 10 young people had to travel some distance to the nearest senior high school or board away from home. Some left school early. Furthermore, 'there was a lot of agitation' about the existing school which had 'the most run down buildings you've ever seen, deplorable' (Principal) and 'really poor outcomes' (Department of Training officer). After a prolonged campaign from the local community. Years 11 and 12 were added in 1995, along with a A\$6 millionar building upgrade. The timing of this development coincided with the strong emergence of an explicit VET agenda in Australian policy.

The new Principal, appointed in 1994, immediately 'headhunted' the expertise of a VET co-ordinator from another town. The Co-ordinator argued that the school should offer VET programmes which were distinct and scheduled separately from the general educational offerings, a practice which, he says, was 'raging' at the time. The Principal resisted this for a number of reasons, not the least being that with an anticipated total senior school of approximately 125 students (it is now 185+), discrete specialist vocational courses would impair the viability of tertiary admission oriented general programmes which require a 'critical mass' of students. Furthermore, he argued that discrete VET programmes tended to be used as a dumping ground for students with behavioural problems. The Principal also argued the case for a broad general education which would contribute to producing adequate citizens not just adequate employees, otherwise, all 'we're turning out is factory fodder that ... have got the political skills and ... understandings of society and of the environment of 14 year olds.' Nevertheless, he admitted that

> [VET is] the flavour of the month – if you want to pick up your government grants and all that sort of thing, you've got to play that game a little bit. I don't really think that it is the role of schools to train people for jobs but you know [what] the current political climate [is] and educationally its flawed. Schools are not the place to teach people how to do jobs, but schools, nevertheless, have got an obligation to satisfy society's need for productive workers.

And 'play the game' they did, and do exceptionally well, with all the confidence and focus of the community's other entrepreneurs.

All Year 11 and 12 students study six subjects each year. For students aiming to take Tertiary Entrance Examinations (TEE) at least four of their subjects each year will be directed towards the tertiary exams. Of 60 students completing Year 12 in 1996, 36 took this route and almost 30 proceeded to university education. Non-tertiary bound students are strongly encouraged to take four core subjects: English, Mathematics, Computing Fundamentals and Work Studies and select two other subjects. The list of choices includes both general and vocational subjects such as Catering, Food Production, Jewellery, Furniture Woodwork, Arts and Design, Photography, Small Business Management and Enterprise. All students are able to take Structured Workplace Learning (SWL) although they must first enrol in a course in Work Studies.

In many schools in our research project, the general and tertiary education oriented programmes in post-compulsory schooling are considered of high status and their 'purity' is fiercely protected from the down market image of the VET programme. In dramatic contrast, in Margaret River, the TEE option appears sufficiently secure for the school to bring a strongly vocational slant to the post-compulsory years. In its VET courses the school set about carefully crafting spaces in which an enterprising youthful identity might be designed. The school decided that

> [all] upper school students would have access to a comprehensive general education that would best prepare them for further study, employment, enterprising self employment and citizenship. We want to instill in students a sense of empowerment, that sense of I can do what I want as long as I apply myself.... Our idea of vocational education is not just about the skills list.... It's about mentoring our young men and women ready to take a place in society.... It's a holistic education, a general education, it's not specific.

This image of a school connected well with the local middle-class aspirations for their children to have a university oriented 'general' education with all the cultural capital which that entails. It tapped into the concerns of the local employer community about the lack of a 'work ethic' among the town's youth. Finally, it drew, depended and fed upon the town's construction of itself as the entrepreneurial but socially responsible 'village'.

There is a considerable emphasis in all the VET courses on 'enterprise and small business' with small groups of students managing various parts of the school's farm, or undertaking their own projects. Consider, for example, *small business management and enterprise*. At the beginning of the year their teacher designs the course around the interests of groups of students. Of the seven Year 12 students enrolled in 1996, four girls worked in viticulture and they ran the vineyard on the school farm for that year. Their work included organizing the picking of grapes, titrating the grape juice, designing a wine label- and producing a wine for which they won a local competition. Two boys worked in horticulture including building their own facilities, developing a market and selling the products. The school brings in mentors from the local community to support students in their projects, since the teachers themselves rarely have the specific skills needed and, of course, students have access to ready markets in their community. Students have also set up a web-based accommodation guide, which begins:

The place to look for Bed and Breakfast, Chalet or Cottage. Accommodation in one of the best wine producing and surfing areas in Australia. These establishments are helping to support our school, enabling us to provide a better education for our youth. Please quote our internet site when making bookings. If you would like to be listed on this page, contact the school to discuss terms. (http://www.mrshs.wa.edu.au/accom.html)

These sorts of practices are grounded in particular views of an ideal, enterprising youthful identity which is both 'individualized' and 'standardized' (Beck, 1992). In global economies the supply and demand for 'individualized' and 'standardized' (Beck, 1992) capacities, attitudes and resources assume high levels of importance in shaping the life options and chances of individuals. Beck (1992) argues that in 'reflexive modernization' individuals are increasingly released from prior groundings in the 'conscience collective' of class, gender and family relations (p.87). These 'tend to dissolve' in a 'surge of individualization'. Here there is a sense in which individuals 'inside and outside the family' must become makers of their own destiny. The penetration of market relations and of abstract systems into every aspect of life compel the individual to choose. On the other hand and at the same time they promote forms of market and institutional dependency – forms of 'standardization'. So, we see 'livelihood mediated by the market as well as . . . (by) biographical planning and organization' (p.130). For Beck then these processes of 'individualization' are carried by, and indeed, carry processes of 'standardization' (1992).

These processes create a range of new imperatives with which individuals, institutions and localities must engage. In Margaret River this engagement is evident in the school customizing itself as a responsible member of local employers networks, helping them to design 'job ready' young people. At the same time it also responded reflexively to the hopes of young people for access pathways to labour markets – local and beyond.

Manufacturing the village school in a globalized village

The metaphor of the 'nurturing village' is used constantly in the school. The VET Co-ordinator asserts, 'A lot of people see this small community as worth protecting.' In an email to a VET site, the Co-ordinator describes features of the school's structured workplace learning (SWL) programme, and the composition and role of the Committee, (consisting of 'regional entrepreneurs' see Lowe, 1993) set up to oversee it.

> One other bonus is the amount of new businesses recruited by these committee members . . . they really are ambassadors for our program/school and also do a lot of explaining regarding SWL to new employers. . . . This is possible because we are a closed town so to speak – isolated by distance, socially cohesive and just about everyone knows everyone as well.

His notion that Margaret River is 'a closed town' seems to be contradicted by the digital and migratory flows that are part of the school's programmes. Both the school and community regularly connect globally via the web – one web search for 'Margaret River' produced 2829 listings. Further, students' mobility patterns for their workplace learning show that flow is an expectation and feature of the programme – as is connecting to certain forms of professional expertise. Indeed, it is seen by some as good training for their sense of themselves as potentially globally mobile workers.

Students have to use their school holiday periods for Structured Workplace Learning and may travel some distances. For example, one young woman wanted to increase her understanding of nursing,

> . . . and so we put her out and she has done two years work of work base learning, given up her holidays to do it, roughly five weeks a year. At the end of Year 12 she has [been] all around the south to Woodside Maternity Hospital in Fremantle *[300 km north]*, down to Augusta, Margaret River itself and Busselton. So what she's actually done is completed fourteen subjects which is two bonus subjects including four TEE for university entry and two units of the industry specific work base learning course in health and community services. She passed with flying colours . . . and so basically she . . . hasn't had a holiday but sees it as really worthwhile.
>
> (VocEd Co-ordinator)

This student is quoted on the school's website, promoting the SWL programme.

> Witnessing a birth got rid of any doubts I might have had about whether I was suited to being a Registered Nurse/Midwife. I now know this is exactly what I want to do

A boy, particularly talented in science, gained a SWL place at BHP where 'he was fortunate' because 'they had a bit of a problem with the acidity in their effluent ponds'. BHP flew in geophysicists and geologists from all over the world to assess the problem. As a result, in one week, 'he was immersed in the work of an incredibly educated, focused, professional group of people, both men and women.' The school then secured the first placement ever with a particular exploration company which flew him to their uranium mine in the north of the State some 3000 km from Margaret River, boarded him for two weeks and then flew him back. The company has now offered him paid work through his university holidays.

> Now he brought back to us a knowledge of what it is like to work in camp, but what he also said is, I know what university to go to, I know what course to do, I know what to specialize in. He'd been immersed. He was around mentors who were doing what he wanted to do.... I suppose this lad is now more focused. He's now applying for scholarships and using his work place learning, his vocational education, to support his university entrance. He [was able to] pick up vocational education because down here we run everything... 'on the grid'. (VocEd Co-ordinator)

These networks between the school, the business and wider professional communities have been carefully built. They are part of a long-term manufacturing strategy. 'Basically we have a curriculum on one hand but we also have an agenda so that our students are employed locally and that our town retains its youth.' In 1995, one hundred local businesses in the Shire were contacted by the school. They were asked to participate in the school's pilot structured workplace learning programme and to complete a survey which, they were told, would influence the formation of the course. Many of the students in the school's more vocationally oriented courses and SWL are the young people described earlier as lacking the 'work ethic'. The school assured businesses that the students were serious about the programme by pointing out: 'The students have shown how keen they are by being more than willing to give up their holidays to be involved.' The school has also created the spaces to work on 'the look', the aesthetics of the job-ready young person in order to develop and maintain connections to the aesthetic sensibilities of the tourist economy of Margaret River.

These practices have been successful in the school's terms. For example, several teachers recount the story of a student with a Social Security appointed guardian and a series of convictions, who was a serious behavioural problem at school. 'It's been a tumultuous time for all of us involved', but he has now graduated from Year 12 moving immediately into an apprenticeship he found for himself.

When I first asked Doug and Paul to place him, I'd already tried six employers and because of his convictions no one was interested. Doug and Paul were hard lads themselves when they were younger and they said 'yes, we'll take him on, but if he steps out of line you've got to understand that he's going to be hammered back into reality quickly.'

This experience was, according to the school, the 'making of the man' because,

he's got a fantastic work ethic...and it was Doug and Paul down there who actually took the time to be involved with him.... [W]hat they basically gave him was an introduction, for the first time in his life, into the adult world and the responsible side of it, not the drinking, the booze, the drugs side of it.

At the annual graduation ceremony this young male said of his experience:

On my work placements with Doug and Darren...they treated me like a human being. Doug and Paul have worked for most of their lives and set themselves up in houses, blocks of land, car and boats. I looked up to them because of that. I'm going to work my arse off so I can have all of that. I will be laughing when I set myself up in a few years and I will thank Doug and Paul for showing me the path to go down.

Such stories are part of the school's promotional culture – shared with students, parents, the local community and others far away. Two years after its formation, the programme at Margaret River is widely regarded as an example of 'best practice', it has won a number of state awards, and the VET Co-ordinator is often asked to act as an expert SWL consultant to other schools. The school charges the price of two relief teachers for each day he consults.

From the start, the notion of a 'partnership' between school and business community in the education of Margaret River's youth was emphasized by the school. According to the Principal,

In terms of supplying labour to the local market, it [is something I'm] really keen to see and we've been trying to market our school within the community as the place to go when you want to employ people and we really have been quite strong. I mean the structured work base learning that we've done...has allowed us to get out to employers and say, hey look, this is better, this is a much better, much more sophisticated model than the old work experience, this is real and significant learning.

Employers are 'empowered' by the school to assess and grade the student in 30 generic skills chosen from a list provided by the Secondary Education Authority. 'When you start saying to employers, we'll do the teaching and you do the evaluation, their eyes light up.' School promotional material woos and flatters the business community.

> Employers are perceived by the school to be the best people in the community to teach students the 'work ethic'.... One of the lines which I use is that we can't teach the work ethic from an ivory tower... [moreover, employers] know they are making a difference in the lives of our community's young adults and they believe in what they are doing. It's a simple hook really.'
>
> (VocEd Co-ordinator)

The school prides itself on the highly professional approach to the programme, 'we're dealing with professional people so we must deal with it professionally.' It is very sign sensitive. All booklets, letters and information sheets are of high quality. Students on work placements are visited at least twice and the Co-ordinator always has a bottle of school wine ready to give an employer in case of a mistake or misunderstanding. At the end of each placement, students send out a thank you card, with a photo of the student with the employer. The VET Co-ordinator also sends out letters of thanks to employers for their 'continuing support of our community's young adults'. Employers are encouraged to continue their participation in the scheme by being acquainted with the success of the previous years programme and they are informed that the following year's students are ' ... looking forward to learning the "work ethic" from local employers such as yourself'. Business people often place these cards on show next to a sticker, prepared by the school, which states that the business actively supports the SWL programme and provides 'vital training for our community's young adults.'

Some businesses have been 'persuaded' to join the programme by the efforts of the Workplace Learning Committee members. When there was an unusually large number of students requesting positions in the electrical field one year, the manager of one of the largest hotels, also a committee member 'let it be known that sparkies working for the hotel should be involved in the programme. The next day saw three very keen contractors ring us up to enrol.' Other employer participants may have been encouraged by the school's reading of the benefits to businesses of partaking in the SWL programme, which included: 'lift the public profile of your business and receive local community recognition for your active involvement in the program' and 'make the right recruitment decisions'. And in this they are not being sold short. At one graduation, the VocEd Co-ordinator quoted from one youth's report on his work experience:

> A role model for me from workplace learning has been KF. He has taught me about hard work and how much it pays off in the end. He gets up very early every morning to get everything ready for the day. He will never settle for second best when it comes to what he sells. He hand picks all the meat he wants and he makes all his own hams and gourmet food, so the level of quality is just how he wants it. I have learned that if I take pride in my job, work hard and become good at it, I will have no trouble finding work and job satisfaction.

Certainly, SWL is a part of the way in which the school markets itself and it students to local employers. However, as with all such image creation, it glosses over or ignores those who are losers in this process. Students who feel displaced, alienated or fragmented by the programme are unheard by it. The students who previously left school at the end of Year 10, have lost the opportunity to undertake 'work experience' since it was dropped from Year 10 in favour of the Year 11 and 12 SWL. For the 5 per cent who still do not 'come back' after Year 10, there is no opportunity to gain work experience in school. Some students who come back, only really do so for the SWL; 'they didn't like that, they wanted to do their work experience in Year 10, get a job and get the hell out of here . . . they're cheesed off at the end of Year 10, they don't want to be here.'

The fact that participation in SWL requires students to give up their school holiday is heavily promoted by the school as evidence of the student's commitment.

> Plus, if you are keen, you'll do it, and that's what the employers really want. They want a keen kid and that is really showing them that the

kid is keen. We have some of them who say no I don't want to do it. You can look at it as an indication of their attitude. Because those kids who are prepared to give up their time are the ones that are picking up the jobs.

(Deputy Principal)

Some, however, resent this. One young male believed that SWL should be undertaken in school time instead of the holidays. He claimed that many of his school friends felt likewise but had taken the course after being coerced to do so by the Deputy Principal and/or parents. Not all students had succumbed to pressure. Another would have taken the course if he could have undertaken SWL during school time but withdrew, 'Because I had to give up most of my holidays and weekend to do that which I wanted to spend surfing.'

The quality of SWL placements also varies widely. The following examples of one young male's 'good' and 'bad' placements represent typical student experiences.

I went out to Bunyip Galleries . . . that's a fine furniture gallery. Went out there in the workshop and they had a first year apprentice out there and they couldn't really give me anything big to do, because he didn't do much, like he just did what he was asked. So I did a lot of timber stacking and cleaning, and just nothing too big. A lot of sanding or whatever.

In contrast,

I went to the upholstery, Patterson's Upholstery. That was good to look at because I didn't really know much about it, but there might be a bit of woodworking involved in it, like framed furniture and that. And there was a bit. It was quite good, they showed me heaps of stuff about it.

Despite these drawbacks SWL has developed a positive reputation among the students. But, as the following quote shows, it has been forcefully sold.

Interviewer: How many year 11s would be doing structured work based learning?

Student: At least half of them because Mr Cullen was forcing it onto some people, like really trying to make them do it.

Interviewer: Why?
Student: Because we've got the best system in the country.

Conclusion

This chapter is informed by a view of globalization which attends to the changing relationships between globalizing economic, social and cultural influences and place, institutions and selves. Its focus was two-fold – first on local expressions of global trends and processes, and second, on the ways in which a locality and a school manufactured themselves for the purposes of enhancing their life chances and choices. The manufacturing metaphor suggests an active and ongoing process which is 'reflexively monitored' (Giddens 1991) by participants in the process. The sense that something is manufactured provokes a further sense that this is something in a competitive relationship with other manufactured objects, processes and practices, and 'must' thus also be marketed. The manufacturing metaphor also points to the increasingly rationalized processes by which the individuals, institutions and localities which are involved in VET produce their identities in response to the circumstances in which they find themselves. They do so by drawing on increasingly sophisticated, rationalized and aestheticized processes of reflexivity in order to position themselves favourably in relation to other places and participants in global economies of signs and spaces.

We have shown how one small rural location in Australia is consciously manufacuring its identity in transnational flows, the expertise it deploys to do so, the manner in which aestheticization is integral to its place marketing, the way networks are mobilized to assist and the winners and losers which emerge as the locality is redesigned. With regard to the school's VET programme we have shown how it mobilizes information and communication structures and economies of signs to facilitate the training and the management of young people's identities to ensure they become 'job ready' and enterprising young people. A customized and well designed VET programme is a key element in the manufacturing and marketing of this place, this school and these identities.

This narrative is largely about reflexivity winners and how they have manufactured their winning status and seek to sustain it by producing and consuming local youth, and by marginalizing disadvantage and 'unproductive' differences within the locality. As we said earlier, 'winning' or 'losing' is influenced by 'access to productive capital or production structures' and to securing a place in the new information and communication structures of global economies of signs and space. Margaret River is clearly rich in the neccessary natural, cultural, social and financial capital to enable it to respond productively in this context. The reflexivity chances and choices of many of its young people are significantly enhanced as a consequence. Let it be clear though, we do not offer this case as an example of 'best practice' for emulation. Rather, it is a case about the mobilization and sustaining of advantage through the servicing of the advantaged. However, as our wider research project is showing, for those localities with few such advantages, warding off the threat of 'permanent disadvantage' in contemporary times is a much more arduous, less glamorous project (for example Willis and McLelland, 1997). They have the cruel task of grappling with the ugly signs and spaces of globalizing processes in which no one accepts responsibility for manufacturing impoverished localities, customizing residualized schools and designing young unemployed.

Note

1. This project is funded by the Australian Research Council and is being conducted by Jane Kenway, Peter Watkins and Sue Willis, with Peter Kelly and Robin Meulebach as researchers in Victoria, and Peter McLelland and Judy Berman in Western Australia.

7
Development, Democracy and Deviance in Contemporary Sociology of Education

Lynn Davies

Three of the most important strands in sociology of education today are arguably sociology of development, sociology of democracy and sociology of deviance. They are not often put together, but global trends suggest a new combination of thinking which would lead to a more proactive role for sociologists of education. A sociology of development explores why a country is at a particular 'stage' of progress, stasis or regress; a sociology of democracy traces the discourses and policy trends which surround a political movement; and a sociology of deviance analyses the social values in any society by which normality and its opposites are delimited. The imperatives are that there is still little consensus about how a country should attempt to develop in the future; there is nonetheless an international movement towards democratization in many spheres of public life; and there is a continuing violence and lack of peace which threatens both of these, development and democracy.

I take the view that the function of sociology of education is both to provide analytical tools and to promote practice in education likely to enhance the 'progress' of a society. The failure of sociology of education to influence policymakers in many countries has been not just its unpopular critique of government but also its perceived lack of immediate practicality in the face of huge global shifts in the social and power order. Sociologists of education have two immediate tasks: to locate the power of the individual, group or country within the new global order; and to find a value position which is internationally valid and transparent, through which persuasively to engage in their critique of educational policy and educational action. This chapter therefore attempts to provide a way of reconceptualising macro and micro, structure and agency, which can simultaneously explain change (or stagnation) at the system level and acknowledge power for social actors at the individual or group level. To do this, it draws on the newer fields of chaos and complexity theory, and contextualizes such a systems approach through human rights theory and practice.

What brings together sociologies of development, democracy and deviance is of course the age-old sociological question *'who defines?'*. First, by what and whose criteria is a country said to be 'developed', 'developing' or 'under-developed'? Second, what are the definitions of 'democracy' by which a government or an institution can organize and legitimize itself, or an opposition can claim rights? Third, who has the power to define certain behaviours as normal and, therefore, to define other behaviours (and, by extension, other people) as deviant?

These questions have often occupied different branches of sociology. In development terms, the debate has been round the shift from modernization to dependency theory, from the traditional explanation of third world poverty as its failure to 'become modern' on Western terms, to the neo-Marxist analysis of global inequality as resulting from the enforced dependency of developing countries on their richer counterparts through the history of neo-colonialism and exploitation. More recently, these more economic analyses have continued in the critiques of neo-liberalism and of structural adjustment policies pursued by the major banks and agencies. Writing on democracy has on the other hand naturally sprung from political theory and political philosophy as well as from policy sociology and from work on equity and social justice. Deviance has continued to be the realm of interactionist sociology, borrowing from criminology in its aetiology of the 'deviant' and from phenomenology in its exposition of the social construction of everyday norms and of identification of 'the other'.

It can be seen that not just a conjoining of macro and micro, but also of economic, political and social theory, becomes important. The World Bank has identified the trends it expects to have profound consequences for education across the globe over the next 25 years.

The key factors are expected to be democratization, the swing to market economies, globalization, partnerships between the state, parents and communities and technological innovation'.
(*Times Educational Supplement*, 16 April 1999, p.20)

Any sociologist of education can look at that list and perceive the inherent tensions and contestations: do market economies threaten democratization? What happens to the voice (and language/s) of parents and communities under globalization? Does technological innovation promote equality and communication or does it further polarize already divergent groups or countries? And should the World Bank continue to be the key reality definer? Such questions require the forging of a number of arenas of sociological theory, brought together under this concept of the power to define.

Another underpinning concept is also that of *discourse*. Discourses of development range from human capital theory to green movements, from conscientization of the peasants to neo-liberal market ideologies. They are traceable – and often juxtaposed – in government documents, five-year plans, ministerial pronouncements and the mission statements of non-governmental organizations. A variety of discourses of democracy are similarly found in such national documentation, but also in the policy statements from international agencies as far apart as UNESCO and the World Bank. Multi-party states, freedom of opinion and opening up of markets can all come under the heading of democracy (a range of definitions is discussed in Davies 1999a). Discourses of deviance are often to be found in the moral sphere, from religious groups as well as peace organizations; more threateningly, they are also to be found in nationalist movements, through which freedom fighters are distinguished from terrorists, and reclamation is distinguished from invasion.

In all three fields, definitions and discourses are codified in the current striving for *indicators*. Through lists of identifiable measures, countries can be compared on GDP, mortality rates and military spending; on degree of democratization, the Gini coefficient of resource distribution and on access to information; and on indices of corruption and abuses of human rights. The theorising that ensues is based on correlations and on attempts at causation: is a country able to develop because it is democratic, or is democracy a luxury that is possible once a country has reached a sufficient level of economic development? Is corruption a result or a cause of poverty and stagnation in growth? Clearly there are self-reinforcing cycles. The choice of indicators are of course not in themselves value free, and have changed over time: in the mid 1980s, one would find indicators of development such as 'agricultural production per male agricultural worker'. Human Development Reports now not only avoid gender bias but include interesting measures such as the 'profile of human distress' and the 'soldier-teacher ratio'. Deviance and development are brought together not just in the corruption indices but in comparison of issues such as pollution and of 'total number of adult reported rapes' (UNDP 1995–99).

One important benchmark and set of indicators which cut across development, democracy and deviance are of course the international conventions on human rights. Most countries are signatories to some or all of such conventions, whether the original 1948 UN Declaration of Human Rights, the 1989 UN Convention on the Rights of the Child or more regional versions such as the 1981 African Charter on People's Rights. What distinguishes countries is whether they have ratified these conventions in their legal systems and therefore whether the conventions are really influencing social and educational life. The DfEE in England and Wales certainly has not ratified in any legal sense children's right to participation. I will return to the importance of a human rights framework later in the chapter.

Development, democracy and deviance in education

If we look at development, democracy and deviance in the realm of education at present, we can see a number of equally urgent research and policy agendas. In terms of development, first, there is the continuing question of how or whether education can aid development (however this is defined). The research is still contested and shows no clear linkages: if there is a correlation between level of economic development and number of mean years of schooling, the latter may be a result of development rather than a cause. Some studies indicate that schooling may help farmers to be more productive; other studies show no link between schooling and productivity (Bennell, 1999). Literacy is seen as a universal good, and as an indicator of human development would demonstrate links with equity, particularly for women, minority language speakers and those in rural areas. Yet on indicators of economic development, associations are harder to establish: much depends on the types of literacy, their usage and their sustainability. The current drive in England and Wales for a heavily prescribed and orchestrated literacy and numeracy hour, supposed to reverse the decline in competitiveness, may be less good an economic investment than fostering a learning culture, situational literacy and recognition of multiple intelligences.

Another significant link between education and development is the renewed interest in UK of development education. Formerly concerned with 'other' countries, the Department for International Development has established a working party to promote this in schools in UK, working with organizations such as the Development Education Association. This ties in with concerns about global citizenship and environmental issues, and in that sense may not seem a radically politicized avenue. Yet if such an education enables young people to start to challenge foreign aid policy and in particular military policy in terms of sales of arms to doubtful regimes, then it may be seen as threatening. Equally radical may be the exercise of thinking about whether the UK is itself really developed. A reverse use of indicators is in the revealing exercise of '*How developed is your school?*', which uses development indicators such as literacy or energy consumption, as well as access to information and basic freedoms, to enable children to explore how their school would fare if measured in a UNDP human development report (Davies 1999b). At least two Birmingham schools are currently using this as part of their development education curriculum. It is interesting translating the 'index of corruption' into an analysis of how teachers and pupils use power, and translating 'military expenditure' into a measure of the time and money spent on discipline and the use of conventional teacher weapons.

In terms of democracy, secondly, there are the linked concerns of *education for democracy* and *democratic education*, that is, whether schools can educate tomorrow's citizens to create a more democratic society, and simultaneously whether there can be processes within a school or college whereby students can practise the exercise of democracy and be citizens of the school (for example, in UK, Carr and Hartnett 1996; in USA, Apple and Beane, 1999; internationally, Harber and Davies 1997). In 2002 in England and Wales, the citizenship curriculum will become compulsory for secondary schools, and advised for primary schools (QCA 1998). Linked with a resurgence of books on citizenship education (I located over 50 in a recent review, Davies 1999c), the policy has set in train a rash of conferences and workshops on citizenship, together with new training courses for teachers. Various organizations such as the Children's Rights Office and the NSPCC are interested in how UK compares with other European countries in terms of pupil citizenship of the school, and have instigated research which explores the formal legislation of a country on pupil democracy and actual practice in schools and classrooms. The findings are demonstrating a much clearer level of legislation about pupil involvement in countries such as Denmark, Sweden, Germany, Holland and Austria, with student councils as compulsory and pupils legally represented on governing bodies or curriculum committees (Davies and Kirkpatrick, 2000). As said, the DfEE recommendations fall short of such legislation, and it remains to be seen whether non-statutory advice about pupil involvement will generate an insistence on listening to pupil 'voice', and the degree of sophistication in the democratic process so apparent in European schools.

In deviancy terms, thirdly, there is the renewed examination of violence, now including not just bullying, but also violence by teachers in terms of corporal punishment in many parts of the world, as well as the more horrific violence and use of guns in schools in parts of South Africa and USA. I have argued before for the use of deviancy theory to examine the work and behaviour of teachers, and generated typologies of teacher deviance (Davies 1990; Davies 1993); in USA too, there is recognition of schools as perpetrators of *systemic violence* (Epp and Watkinson 1996). In England and Wales the government concern (as well as demonising teachers through Ofsted) is with pupil 'behaviour problems' and the renewal of 'behaviour support units' in which to 'treat' or contain the disaffected. Yet in this round there is perhaps more official recognition than hitherto of the role of the education system itself in generating alienation, and the effects of the stranglehold of the National Curriculum. There is also more support for learning conflict resolution and mediation skills in young people, and for staff as 'learning mentors' who would act as advocates of children rather than simply definers of behaviour. A renewed and refreshed sociology of deviance would move beyond simple labelling theory and deviance amplification spirals to encompass the links between national deviance (for example from international conventions) and teacher and pupil actions.

Jamil Salmi (1999), for example, provides a very interesting typology of violence using four categories: direct violence (for example, homicide and massacre); indirect violence (for example, violence by omission: lack of protection against poverty or accidents); repressive violence (denial of human rights); and alienating violence (racism, living in fear). These categories can be used to examine violence along dimensions of time, space and ideological boundaries, as well as to identify harmful situations in democratic countries where, theoretically, human rights are protected by the rule of law. Applied to education, schools can evidence firstly direct violence in the use of corporal punishment; indirect violence in terms of continuing illiteracy linked to poverty and of discrimination; repressive violence in the form of denial of human rights or of access to information; and alienating violence in terms of the culture of fear, testing and examinations. Conversely, the typology can of course enable us to see where schools act as a direct influence to overcome violence and improve human rights, using peace education, challenging authoritarian governments (as in Korea and Thailand), giving young people skills for productive employment, improving health and empowering underprivileged groups.

I now turn to how to bring together these research agendas and typologies, using the insights of complexity theory.

Theorizing a new sociology of education

The usefulness of the juxtaposition of development, democracy and deviance (the 3Ds) is not just that they share common ground in terms of the 'who defines' question and that they clearly share concerns about human rights. I would argue that they provide a new way into thinking about the perennial concern about linking macro and micro, about structure and agency. Following Giddens' work on structuration (1984; 1990), which argued that structure and action could not form a dualism, and that structure was inherently transformable by agency at any point in time, have emerged concerns to be able to retain *analytical dualism* (Archer, 1995; Willmott, 1999). Without a reification of structure, or returning to determinist Marxist accounts, this means being able to see structure as having a degree of relative autonomy which exists regardless of how actors construe or behave within it. In order to explain how structures act differentially on different actors (sometimes more constraining than others) we have to see a structure as having some independent properties persisting over time and space.

A promising avenue for resolving the issue of dualism is that of the emerging field of *chaos and complexity theory*. Like weather systems, there is the realization that educational organizations may be so complex that they are inherently unpredictable, and their range of developmental possibilities difficult to calculate. Chaos theory provides the recognition that one small event can have huge effects elsewhere – the conventional analogy being a butterfly flapping its wings on one side of the world causing a hurricane on the other. Explanatory variables are exquisitely sensitive to very small differences or initial conditions. Such effects are not completely random, but are the product of a highly complex chain of events and non-linear dynamics. There are scientific and social scientific laws of behaviour to explain broad trends, but they cannot predict the behaviour of individuals. The analogy here is the sand pile: when you pour sand on to a surface through a funnel, it will act according to physical principles to form a conical shape. However, at certain times small 'avalanches' will appear, where cascades of sand form and rush to the bottom. That there will be avalanches, and that in the end the sand pile stays roughly the same shape is predictable, but not the path of an individual grain of sand.

This is not a Foucault-like postmodernism, where everything is relative, and the social world is linguistically constructed. The aim of complexity theory is to make sense of a world that exists objectively regardless of our language games, and has a degree of autonomy outside the people who live in it (Price, 1997). Nonetheless, complexity theory offers a more optimistic view of agency than Foucault, where people have difficulty breaking free of totalitarianisms of the modern era, the discursive formations which govern our lives. Subjectivity is not a creation of language, but objectively real, an emergent property of biological and social life. The key to this is the notion of *self-organizing systems*.

At the same time as chaos, is the acceptance that life is robust – it is continuously overbalancing and correcting itself as we do, unconsciously, when walking on two legs. Complex adaptive systems (CASs) like brains and schools need to balance order with disorder, stasis with turbulence, stability with fluidity. This balance point has been termed *the edge of chaos*. In social organization, people who are trying to satisfy mutual needs unconsciously organize themselves into an economy through myriad acts of buying and selling – this, claims Waldrop (1992), happens without anyone being in charge or consciously planning it. In the same way, atoms apparently search for minimum energy by forming complex bonds with other, making molecules. An important point with regard to human agency is that complexity is a property of a variety of interactions, with the possibility to align themselves into many different configurations. You could have a large number of components, but if there were no possibility to interact, align or organize themselves differently, then this would not be a complex system.

What happens is something called *emergence* – a combination of elements brings about something that was not there before. CASs do not just have high interaction, but generate outcomes which are not linearly related to initial conditions, and have non-obvious or surprising consequences. Culture emerges on a separate level of organization or abstraction from the individuals, organizations or beliefs that constitute it. But it also emerges *in* each individual through socialization, interaction and experience. This is why it is so difficult to pin down something called a 'school culture', let alone make recommendations about its ideal transfer from one institution to another.

There is a sort of Darwinian evolution about this; but there is a difference. Darwinian selection is slow, the product of random mutations very gradually gaining ground. In the emergence arising from complex adaptive systems, this can be relatively sudden, a 'spontaneous order'. Apparently, features such as the eye are difficult to explain through random mutation. Systems do not usually evolve themselves into nothingness, but typically add new features on. Importantly in educational terms, the mechanism for selection is *communicative success*. Some types are more flexible than others and allow for better adjustment to environmental realities. This sounds like the survival of the fittest, that is, in social terms the promotion of the strong or privileged. Yet the point about a self-organizing system is that it seeks balance. This leads to the concept of 'rupture': systems branch and bifurcate, but after three bifurcations, most systems will have exploded into far-from-stable non-linearity. For example, we know that the rich get richer; but if income differences become twice, then four times, then eight, then sixteen times greater between rich and poor, chaos, in the form of non-normative behaviour (that is, riots) is much more likely. The system has to adjust again. Here we see the link to catastrophe theory, where there is abrupt change. This has been applied to war, revolution, prison riots and settlement patterns, as well as curriculum change. Whether one thinks the National Curriculum is a catastrophe is interesting, but it certainly represented an abrupt departure for education in England and Wales.

Between different systems are 'boundaries' and 'boundary conditions', with different types of feedback and feedforward between them. For example, the family produces children; a schooling system is devised dependent on the family being prepared to devolve its responsibility for education; in turn an administrative system is devised to control and supply the schooling system. The family could exist without the schools, but not the other way round. One could not have teachers without learners, managers without someone or something to manage. There is, therefore, a 'threshold' between the two systems, where change clearly effects the next level and where there is asymmetric dependency. Behaviour depends on feedback: does the family still want to send children to school? How do pupils respond to a teacher? Do 'the managed' agree to appraisal or to implement the literacy hour? The significant feature of non-linear dynamics for educational systems and schools is that there is feedback in which internal or external changes to a system produce an *amplifying* effect. A yawn, epidemic or lifestyle can spread through a population. Courtney Brown's analysis of US environmental policy includes data on numerous variables such as environmental degradation, political structure, citizen attitudes and electoral outcomes. It shows how political and policy choices in the USA can produce environmental damage across the globe. Such analyses also show how arms escalation also produces increased tension and the likelihood of war (Eve *et al.*, 1997).

Complexity and change

Complexity theory has great potential, therefore, in our quest for a sociology of development, democracy and deviance – both in its analytical power and its implications for change. 'Structure' and 'agency' can be replaced with the notions of *adaptive system* and *communication*. We can look at both schools and countries as complex adaptive (or maladaptive) systems that rely for survival on feedback, feedforward and non-linear change. This has parallels with Giddens' notion of structures needing agents to reproduce social rules on an everyday basis, but it has greater dynamism and recognition of the importance of timing involved in reproduction or transformation, in terms of the system's current degree of stasis or turbulence. There are semantic problems with the notion of 'structure' in its implications of something static; the notion of a 'system' on the other hand is not the old structural functionalist simple view of a sum of interrelated parts, but something much more fluid and active its search for information.

Admittedly there is still a danger of reifying such a 'system' as existing outside the people who constitute it, yet in the notion of an *adaptive* system, there are the avenues for individual and group influence. These are not 'spaces' in an imperfect structure, but an essential part of the ongoing organization. If, like a brain, a CAS relies on constant feedback loops, then every person in a system is not only capable of contributing but is *necessary* in providing that data. 'Agency' implies the need somehow to 'do' something, but 'communication' – rightly in the information age – simply relies on voice or silence. This gives much more potential than the old role theory notion of 'actors' or the newer versions of 'agents'. You do not have necessarily to 'be empowered' in order to create a butterfly effect. The smallest child provides feedback every minute of the day. The dualism is then of what I shall from here on term '*systems*' and '*voicers*'.

Complexity theory would then be easy with the possibility of 'analytical dualism'. The notion of boundaries and boundary conditions, with 'asymmetric dependencies' between different levels fits well with a view of structures and strata as irreducible at moments of time, from the level of individual, to the school and to the education system. Yet complexity theory provides more potential for understanding gradual and sudden inroads into the workings of the levels. There is, as said, an evolutionary principle, that a system 'learns' from mistakes and successes and has a memory. The difference from a Darwinian theory is the jumps, the sudden emergence, not explainable through random mutation. Marxist theories of control are containable within complexity theory, given the emphasis on different levels in a system, and different dependencies; that the revolution by the proletariat did not appear is also explicable, given that simple cause-and-effect and fluidity in boundaries are also features.

Where chaos and complexity theory needs development in sociological terms is in a theory of power. Significantly, the control of complex adaptive systems is often very dispersed and decentralized. Brains have no master neurone and economies have a frustrating tendency to defy attempts at centralized control. Is this then an apologia for neo-liberal free market ideologies? It would be, except that free markets are of course not free, and still function in the interests of some group or some enterprize. One needs to compute into the model of a human complex adaptive system all the human emotions and patternings of greed and fear as well as love and satisfaction. (Incidentally, ants are at a greater degree of social evolution than humans, and are more skilled at non-violent conflict resolution.)

Complexity theory was originally a theory from maths and physics, and has itself to be 'adapted' to be applicable to the social world. This is not to anthropomorphize a 'system' – it is just that we tend to describe this in human terms of intentionality, a system 'trying' to survive, in that this is how we view ourselves and find it difficult to describe any other way. As McFadden (1995) argued, we need a theoretical framework which allows the discussion of both agency and social structure without rationality being ascribed to the system. Nor is it a return to the notion of a society as an 'organism'. Giddens rejected naturalistic analogies; and as Willmott confirms, education cannot be thought of as a magnetic field of forces, nor as analogous to the lungs of a body/state: 'such naturalistic or biologistic thinking would now be laughed out of sociological court' (1999: p.6). Yet complexity theory, while beginning from biological and physical modelling, does not simply provide parallels and analogies for the social world. In its merging of the social and the physical, in the effects of human agency on the natural world in a complex system, it has explanatory and predictive as well as merely descriptive value.

Communication, knowledge, memory and modelling

Giddens and structuration theory have been criticized as being relatively silent about the likely direction of social change, or analysis of where change is possible (Shilling 1992). While complexity theory by definition would have even less precision about change, (and in that sense cannot be accused of being a 'grand theory' or narrative) it has suppositions which could be tested empirically: that intentionally increasing the amount of communication and feedback in a system would lead to creative turbulence and emergence. This is not just the tackling of Bernstein's (1990) 'relay' of power and meaning, the pedagogic discourse, but (and largely ignored by Bernstein) the reverse flow of information from the subjects of the discourse to the teachers, the mutual *exchange* of (albeit different formations) of 'knowledge' and information. Oppressive class relations will not be altered simply by changing teaching methods, transmission codes or language, but by enabling sufficient channels in a school for articulation of the student voice – and building on this voice. This of course is risky, and requires new modelling; but schools which have, for example, experimented with student councils, with pupils being involved in, say, teacher appointments, have expressed surprise at both the capabilities and creativities of pupils. The key point about feedback is that it must be acted upon: it is not enough to 'give students a voice' and then ignore the implications.

As Willmott admits, Giddens' notion of 'discursive penetration' is an important corrective to the extremes of structural Marxism and normative functionalism, for actors are knowledgeable in their day-to-day activities. But he claims that 'they are not as knowledgeable as Giddens would have us believe'. The aim of sociology is to provide objective accounts of social reality than can and indeed do conflict with actors' accounts – for example, objectively false accounts of working-class opportunities, or reasons for unemployment.

> Yet even if all of the unemployed had full discursive penetration of the capitalist social relations that are responsible for their inability to find work, such knowledgeability may be of little import, for collective action may not issue in the sorts of structural change that is required to provide full employment.
>
> (Giddens 1999:16)

This is the Freirian dilemma, in developing country terms: does the 'conscientization' of the peasants, and their recognition of their domination, actually result in a change in those oppressed relations? It may be that people use their new found literacy to simply move up the hierarchy and become part of the dominator elite. Knowledge alone does not create change: an adaptive system may simply incorporate new knowledges into new strata (as we have seen with information technology experts). What creates emergence is feedforward as well as feedback, when 'voicers' use their knowledge or literacy to create ripples, individually or collectively, when they *provide* sufficient information to lead to new learning and adaptation for a system.

Interestingly, debates on structuration and the portrayal of change in complexity theory both use the concept of 'emergence', although with different meanings. Willmott argues, unlike Shilling, that structure is an 'emergent' level or stratum of social reality, placing real limits on what teachers do. If, as Shilling asserts, 'change is an ever present possibility' then explicating 'why the majority of teachers teach, why the majority of pupils turn up every day and learn and why the Conservative government was able to steamroller through the National Curriculum remains an impossibility' (1999:9). Pupils and teachers do resist; but resistance carries 'structured penalties'. Such penalties are only possible on the basis of existing social relations (teacher–pupil, headteacher–teacher) – they do not inhere within the properties of the individual concerned. Structure has its own effects, since it remains, despite a turnover of occupants. What complexity theory is interested in (if this not to reify a theory) is a second order emergence: how the actions or voices or 'discursive penetrations' of people somehow combine to create a new emergence, different from the sum total of its constituent parts, and once again, not reducible. As I write comes the announcement from USA that for the millennium, Third World debt is to be written off (albeit in a staged fashion). The pop group U2 is being interviewed about their role in this. It is difficult to grasp the suddenness and full implications such an announcement, still less that an ephemeral music group could have been 'agentic' in this. Yet a very complex combination of different forces and discourses will have combined to create this moment of emergence, shaking the structure of first world domination over third world economic spending.

Key concepts within complexity theory to explain stability and sudden change are memory and modelling. History and tradition are far more powerful determinants of how a society is organized than economic or political 'forces' that 19th-century social theory reduced to social 'laws' (Turner, 1997). Behaviour is determined by memory of past interactions, with a 'feed forward' to control the next set of interactions. This is not to say that organizations should remain the same, or should claim the right to act in certain ways because of 'culture' or 'tradition', but that there is usefully a constant process of analyzing whether or why things worked in the past and what else might be needed in the light of predictions about the future. Institutions need to develop and surface their memories.

CASs, secondly, themselves apparently constantly make predictions based on their various internal models of the world. These are not passive models, but can come to life and 'execute' in order to produce behaviour in the system. Obviously, efficient organizations try consciously to predict by making a business or marketing plan. Models are also often 'inside the head', as when a shopper tries to imagine how a new couch might look in the living room, or when a timid employee tries to imagine the consequences of telling off his boss (Waldrop, 1992:177). Anything that we call a 'skill' or 'expertise' is an implicit model – or more precisely a huge set of operating procedures that have been inscribed on the nervous system and refined by years of experience.

But, as Waldrop asks, where do the models come from? Who programmes the programmer? Ultimately the answer is no-one. This was Darwin's great insight, that an agent can improve on its internal models without any paranormal guidance at all. It simply tries the models out and sees how they work in the real world – and – if it survives the experience – adjusts the model to do better next time. This is the basis of cognition and learning, and hence the hallmark of the 'learning organization'.

A superb example of the power of modelling – and of deviance – comes from the Albanian 'parallel' education system engaged in during the 1990s, arising from refusal to participate in the Serb defined and controlled education system. Kosovar Albanians set up an entire system, from early years to university, which 'paralleled' the official system, and took place in people's houses or cellars, paid for by a tax and by outside donations (Davies 1999d). In Ofsted terms, it would not have been a 'quality' system, but it had a number of agendas. The 'internationalization' of the problem was a key strategy, showing that the status of Kosova was not just an internal question for Serbia. As the historian Noel Malcolm points out, by setting up the institutions of a separate republic, the Albanians of Kosovo have engaged in a strategy of political 'as if':

> To behave as if Kosovo were not part of Serbia might seem, in the short term, sheer make-believe; but if the strategy were persisted in for long enough, foreign governments might eventually feel obliged to admit that they were the ones who were engaging in fiction when they continued to treat Kosovo as a mere region of the Serbian state.
>
> (1998: 348)

This was indeed borne out by the eventual intervention of NATO.

Human rights and transformative deviance

In the end, however, we do not need to privilege either structure or agency, system or communication, and can continue to research at different sites (Shilling 1992). If we see a CAS *as* patterned sets of communications and complex feedback loops, then we can look at micro and macro levels in terms of degrees of difference in both access to information and how far voices are heard and accepted. In the end, it is human beings who control the communication flows; it seems obvious that people are constrained by the communication and discourse available, but that they are simultaneously central to the onward transmission of that communication and discourse. It seems pointless to argue over whether one approach is 'weak' on structure or 'weak' on agency; our question is where communication is located and how control at one level or site impacts on behaviour at another. Seeing 'the labour market' as a complex adaptive system is not to deny human agency; it would form a complex adaptive system precisely because of people's fluidity in their understandings and communication of it, and the possibility to align themselves differently within it. Do gender relations constitute a CAS? Yes, in that, again, there is always the possibility for people to align themselves differently, as has happened continuously in the past; yet whether there has been sufficient turbulence to bring a gender system to the edge of chaos in most countries would be a point of argument, even if feminists might claim some sort of 'emergence'. This is again where deviance and resistance is so crucial.

> What resistance theory fails to capture is the variation in the responses to schooling which arise from the intersection of student and teachers perspectives, perception and expectations, particularly when such intersections involve a variety of modes of masculinity, femininity, class, race and ethnicity. Different combinations of these cultural modes allow different patterns of resistance and action in the school context. An alternative interpretation then of the evidence on student resistance is that students from certain kinds of backgrounds have experiences of schooling which restrict their opportunity to extend their knowledge. The response to this form of schooling for many students is to resist it.
>
> (McFadden 1995 p.297)

Complexity theory is powerful here in two ways: first, in the recognition of the search for knowledge and second in recognition of recombinant phenomena, that is, how deviance is not reducible to a simple class based, or gender based resistance, but draws on complex forms of realignment. This recalls some earlier work on pupil deviance, where I was initially puzzled by the huge range of scripts that girls could draw on, and the lack of predictable alliances (Davies, 1984). When one looks at the creative and infinitely elaborate ways we all have to draw on cultural and social resources, one wonders how patterns become possible, and CASs survive. They are not constantly on the edge of chaos. They survive of course because of mutual dependencies, and sufficient shared communicative competences and communicative histories to preclude the need for constant negotiation and expression. Here Walker's (1993) notion of social structures not as determining 'external objects' but as 'sets of options' is still relevant, even if pedagogic inequality breeds a restricted knowledge base which restricts the options and possibilities that people see for themselves.

This is why we need a new sociology of deviance which comes off the relativist fence to distinguish 'transformative' from 'reproductive' resistance. The latter characterized the girls in this above-mentioned study, whereby their resistance to schooling merely in the end confirmed their position in the working-class order, as well as in the gender order. Resistance studies, in the tradition of Willis (1977) onwards, have tended to focus on such confirmation of class identity. Transformative deviance on the other hand is that which actually changes individual life or collective opportunity. A Swedish colleague and I engaged in a study to trace the 'influence' of girls, distinguishing this from resistance, in attempting to locate means by which girls, acting collectively, and using various sources and resources, are able to effect change in their school or class (Ohrn and Davies 1999). A key concept from complexity theory is that of 'mutants' – those people or configurations who disrupt the 'normal' feedback flows to create 'self-organized criticality'. This is where deviance comes in, as we see the possibility of the creative mutant who starts a process breaking down the previous equilibrium; of questioning a new critical path.

Particularly in linking development and democracy it is inadvisable to regress to relativism. One particular phenomenon of global 'emergence' has been the growth of conventions on human rights. While there are critiques of the universality of human rights, and the accusation that although the UDHR was ratified by the UN General Assembly, the worldview it represents is historically grounded in European traditions, it nonetheless has had huge global implications. Despite sharp differences among delegates from North and South, the 1993 World Conference on Human Rights reaffirmed the universal, indivisible and inalienable nature of human rights, including that of the right to development (Eade, 1998). A political sociology of deviance might examine the real turbulence in a system, but use a rights based approach: one could in fact distinguish not two but three types of deviance, in terms of its effects: those who deviate from the norms of human rights (negative deviance); those who deviate from oppressive rules, but reproduce the status quo in other ways (reproductive deviance); and those who deviate from oppressive rules to claim rights, and in so doing create positive change (transformative deviance).

To judge which is which links with a central feature of democracy and of a human rights approach to development, that of accountability. Leys (1996), in his critical account *The Rise and Fall of Development Theory* concluded that for the survival of poorer countries, a more open global market for goods and capital was required which would have to be more representative of, and accountable to, people (as opposed to wealth) than most current global institutions: 'For all countries of the world, recapturing control over their own destinies requires the re-establishment of social control over capital and the resubordination of markets to social purposes' (p.194). The current *de facto* colonization of Africa by aid consortia, World Bank structural adjustment teams, the UN High Commission for Refugees, the UN Food Programme and a host of other agencies could also be transformed:

> it could give way to a new long-term, open and accountable system of collaboration between domestic and supranational political leaders and public servants, based on principles of mutual interest in creating the economic and social preconditions for a new and more genuine sovereignty... in some sectors more scope will need to be given to markets, in others more attention will have to be paid to the construction of non-market institutions that are resistant to politicization and corruption and yield socially efficient results.
>
> (1996:195)

I would argue that some version of democracy – while not perfect – is the least worst way we know of providing the maximum feedback, openness and accountability. People are legitimately able to voice their opinions, to remove the maladaptive or authoritarian from office, and to question the levels and hierarchies of the system. Those in power have agreed mechanisms for justifying their actions, establishing what people think on a systematic basis and having to adapt accordingly.

Schools are of course smaller CASs, but with the same features: the need for constant feedback and feedforward, and implicitly, the need for a transparent and democratic set of processes which allow for such information flows. Technology can provide management information systems, and sophisticated ways of amassing data on pupil inputs and outcomes; what many schools still lack are DIMS, or *democracy information management systems*, those regularized transfers of accountability, ways of conveying and sharing qualitative information about pupil (as well as teacher) feelings, voices, perceptions, understandings, and, most crucially, suggestions for improvement. Perhaps another definition of developmental democracy *is* self-organizing criticality: processes of accountability are not just revealing information, about checks and balances, but about learning from success and failure.

'Voices' in development

This leads to the need to identify the sites for such accountability. Clearly there are different levels of 'voice', from organizations down to the individual. National development requires a 'dense web' of 'intermediate institutions' (banks, financial and technical services, training, and infra-structure of all kinds,) that the market needs but does not itself provide (Leys 1996). Sklar (1996) has a different classification of 'developmental estates of the realm', the classification of groups that contribute to national development. His theory of developmental democracy parallels Durkheim's identification of 'organic solidarity' in the suggestion that developmental democracy is founded on a powerful norm of political conduct, namely accountability, which is manifest in two ways – first, organized groups of all kinds – social, economic, political, professional, administrative and others – are accountable to each other in accordance with settled rules of interactive conduct; second, groups promote the interests of their members when leaders are accountable to the followers by which they are chosen. But Sklar questions a 'whole system' view:

> In all countries, democracy is manifest in diverse forms, or fragments, which reinforce one another in the production of developmental effects. This conception of democracy 'in parts' is an alternative to whole-system conceptions of democracy that are neither realistic nor scientific, as opposed to ideological.

> (1996: 40)

Such fragments might be freedom of the press, or guaranteed health services, or equal protection of the law, or elements of industrial democracy.

At first sight, this rejection of a whole system approach seems to lie at odds with a CAS analysis. Yet in fact it fits very well. The 'fragments' of democracy are the ways to create turbulence, the dynamism that characterizes a society that develops. The phrase is the 'self-organizing system'. As Leftwich points out:

> to expect that heavy doses of externally imposed conditionality will yield either good governance in the managerial sense of stable democracy in the liberal pluralist sense – let alone sustained economic development... seems naive to say the least. The only social process that can both institute and sustain both good governance and democracy is the process we know as politics which I defined earlier as consisting of all the processes of conflict, cooperation and negotiation involved in the use, production and distribution of resources.
>
> (1996:37)

This perhaps reflects Manji's (1998) argument that the development discourse has served to deflect the more radical, rights-based forms of mobilization that spearheaded the liberation struggles in many countries. There has been a 'depoliticization of poverty', often exacerbated by the work of NGOs claiming to be neutral in their assistance. As Eade (1998) summarizes:

> Instead of exercising their rights to participate in shaping their societies, people are at best offered the opportunity to participate in top-down development projects that all too often act as a vehicle by which their existing rights and values are still further undermined.
>
> (p.9)

If one translates the above into the school, one finds a similar denial of rights, as children are at best offered the opportunity to participate in a top-down curriculum. There has to be a repoliticization of both poverty and schooling, with a rights, not an aid focus.

Trying to catch the rain

One child – identified as deviant, naturally – from some Birmingham research on literacy and truancy was explaining to an interviewer from the Basic Skills Agency his continual absence from school. He reflected his despair in understanding teachers, as follows:

> In some lessons, the words just come at you all the time. You can only get some. It's like trying to catch the rain.

The insight from complexity theory is that all feedback is useful feedback in some way or other, and the powerful image expressed by this so-called illiterate child would be significant information. We should listen to our deviants more – not just for what they tell us about the reasons for their personal mutation, but for what they tell us about the system and how they may be impacting on that system. The sub-title of this whole chapter could well be 'trying to catch the rain'. Just as in a brain, with neurons firing in all directions, schools and nations are a mass of potential information flows, reflecting and bouncing from every cell/participant. The distinction between a brain and a fragile state is not just the degree and speed of the transmission, but that – unlike brains – fragile states and fragile schools choose to ignore vital information. All members are reflectors, and many can be trained to reflect precisely the messages that are fired at them. But a CAS needs deviants, mutants, reflexors who angle things differently, who generate different sets of information and fire them at different recipients. We need a sociology of turbulence, which can explain dynamic change, upheaval and positive emergence as well as what appears to be the collapse of a system.

A three Ds sociology then combines a policy sociology – the analysis of the top-down – and a deviancy sociology – the bottom-up small but transformative effect. We know that power is asymmetric, but also that the exercise of power needs a response from those being governed or controlled. My own field of working with international students, teachers and managers fortunately provides a host of examples of the butterfly effect, ranging from the inspector who returned to their country to instigate a new inspection policy in the Gambia, to the 16-year-old school students' union representative from Denmark who came to a conference in England, whose participants then, impressed by her eloquence and agency, put pressure on DfEE to introduce more democracy into the system. Chains of events must be seen not as 'constrained' by the system, but as moving about, bouncing from one voicer to another, like balls turning on the lights in a pinball machine.

Put simply, then, in order to develop, a country needs creative and positive turbulence arising from a complex communication system; politically and educationally, democracy is the best way we know to ensure that communication; and the study of deviance is a key tool in establishing who holds the power to define normality or chaos, reproduction or transformation. Structuration theory cannot easily explain change and emergence; complexity theory provides a framework to understand education systems and social systems as complex adaptive ones, with the adaptation requiring mutants/deviants and non-linear dynamics. Analytically, complexity theory provides strong explanatory and predictive power; but strategically, education also needs a value component; and a human rights framework is what gives sense and life to the 3Ds of development, democracy and deviance, and locates the type of emergence that we want.

8
The Sociology of Comparative Education

Lawrence Saha

The comparative study of educational systems has a long history. The field can be traced to the early 19th century when it became common for European governments to send emissaries abroad to find out how education was carried out in other countries. About the same time the practice became more structured and of interest to academics, as well as practitioners and policymakers, and the subject of comparative education came into being (Epstein, 1994; Holms, 1965).

The status of comparative education has frequently been debated in academic circles, in particular whether it should be considered an interdisciplinary field of study or a discipline in its own right. Comparative education can be defined simply as the study of the variations in educational systems and processes, and how education relates to wider social factors and forces. In this respect it is an academic and interdisciplinary field of study, and includes scholars from historical, philosophical, sociological and anthropological backgrounds, to name but a few (Epstein, 1994).

Just as comparative education incorporates interdisciplinary interests, it also serves a multiplicity of academic and policy related functions. The comparative study of education has provided a rich source of knowledge about how education functions in different social, political and cultural contexts. In this respect, the search for more than descriptions, but rather for universal educational principals has been greatly enhanced by comparative educational research (Keeves and Adams, 1994; Paulston, 1994). In addition, however, comparative education research has provided the basis for national debates about educational issues in many countries. It has similarly provided the basis for guidelines and models in the development of educational policy and planning programmes. Finally, it has had enormous input into the lending and funding programmes of international organizations, such as the World Bank (Altbach, 1991), and national aid organizations such as NORAD (Norway) and SIDA (Sweden).

This interdisciplinarity of comparative education is also reflected in the methodology used in the gathering and analysis of comparative educational data. Comparative education research has been both humanistic and scientific, and quantitative and qualitative (Keeves and Adams, 1994). A recent survey of research strategies in comparative education, focusing specifically on three journals, *Comparative Education Review*, *Comparative Education*, and the *International Journal of Educational Development*, found interesting shifts in research direction from the 1950s to the 1990s (Rust *et al.*, 1999). While most research published during this period tended to be qualitative in nature, the authors noted an increase in quantitative research from the 1960s to the period 1985–95. The authors also noted that earlier research tended to focus on the developed countries, while research in the same three journals in the 1985–95 period was much broader and focused on both developed and developing countries. The authors conclude that the field of comparative education is 'methodologically fragmented and pluralistic' (Rust *et al.*, 1999: 107). It is clearly a changing field.

One growing feature of comparative education has been its emphasis on Third World education, and in particular, the role that education plays in furthering the economic and social development of these countries (Altbach, 1991). Holms (1965), in the early period of the establishment of comparative education as an academic field, noted its role in educational policy and planning. Against the backdrop of the reconstruction period of the Second World War, he observed that the comparative study of education identified how education could exercise a role in the technological, political and economic development of societies.

Comparative education and the relationship between education and development have not traditionally been seen to be parts of the sociology of education. Sociologists of education have conducted considerable research in developing countries on educational issues related to development. However much of this research has tended to be identified with comparative education rather than the sociology of education. Thus much of the research in the sociology of education and development can be more easily found in comparative education journals than in sociology of education journals. This is a tendency that will probably continue.

Having said this, however, the relationship between education and socio-economic development, in both industrial and less-industrialized countries, has been extensively researched from a sociological perspective. In many respects, this body of research has had considerable impact on third world development policies where education has been involved, especially through the impact of bodies like the World Bank, Unesco and the Asia Development Bank. It is also true to say that the sociology of education and development is among the more interdisciplinary subfields of the sociology of education. Thus much of the research in this field draws upon research in the economics of development, the politics of development and the social psychology of development. In this respect, the field of education and development is rich in its theoretical and methodological contribution to sociology generally. But because this research is comparative in nature, much of comparative educational research is a part of the sociology of education generally.

Theories in comparative education

There are no theories that are unique to comparative education. This is not to say, however, that the field is without theory. In fact researchers have tended to borrow from a wide range of theories, ranging from human capital theory, to critical theory and postmodern theory. Paulston (1994), who noted that the early history of the field was descriptive and inductive, has produced a recent description of the theoretical developments in comparative education. Since the 1970s he argues that the field has become more heterogeneous in its use of deductive theories and methodologies. Furthermore, he points out that the theoretical development of comparative studies of education and development have shifted ' . . . in knowledge framing, from the traditional social, behavioral and Marxist science models to those of language, culture and the interpretive humanities' (Paulston, 1994: 928).

The issues in these debates rested on the assumption that a unitary theoretical approach, or theoretical orthodoxy, within the field was somehow necessary and desirable for scientific legitimacy. However, as is true in sociology generally, theories specify the focus of study, so that theories do not compete among themselves except insofar as the foci of the theories are seen to have high or low priority in research and policy. The view that theoretical approaches might be complementary rather than competitive began to emerge in the late 1980s (Keeves, 1988), and an argument for paradigmatic pluralism in education research generally was put forward at the end of the century (Husén, 1997).

In this context, the following sections provide a brief coverage of the main theoretical paradigms, both their strengths and weaknesses, which can be found in comparative education at the end of the 1990s. These theories are presented under four major paradigmatic headings, called perspectives: neo-liberal perspectives, radical perspectives, critical perspectives and postmodernist perspectives.

Neo-liberal perspectives

Perhaps one of the most dominant theoretical perspectives has been human capital theory. Human capital theory postulates that education contributes to socio-economic development by improving the quality of human capital, and it directs attention to the study of improvements in human productivity through education. Sociological research guided by human capital theory tends to focus on various forms of rate-of-return or cost-benefit analyses. From this perspective, sociological research into the relationship between education and development overlaps considerably with economic research.

A second dominant theoretical perspective in the study of education and development, and one that is more sociological, is modernization theory. Modernization theory assumes that education promotes socio-economic development by creating people who will hold modern values and thus behave in a modern manner. Sociologists who take this perspective tend to focus attention on the attitudes, beliefs and behaviours of individuals, and they argue that a primary purpose of education is to foster the acquisition of a modern outlook by individuals in society.

Both the human capital theory and modernization theory reflect a neo-liberal ideology and since the mid 1950s have dominated much research and policy in the education and development field. They also have been extensively criticized for being largely Western-centered and too capitalistic in orientation. (For a thorough criticism of these theories, see Fägerlind and Saha, 1989.) Still within the neo-liberal framework, the theoretical perspective which has emerged in the last decade, and which looks like dominating much of the research and policy in the education and development field is globalization theory.

Globalization theory, and its variations, assumes that the local, regional and national boundaries of social institutions are breaking down and a 'new order' of international competition based on flexible production is emerging at a world level. With respect to issues related to education and development, globalization theory focuses attention on the acquisition of flexible worker and management skills. The idea behind this theoretical approach is that in the new global environment, flexible and life-long education assume greater importance so that a country's workforce is able to make quick and effective adjustments to the development of new technologies and meet new industrial needs.

Radical perspectives

A second group of theories that are important in the sociology of education and development take a more cautious approach regarding the role of education in the development process. Those who use these theories to analyze the development process focus their attention on inequalities in society as a measure of development itself. They regard education as much a cause of those inequalities as well as a way of overcoming them. A primary concern with theorists within this perspective is how to reform education based on Western capitalist models so that the perpetuation of privilege and wealth through the education system does not continue. Two theories which fall within this perspective, and which are to some extent still influential in the education and development field, are conflict theory and dependency theory.

Conflict theory, like modernization theory, is eminently sociological. It has its sociological roots in the writings of Weber and Marx and is based on the assumption that conflict is a normal condition of society, and that conflict has its origins in the domination of one group or groups by another group or groups. For Weber these groups can be defined in terms of class, status and power, whereas for Marx they can be defined in terms of economic class alone. The Marxist version of conflict, both in its original orthodox form or in its newer manifestations in reproduction and resistance theory, assumes that conflict is manifested in forms of exploitation and oppression.

Conflict theorists have as their ideal model of development the attainment of a society which has a high level of equity, an open opportunity structure and no discrimination or exploitation. In order to bring this about, an educational system that breaks the cycle of reproduction is needed. This implies the possibility of schools that are ideologically and culturally integrated into the subgroups they serve, and also the possibility of some level of affirmation of action in schools to encourage students from disadvantaged or oppressed backgrounds.

Dependency theory shares many of the assumptions of conflict theory, except that the major focus on development is on the attainment of self-determination, and social and economic sustainability. Those who adhere to dependency theory argue that an obstacle in the development process is the social, cultural and economic dependency of one society on another. Thus a major source of the absence of development lies outside a society and on external rather than internal factors.

Given these assumptions the role of education is much the same as for the conflict theorists. As long as the educational system operates in the interests of maintaining dependency, it will serve as an obstacle to development. Education can reinforce dependency by producing graduates who will be more committed and oriented toward success in jobs and careers which are not in the best interests of their own society. In a similar fashion, their political views are such that they are committed to maintaining liaisons with external political figures. Therefore, from within the dependency perspective the main role of education is to help break the dependency cycle. One way of promoting this break is through consciousness raising and political mobilization, and a sense of citizenship which values autonomy and sustainability rather than dependence.

The critical perspective

A critical approach to issues of education and development actually incorporates two theoretical paradigms, namely that of critical theory and that of post-colonial theory. These approaches are not often overtly espoused in education and development research. Nevertheless, they do appear implicitly in much of the education and development literature.

The basis of critical theory implies 'uncovering hidden assumptions and debunking their claims to authority' (Abercrombie *et al.*, 1994: 94). The theory traces its origins back to the writings of the Frankfurt School which was concerned with unmasking forms of oppression in society and, thereby, bring about the emancipation of members and groups. Those who adopt this theoretical approach in the study of education tend to see schooling as a source of oppression, primarily through the 'hidden curriculum' and the process of 'deskilling'. The consequence of these forms of oppression is the perpetuation of the exploitation of the disadvantaged in society.

The model of development which the critical theorists espouse is the construction of a society in which there is freedom from exploitation and hidden sources of oppression and exploitation. This can be achieved, it is thought, by introducing into the curriculum the learning of empowerment skills, which includes citizenship and civic education. In the development context, the writings of Paulo Friere and the notion of 'conscientization' has been seen as a key concept in this liberation or 'unmasking' process (Friere, 1970, 1973). In the third world, literacy programmes and various forms of popular education are manifestations of this type of application of critical theory (Evans, 1997).

Somewhat related to critical theory, and still within the critical paradigm, is post-colonial theory. The notion of post-colonialism is probably best traced back to the publication of Said's *Orientalism* (1979) where it was argued that only by understanding oriental culture as understood and experienced by orientals, can one understand the European culture which produced it. Thus the post-colonial perspective has entered into the education and development literature in attempts to free the school curriculum in many third world countries from the cultural dominance of outside influence. Thus a focus on national culture, national identity, national consciousness and national self-confidence are all a part of the application of a postcolonial perspective to education and development.

Postmodernist perspectives

The final theoretical approach which sometimes is found in sociological studies of education in development is that of postmodernism. Post-modernism is an intellectual perspective that holds that the dominance of an overarching belief in 'scientific rationality' and a unitary theory of progress and development has come to an end. In its place is a stronger reliance on culture, signs, images and a plurality of viewpoints about social forces and social change. In this respect, postmodernists question whether rational thought and technological advance alone can guarantee development and progress.

The postmodernists adhere to a high level of social and intellectual pluralism and high tolerance. In this context, the postmodernists are similar to the critical theorists in that they seek the liberation of intellectual pursuits from the dominance of the 'modern' set of cultural beliefs, such as theories of development and progress. The postmodernists instead advocate a plurality of ideas, with no clear policy implications for the state, because under postmodernist conditions, the state loses control over knowledge. Thus for the postmodernists, it does not make sense to speak of development in the conventional 'modernist' sense. The role of education in a development context, then, is to subject all knowledge to criticism (deconstructionism) and accept a plurality of knowledge systems.

These theories, to a greater or lesser degree, represent the various approaches which one can find in the education and development literature, in both Western developed countries as well as third world countries. Each theoretical approach contains its own set of assumptions about development, and how education should be structured to attain development goals. During the 1960s and 1970s the dominant paradigms were the human capital and modernization theories. However, as we enter the next millennium, there is much more a plurality of theoretical approaches, each providing its own unique strategy for the utilization of education in bringing about development objectives.

The three dimensions of comparative education and studies of development

In addition to theoretical perspectives, the link between education and development needs to be seen in terms of three sociological dimensions, namely, the economic, the social, and the political. This in itself represents a departure from the conventional view of education and the development process, namely that development was primarily an economic matter. However, in recent years there is an increasing acceptance that the contribution that education makes to the development process is much wider, and incorporates not only the economic, but also the social and political. The following sections will treat each in turn.

The neo-classical view: education and human capital

The most common understanding of education's role in the development process is in terms of its contribution to economic development. Models of economic development have been dominant since the emergence of the 18th-century theories of progress put forward by Adam Smith, John Stuart Mill and others. Theories of economic progress agree that one, but not the main, component of progress is the human dimension, that is, the quality of the working population, which in turn contributes to economic development.

The underlying assumptions in this link between education and economic development are best articulated by human capital theory, whereby any improvement in the health, skills or motivation of the workforce are seen to improve the productivity of workers. Insofar as education brings about improvements in the quality of the human population, it is seen as a major contribution to the economic growth of a country.

Contemporary economists who hold this view are able to cite considerable evidence which they regard as supportive, for both agricultural and industrial workers. For example in rural areas, two surveys of the literature have identified 31 pre-1980 studies and 14 post-1980 studies which supported the notion that increased education led to increased agricultural productivity. In the earlier survey of 31 studies, Lockheed and her colleagues (1980) concluded that farmers with an educational attainment of four years increased their productivity by between 7 and

10 per cent. Building on the earlier survey, Moock and Addou (1997) found an additional 14 studies which, even when taking into account critiques of these studies, clearly supported the notion that, beyond a threshold level, formal schooling improved agricultural productivity. Although it is difficult to locate studies of the impact of education on factory worker productivity in single countries, the evidence suggests that higher levels of education do result in higher levels of worker productivity. Haddad *et al.* (1990) suggest that one consequence of higher levels of education is the opportunity to change to jobs with higher skill demands and incomes.

Using the rate-of-return approach, Psacharopoulos (1985, 1994) has provided perhaps the most comprehensive evidence that investment in education does result in forms of economic growth, irrespective of the type of society. If one assumes that economic development can be defined in terms of rates of return, then his studies over the past several decades merit attention. Beginning with the study of 32 countries in 1973, Psacharopoulos, by the mid 1990s, was able to produce rates-of-return to investment in education for 78 countries. His findings show that in developing countries the social rates of return to primary schooling were between 17.9 and 24.3 per cent, depending on the region. For secondary schooling and higher education, the comparable rates were 12.8–18.2 per cent and 11.2–12.3 per cent respectively. These figures were higher than the respective 14.4, 10.2 and 8.7 per cent returns for the OECD countries. Nevertheless, the consistency in the direction of the figures makes it clear that education brings about positive economic returns to society as a whole (Psacharopoulos, 1994).

However, these rates of return concern the benefits of education to the economic development of society as a whole. What about the benefits to the individual? In this respect Psacharopoulos' findings are even more interesting, for the rates of return to individuals are on the whole greater than to society, and the discrepancies are greater for the higher education level than for the primary school level. Therefore, while it is appropriate to focus attention on the social rates of return to investment in education, it is also important to keep in mind the individual rates of return, as the latter may occur partly at the expense of the former. Nevertheless, in terms of economic development, the research of Psacharopoulos makes it clear that education plays an important role. In fact, this comparative approach makes it possible for Psacharopoulos to conclude that in developing countries investment in primary education, the education of females and the academic curriculum will make the highest contribution to economic development.

Although this approach to the analysis of the link between education and development has been criticized (Bennell 1996), the comparative analysis of education has made significant policy inputs into the priorities of educational expansion in both developed and less developed countries. These are most apparent in the World Bank 1995 policy review, *Priorities and Strategies for Education* (World Bank, 1995).

Alternate economic models of education

For over three decades some economists have suggested that the relationship between education and development is not as straightforward as implied by the neo-classicists and the human capital theorists. In the late 1960s Coombs (1968) argued that the expansion of government funded educational facilities would not necessarily lead to economic growth, but could result in an economic burden brought about by the costs of sustaining larger but possibly inappropriate educational structures. More than a decade later Coombs (1985) concluded that the relationship between education and economic growth was more complex but not appreciably different from his original argument.

Other comparative educationists agreed with this view. Weiler (1978), for example, questioned the notion that educational expansion would automatically lead to economic growth. He argued that issues of equity, the relationship between education and work, and educational reform were among the three most important issues related to choice in educational policymaking. In effect, he agreed with Coombs that investment in education will not necessarily lead to economic growth.

In a similar manner, Blaug (1985) argued that the effects of education on economic growth are not linear and straightforward, and that other social factors sometimes intervene to produce unintended results. He suggested that economists should direct their attention to the 'screening hypothesis', the 'incomplete employment contract' and 'labour market segmentation' for expanations as to why educational expansion had not always resulted in the level, or type, of economic growth desired. In this respect, Blaug's more critical approach to the relationship of education to economic growth was consistent with the sociological arguments put forth earlier by Dore (1976), that the unrestrained drive for more education in any country could result in a dysfunctional overproduction of highly trained educated persons. This he saw as particularly relevant for developing economies where the needs for human capital were not always the same as in developed countries.

There are at least two alternatives to the human capital perspective in conceptualizing the relationship between education and economic development (Easton and Klees 1990; Klees 1989). The first is the institutionalist approach whereby focus is directed to the patterns of social behaviour which shape supply and demand for education (rather than the reverse), and the use to which it is put. In this context labour market segmentation and internal labour markets have been seen as important explanatory variables for the difficulty of investment in education to bring about the desired development results (Easton and Klees 1990; LLamas 1994; Tueros 1994). The second alternative is the radical economic perspective, or neo-Marxist political economy, which focuses on the ways that education leads to the reproduction of social inequalities, and the detrimental effects that these processes have on economic growth. Authors such as Bowles and Gintis (1976) and Carnoy and Levin (1985) have suggested that investment in education can and does have negative effects on economic growth. The failure of educators and economists to take these factors into account lead to educational policies which result in more problems than are solved. In other words, the effects of educational expansion are not self-evident, and do not necessarily lead to economic growth (Dronkers and van der Ploeg 1997).

Summary

Comparative educationists and some economists now agree that educational expansion will not necessarily lead to economic growth. Although the belief in the contribution of education to the improvement of human capital continues to survive, the structure of the labour market and the social and cultural context within which this expansion takes place, are also seen as important. In this context, the questions of the type of education, for which target population and for what kind of development must be taken into account. In this respect, the economic dimension in the relationship between education and development is highly complex and remains of considerable interest to comparative educationists.

Education and social dimensions of development

The social conditions of some parts of the world have not improved much in the final three decades of the 20th century. The problems of illiteracy, under-education, poverty, lack of housing, and indeed meeting the basic human needs, have remained high on the agendas of governments and international organizations, especially in the developing countries. However, in spite of the fact that primary school enrolment in the developing countries more than doubled between 1960 and

1990, about 130 million children remain without primary schooling. Furthermore, although illiteracy rates have declined since 1970 from 55 to 35 per cent, the increase in population has meant that the actual number of illiterates in these countries has increased from 890 to 948 million (Ahmed, 1997).

Research in comparative education has made a considerable contribution to better understanding the role that education plays in improving these social conditions in the process of change and development. Furthermore, when these social needs are not met, the effects of economic development on a country may be attenuated, or blocked altogether. Thus it is essential to take into account the ways that education may or may not influence social factors to obtain a broader perspective on the overall relationship between education and development.

Education and becoming modern

Comparative educational researchers have regarded education as a principal agent for improving the quality of life, and there is hardly an aspect of social life that has not been explored by them. (See, for example, Parker and Epstein, 1998.) The underlying assumption is that education opens up minds to wider intellectual and material horizons, and produces basic attitudes and values which makes change and a modern society possible. The most important theoretical perspective, which has driven this approach, has been modernization theory. Much of the research on education as a modernizing agent has been based on the definitions and measures of Inkeles, who first attempted to operationalize the notion of the 'modern man' (Inkeles and Smith 1974).

Comparative researchers have generally accepted the description of Inkeles and Smith of a modern person. For the latter, a modern person exhibits the following characteristics: (1) an openness to new experience; (2) a readiness to social change; (3) an awareness of diversity in attitudes and opinions, but the disposition to hold one's own views; (4) being fact-oriented in forming opinions; (5) a focus on the present and future rather than the past; (6) a sense of personal efficacy; (7) oriented to long-term planning; (8) a trust in social institutions and in individuals; (9) a high value on technical skill; (10) a high value on education; (11) a respect for the dignity of others; and (12) understanding the logic underlying production and industry.

Numerous studies during the 1960s and 1970s supported the modernization hypothesis. For example, Lerner (1964) found that Middle Eastern adults who had attained at least a secondary school education had higher levels of psychic empathy, that is, the ability to adjust efficiently to continually changing environments. Similar findings were found in Mexico (Kahl 1968) and Brazil (Kahl 1968; Holsinger 1974). Using political interest and awareness as an indicator of modernization, Almond and Verba (1965) found that higher levels of education resulted in higher levels of political interest among respondents in the United States, Great Britain, Germany, Italy and Mexico. Inkeles and Smith (1974) found strong correlations between educational attainment and individual modernity in their study of adults in Argentina, Chile, East Pakistan (Bangladesh), India, Israel and Nigeria. Subsequent studies by Verba *et al.*, (1978) and Inkeles (1983) have reinforced these earlier findings. Finally, Delacroix and Ragin (1978) argued that the school is a domestically based modernizing institution while the mass media may or may not be. In their study of 49 less developed countries, they concluded that the school had the potential to modernize without Westernizing, and that countries with strong state-sponsored programmes (mobilizing regimes) used education as a modernizing agent more effectively than less controlled programmes.

A critique of the modernization hypothesis

The most fundamental critique of the modernization hypothesis is whether the process of becoming modern is incompatible with traditional attitudes, lifestyles and behaviour. Furthermore, there were researchers who did not believe that schools were inherently modernizing. From a theoretical perspective, the traditional–modern dichotomy was challenged from the beginning by Gusfield (1967), and more recently by Preston (1996) and by Smolicz (1998). Empirically, Armer and Youtz (1971) were among the first to suggest that under certain circumstances, schools and the curriculum could have a traditionalizing rather than modernizing effect. Studies of Koranic schools have supported this notion. For example Wagner and Lofti (1980) found that Koranic schools do inhibit the acquisition of modern values. Schools seem most successful as traditionalizing mechanisms in countries which have most strongly resisted foreign domination, such as in Morocco, Nigeria and Indonesia (Wagner 1985).

Additional criticisms have also been made. For example, it has been argued that the 'modernizing' impact of education is simply a reflection of the fact that Western-type schools, which teach a conventional curriculum, transmit knowledge upon which measures of modernity are based. Thus, by definition, Western-type schools are modernizing schools. Similarly, it could also be the case that the relationship between education and modernization is the result of the self-selection of parents and students, particularly in less developed countries. Predispositions to modern values become the motivating factors for school attendance, with the result that schooling and the acquisition of modern values are the result of a common determinant (Fägerlind and Saha, 1989).

Although it is argued that a country characterized by modern values will benefit in terms of the quality of life of those within it, the transmission of modern values through education can also create unintended consequences. This has been most obvious in the case of the brain drain of educated and 'modernized' individuals from the less developed to the more developed countries of the world. This phenomenon has been recognized for both those who have been educated internally, as well as students who have been educated abroad but who do not return to their home countries (Broaded, 1993).

In conclusion, then, the role of education in bringing about the social development of a society is not straightforward as the original hypothesis suggested. Comparative and international educationists have recognized this fact and their research on the factors which determine the direction of education's impact is contributing to the sociological understanding of the relationship between education and society.

Education, citizenship and democracy

Comparative education researchers have always recognized the relationship between education and the political life of a country. In the past, their concern has covered a wide range of processes, including political integration, political socialization and political leadership. In recent years this concern has focused on the issue of citizenship, particularly since the collapse of the Soviet Union and the Eastern European socialist countries. However, the attention given to citizenship has become part of a global concern, being found at the forefront of research in both developed and developing societies. Part of this concern can be traced to issues of democracy itself and the importance of active citizenship for a democracy to function smoothly.

Education, political socialization and citizenship

In order for members of society to participate in the political life of a country, they must be socialized into its political culture. Schools have always been seen as a major agent for this process. (See, for example, Braungart and Braungart 1997; Ichilov 1994; Niemi and Junn 1996; Renshon 1977.) However comparative education researchers have documented the differences between countries in the extent to which schools play a role in political education.

This is particularly the case with civic education in democratic countries. For example, Torney-Purta and Schwille (1986) argue that it is impossible to impart consistent civic values in industrialized countries, because many necessary values are in fact incompatible. Some industrialized countries, such as the United States and Britain, emphasize individual success, while others such as Japan, Greece and Germany emphasize security. Indeed, Hahn (1998) documents how the notion of citizenship and level of interest in politics varies between secondary school students in five countries, with interest being higher in Denmark, Germany and Britain, and lowest in the Netherlands, with the United States in the middle.

None of these findings suggest that being schooled in civic values and the ideals of citizenship guarantee compliance with current political regimes or the political *status quo*. In some countries, schools seem to socialize students to favour change rather than to promote stability, in spite of the official curriculum of the school or national ideology. In a comparative study of Columbia and the United States, it was found that American students held favorable political dispositions toward their government, while the opposite was true for Columbian students (Nathan and Remy 1977). In a similar manner, Harber (1984) found in his study of the Hausa in Nigeria that the political values taught in school may openly conflict with those of the political leadership. One reason for this is that while political leaders may wish to encourage democratic values through the educational system, the bureaucratic structure of the system supports authoritarian rather than democratic values (Harber 1997).

Education, democracy and nation-building

The notion of democracy has enjoyed considerable attention among comparative education researchers. Even though there are variations in the meaning of democracy, it is widely accepted that education is a primary agent for the transmission of democratic values and, therefore, for the establishment and maintenance of democratic political regimes. Indeed, it has been argued that the same attitudes and values which contribute to the existence of modern societies, are those which makes strong democracies possible (Inkeles 1999).

It has been argued that the relationship between economic development and political democracy is better understood than that between education and political democracy. In a large comparative study of 107 to 148 countries (depending on the aspect of the study) Benavot found that direct changes in political democracy over time could be explained significantly by the expansion of education, and in particular higher education (1996). Thus not only does education '... enhance the political competencies and skills of individuals, makes them more conscious and effective political actors, and increases their political participation', but higher education creates political elites who can exercise leadership legitimately (Benavot 1996: 402).

The irony of the relationship between education and democratic political development is that the increased political sophistication of citizens may make it more difficult for political leaders to govern. Inglehart (1996) found in his analysis of 21 countries that education and economic security are bringing about an intergenerational shift in respect for authority. This decline in respect for authority is in turn making the task of governing more difficult for political leaders. The creation of politically autonomous individuals who are more likely to become involved in political action will put demands on leaders for responsive democratic institutions. However, as Inglehart notes, it could also result in greater political apathy and civic indifference.

It is in this context that comparative and international education researchers have become more focused on issues related to education and democracy. McGinn (1996), for example, has argued that comparative and international educational researchers do make an impact on increasing public participation in social and economic life. In this respect, the comparative research on forms of civic and citizenship education is demonstrating yet another important dimension of the relationship between education and development. In this case, it is the political dimension which is affected.

Conclusion

Comparative and international education are both expanding fields. As the world becomes more complex, and at the same time comes under the influence of global social and economic tendencies, the comparative study of education's role in these processes becomes increasingly important for both understanding and policymaking. Furthermore, the epistemology and methodology of comparative studies is very much a part of the social sciences. In this respect, the comparative study of education, as described in this article, is very much sociological, and a growing part of the sociology of education.

There are many issues that have not been discussed in this article, not because they lack importance, but rather because the focus has been on a dimension of research that is likely to remain important well into the next century. Clearly the study of gender and sex differences, adult education, agricultural and vocational education will continue to merit attention in this regard (Saha 1995). These topics, however, will be a part of the larger issue of how education is related to the economic, social and political changes, and development that will characterize the 21st century.

Finally, the comparative study of education has shown how varied are the roles and structures which education takes in different cultural settings. Comparative education has provided sufficient evidence to dispel any assumptions about there being a single model of education appropriate for all countries. Education is a major agent for the economic, social and political improvement of society, but only if it is adapted and used in a manner appropriate to the cultural context of a particular country.

9
New Class Relations in Education: the Strategies of the 'Fearful' Middle Classes

Stephen Ball and Carol Vincent

This chapter is part of a broader effort within the sociology of education to write social class back into the analytical problematic of the discipline. Social class has been the subject of considerable debate and development in mainstream sociology in recent years. However, to some extent research in the sociology of education has failed to keep abreast of or take into account empirical, methodological and theoretical developments in class analysis in mainstream sociology. We intend to demonstrate that pronouncements about the 'end of class' are premature. Marshall (1997) suggests that 'we may have mistaken changes in the *shape* of the class structure for changes in social fluidity or the degree of *openness*' (p.5 emphasis in the original).

Class relations in education may differ in some ways from those prevalent in the past but they have by no means disappeared, and as Marshall (1997, p.56) notes, education is the area most often referred to in order to refute claims that the influence of class on individual life chances is in decline. More broadly, Crompton (1998) in the conclusion to her book on current debates on class and stratification comments that 'the concept of "class" – in all its many manifestations – remains essential to the understanding of our contemporary social condition' (p.229) or to quote (Reay, 1998) 'despite a pervasive denial of class status, there are emotive intimacies of class which continue to shape individual's everyday understandings, attitudes and actions' (p.267). Material, discursive and psychological class differences remain a crucial explanatory component of persistent social inequality, and all of these are factors in the complex ways in which class is constituted. None of this, however, is intended to deny or marginalize other dimensions of inequality and their complex, 'messy' connections with social class (Savage and Butler, 1995, p.346).

In this chapter we want to indicate how current social and economic conditions underpin a reworked but also re-emphasized agenda of class differentiation in education (Brown, 1997; Jordon, Redley and James, 1994; Lash and Urry, 1994; Pakulski and Waters, 1996 and Savage *et al.*, 1992). We agree with Savage and Butler (1995 p.347) that 'exploring continuity and change simultaneously' is necessary to reconcile the arguments of those who emphasize long standing patterns of inequality *and* those who point to their transformation as a result of fundamental social and economic change. In particular in this chapter we will consider the point noted by Reay (1998) that 'current educational research has revealed an increasing middle-class policing of class boundaries...' (p.265). We will refer to a number of studies which indicate in particular the interventions of middle-class parents into education practice to defend and further their class interests. These appear to be 'parents who get what they want', as Birenbaum-Carmeli (1999) puts it. In addition, but very briefly, informed by the theoretical work on 'the new middle class', we will argue the need for a more careful and detailed analysis of intra-class differences in education. To be clear then our focus is on the middle class(es) rather than social class generally and more particularly we address the strategies of class reproduction of these middle class(es).

Our concern here is not with debates about the meritocracy or otherwise of the education system in the UK. However, as should become clear, we are taking seriously the view of many middle-class respondents in our research studies that ability is not enough to ensure the success of children (or of their children) in the education system (Gewirtz, Ball and Bowe, 1995 and Vincent and Martin, 1999; see also Jordon et al., 1994 and Marshall and Swift, 1997). As Savage and Egerton (1997) found individual ability is not the decisive factor in the social reproduction of service class occupational positions: 'the overall advantages of the service class over other social classes...exist both with and without controls for ability' (p.667); although there are gender differences embedded in this relationship. Savage and Egerton (1997) also report that the perpetuation of the class privileges of daughters were much more heavily dependent on their ability scores than was the case for sons – 'middle class men have more resources to draw upon' (p.667); they mention material advantages, social networks and cultural capital but the notion of resources remains vague. Commenting that ability alone is inadequate in accounting for class reproduction, Savage and

Egerton refer to the role of 'other mechanisms'. Here we explore some of these 'other mechanisms'.

The end of class?

There is certainly overwhelming evidence of global economic changes which have both made more permeable and reordered class structures. However, Pakulski and Waters (1996) go further and see the 'new times'/ high/postmodernity (or whatever) as having changed the basis on which inequality is constituted. Thus, they argue, 'advanced societies are riven by unacceptable divisions of inequality, conflict and domination that are often marked by coercive or exploitative practices. However, they can no longer be sheeted home to class and any insistence in sociology that class should be our primary focus will divert attention away from these conditions' (p.viii). To some extent this is a sociological truism but whether it can allow us to talk about the 'death of class' or to relegate class to the side lines of social analysis is a different matter. Some theorists have suggested that political claims for cultural recognition have supplanted calls for economic redistribution but this is by no means uncontested (see Fraser, 1997a; Fraser, 1997b; Phillips, 1997 and Young, 1997, for discussion). It is certainly the case that attention has moved away from the grand narratives of class to other inequalities, but much theoretical and empirical attention has been paid to exploring the interconnections, especially of gender and race, with class (for example, the collections edited by Blair and Holland 1995 and Mirza 1997; Savage and Butler 1995).

However, as we see it, these debates have led to an unfortunate neglect of class analysis in educational research, a view shared by Bates and Riseborough (1993) and a number of other researchers in the sociology of education. Nonetheless, the UK class structure, as elsewhere, has changed. Perhaps the most dramatic aspect of change is the rapid expansion of 'middle class groups'. By 1991 approximately 55 per cent of the workforce consisted of white-collar workers and 30 per cent of workers were employed in professional and managerial occupations; double the proportion in the mid 1960s. Set against and in relation to the growth of the middle classes is an increase in income inequalities and in poverty (Joseph Rowntree Foundation, 1995). In relation to these changes researchers and theorists have addressed the middle classes in two different ways: either in terms of the advantages and interests of these people as a whole, as against others – the working class; or, increasingly, by focusing upon the internal fragmentation of the middle classes and patterns of differentiation, division and exclusion which produce and reproduce middle-class fractions (Bourdieu, 1986; Lee, 1993 and Savage *et al.*, 1992). As noted we want to give some attention to both approaches.

Class in context

Class relations and class practices in education both respond to and contribute to economic change and labour market structure. We want to suggest that the contemporary educational perspectives and practices of the middle classes are shaped and informed by a set of fears and concerns about social and economic reproduction. As Brown (1997) explains it:

> The declining faith in the ability of employing organizations to offer secure long-term employment, or to meet their expectations of career advancement, will lead to an increasing emphasis on academic and professional credentials as an insurance policy in the same way that people insure themselves and their homes against adversity...the acquisition of material property is correctly understood by the middle classes to be a 'risky business'...
>
> (pp.740–1)

This is a recurring theme in our recent and current research on parents and parental choice (for example Ball, 1997b). Parents often spoke about the increased competition and risk in education and the labour market for their children compared with their own experiences.

> ...his Dad and I we sort of sat down and said the competition out there, it is a hell of a lot stiffer than it was when we were his age. You might be good but there are people out there who will be better than you, obviously if you stay on at school you know what competition you will be up against. (Mrs P. quoted from an ESRC funded project 'Education markets in the post-16 sector of one urban locale' 1995–97 conducted by Stephen Ball, Sheila Macrae and Meg Maguire, award no. L123251006)

> Life is going to be harder for them than it was for us. In a way you've got to fight to push them to get what's best for them. I suppose it's a slightly selfish thing as well, it's nice to think your kids are doing OK, and they're nice kids and they're doing alright. But I think life is

going to be harder for them than us, and you've got to make sure that they've got the best opportunity there is basically. (Mrs R. quoted from an ESRC funded project : ' "Little polities": schooling, governance and parental participation', 1997–99, conducted by Jane Martin, Stewart Ranson and Carol Vincent, award no. R000 23 7123)

One particular, and very material, aspect of this new politics of uncertainty is the dramatic change in the trajectory of economic growth and patterns of employment which provided the basis for the massive postwar expansion in the middle classes and the creation of the so-called 'new middle class'. For some, their 'imagined futures' and those of their off-spring, are now under threat from the 'unmanaged congestion' and 'intensified positional competition' (Hirsch, 1977) in the old and new professions and in management positions (Jordon, Redley and James 1994, Jordan 1996). The nature of 'career' in management and the professions has itself changed. Increasingly senior managerial and professional jobs are subject to systems of performance related pay and fixed-term contracts (Butler and Savage 1995). We are now used to thinking about 'serial' or 'portfolio' careers. In Sweden, Jonsson (1998) reports tendencies of convergence between certain conditions of white collar and blue collar jobs. Also, in the UK, there are instances of a 'surplus' of qualified professionals in fields like architecture and the law – in the early 1990s 40 per cent of qualified architects in the UK were unemployed. This congestion is exacerbated in the UK by changes in participation rates in Higher Education. The expansion of higher education has raised the participation rate from 12 per cent in the 1970s to approximately 34 per cent (1996–97, Social Trends 1999); with a concomitant increase in graduate unemployment – 6.9 per cent in 1987 rising to 14.5 per cent in 1992 (quoted in Brown, 1997). Thus, a key aspect of the uncertainty among the middle classes is the idea that higher education, once their exclusive privilege, is now being assailed by 'intruders from below' (Ehrenreich, 1989). This leads to an increased emphasis by middle-class choosers on 'principles of division' (Bourdieu 1986 p.479) between HE providers (Reay *et al.*, 1999). Middle-class parental uncertainties about the earlier stages of education are further reinforced by doubts about the effectiveness of state schooling, fuelled by media and Ofsted reports of 'failing schools', declining standards and inadequate teachers. One effect of this has been a loss of support among the new middle classes for efforts to democratize education and social policy. Education is being 'transformed back into an "oligarchic" good' (Jordon, Readley and James, 1994, p.212) or what Thurow and Lucas

(1972) call a 'defensive necessity'. There are, we suggest, a number of strategies on the part of middle-class groups which aimed at preserving their family's positional advantages.

Class strategies

What we want to do here is to establish or co-ordinate a focus of analysis which offers an account of social class related patterns in educational outcomes which is located neither in home differences (childrearing practices, achievement orientation, linguistic socialization and so on) nor in the classroom (teacher or curricular biases, linguistic patterns, authority patterns and so on) nor in differences in measured ability but rather is to be found in the interactions between home and school, in the class strategies of parents.

With some degree of simplification we suggest that these class strategies can be broken down into two distinct but interrelated categories of activity: *choice* and *voice*.

Choice

One of us (SB) has argued extensively elsewhere (Ball, 1993, Ball, 1997a) that middle-class anxieties about social reproduction and the mainten- ance of social advantage are key features of the politics of social mar- kets. That is to say, middle-class parents, on the whole, are familiar with and comfortable with the mode of consumption now operating in the state education system (and other social markets), and further, they are particularly advantaged by it. The market form valorizes certain types of cultural and social capital which are unevenly distributed across the population. The use of these capitals in choice-making and choice- getting enables certain social groups to maintain or change their posi- tion in the social structure. School choice is a critical point of cultural investment in the symbolic economy. Schooling, of certain sorts, is an effective means of storing value for future realization. As a form of signification, certain sorts of schooling generate surplus meaning; '... the circulation of value can only occur when values take on objecti- fied form through some specific instance of representation' (Lee, 1993, p.162). Thus, for many of the families discussed here choice of school is a reinvestment or strategy of reconversion to conserve or enhance their class ranking.

One element of this is the maintenance of exclusivity. As Kenway (1990) puts it: 'In class *relations*, consumption is part of the process of social distancing and closure, helping to define "us" and "them".'

Parents seek to place their children with others, or mainly with others, who are like them. In doing so they seek to achieve a *class fit* between the habitus of home and institution and avoid social mixing. In Bourdieu's terms: 'The agents only have to follow the leanings of their habitus in order to take over, unwittingly, the intention immanent in the corresponding practices, to find an activity which is entirely "them" and with it, kindred spirits' (p.223).

> Mrs Jeynith: Hutton, I don't know... my husband and I felt very keen that she should go into a school where there is a high percentage of children coming in from homes where parents are educated. Now Northwark... a lot of parents are educated, and the children do have a sense of discipline and good behaviour, and so... I suppose it's not very good to speak of this in terms of being class conscious, but really we felt that she should mix with children who come from good homes... and... I don't know, we couldn't really work it out, which school might have a higher concentration of children... she should move around with children from disciplined homes.
>
> (quoted in Ball, 1997b)

A middle-class mother in the 'Little Polities' project whose daughter attends a relatively successful multi-racial girls comprehensive in London discussed the difficulties of choosing a school for her son. She spoke about her fears of the local comprehensive which has a poor local reputation.

> I think there's a whole band of people like myself who wouldn't naturally send their children privately... and would if there was an establishment that was a little bit better than what we've got, I think they would readily support it... I think Durham school has got a wonderfully committed staff, but it, and you know, it probably doesn't sound very politically correct to say this, but at the end of the day what you're, I mean my child is proficient in English... and I'm particularly passionate about literature and the English language and I want that fully developed. I'm not saying that that can't happen, but then I think a school like Durham that embraces so many cultures has so much to give, but I also want my child's English extended, and whilst you know, he is mixing with children who haven't that level, I mean OK in other areas yes, wonderful, but you know, I want that side of things developed... I think that's an issue that has to be addressed because it's one that sounds, very you know,

and we had, the primary [school] PTA organized for the head of Durham to come along, and I said the same point there, risking my neck...but I knew it was in a lot of parents' minds and I felt awful saying it, and I said, you know, this isn't and I'm not the pushy white middle class parent, well, I suppose am, but you know, that's an issue that has to be looked at.

(Trisha, white mother, 'Little Polities' project)

One of the results of the pursuit of exclusivity is a trend towards polarisation within the education system and other social markets as the choices of the socially advantaged allow 'new narrower mutualities and clubs' to form, excluding other social groups (Jordan, 1996, p.241).

Recent research has identified a tendency for schools in competitive local markets to be acutely aware of the need to secure both a high level of subscription from new pupils and a high-ranking position in the league tables, and thus to tailor their provision to the perceived concerns and desires of middle-class parents. Thus, especially within a market setting, it is not always necessary for the middle classes to act to get their way. Reay (1998b) describes events in an English comprehensive school, Fletcher in which a science department commited to mixed ability teaching, with a successful examination record, is required by the headteacher to reintroduce setting (tracking) as part of a concerted effort by the school to recruit more middle class parents. Mixed ability, the Head argues, is regarded by middle-class parents as not serving their children's best interests. Internal debates at Fletcher were circumscribed by the 'strong authority of the principal' and a separation of issues of equity from those of excellence. Tracking or setting, as against mixed ability teaching, is a particularly pointed issue which sets educational and social issues against those of exclusivity and social advantage.

Similarly, a study of grant-maintained schools conducted by Halpin, Power and Fitz (1997) indicated a reinvented and invigorated traditionalism in these schools; one that was based on a perception that this would appeal to middle-class parents. As well as moves intended to signal academic rigour (for example plentiful homework, emphasis on exam performance), greater differentiation of the children (through for example, setting and streaming), there are also signs of growing deployment of signifiers of traditionalism (strict uniform policies in particular) (see also Gewirtz *et al.*, 1995 and Woods, Bagley and Glatter, 1998 for similar developments in the maintained sector).

As Bourdieu and Boltanski, 1981 pp.220–1) put it: 'The education market has become one of the most important loci of class struggle. Education itself is changed by all this.' It becomes in Labarea (1997) words 'an arena for zero-sum competition filled with self-interested actors seeking opportunities' (p.32). All of these might be seen as a part of what (Beck, 1992) describes as the reflexivity and individualization typical of 'risk societies'.

Voice

The other set of strategies to which we wish to draw attention can be grouped under the heading of 'voice'. By this we mean the way in which parents formulate and express their views and opinions to a school, and the ways in which they interact with the institution once their choice of school has been made. Do middle-class parents use their voice to protect and defend the interests of their children? Raftery and Hout (1993), writing about educational inequalities and education reform, suggest that this is the case. They argue that:

> To try to advance merit and retract class advantages as a basis of selection in a system that remains highly selective is likely to rankle too many entrenched interests. Those who lose privileges could be expected to fight to retain them.
>
> (p.60)

If this is so, what are the issues on which middle-class parents exercise their voice, and what strategies do they use to do so?

In the US, a number of studies have revealed the opposition of affluent white parents to detracking programmes. Stuart Wells describes the findings from her study as follows:

> Within each of our ten schools, when educators penetrated the ideology that legitimates the track structure (and the advantages that high-track students have within it), elite parents felt that their privileges were threatened. We found that local elites employed four practices to undermine and co-opted meaningful detracking efforts in such a way that they and their children would continue to benefit disproportionately from educational policies. These four overlapping and intertwined practices were threatening flight, co-opting the institutional elites, soliciting buy-in from the 'not-quite-elite', and accepting detracking bribes.
>
> (Stuart Wells and Serna, 1997, p.728)

In an earlier paper based on the same study Stuart Wells and Oakes (1996) argue that, what they call 'efficacious parents of high-achieving or identified gifted students will demand greater differentiation between what their children learn and what is offered to other students' (p.138). All of this is mirrored in Lipman's (1998) study of schools and school restructuring in Riverton, USA. In particular, in her case study of Gates High School, Lipman identifies the work done by Riverton's upper middle-class interests to 'limit and define restructuring through their opposition to the heterogeneously grouped Study and Research Methods class and their ability to reinstate their children's separation from low-achieving African American students' (p.170). Gates was 'a microcosm of the interplay of competing interests' (p.142) in the school district. As Lipman goes on to say: 'The web of race and class in these power relations was difficult to untangle' (p.170) but 'Elite white parents did not seem to object to high-achieving, mainly middle-class African Americans in honors classes' (p.171). Essentially at Gates certain issues and areas of debate about restructuring were 'off the agenda' – 'silences and omissions' existed. As at Fletcher School mentioned earlier, 'equality and educational excellence were framed as competing and separate interests' (p.170) within the school, the school district and the community.

A similar widespread middle-class resistance to privilege threatening changes – like detracking or racial integration programmes – is reported by Kohn (1998) who describes parents who act in this way as 'in effect *sacrificing* other children to their own' (p.571). That is, the 'personal standpoint', self-interest, aggregative principles predominate. The self-interested parental chooser is in Barber's (1994) terms: 'oblivious to that essential human interdependency that underlies all political life' (p.25).

Another example of 'intervention' comes from Australia, and another Riverton, a Queensland primary school. Hatton (1985) describes the activities of the Parents and Citizens Committee (P&C) – 'a very powerful body' (p.260) made up of upper middle-class parents. Successive principals at Riverton were unable to 'handle' the P&C who were active and effective in blocking a number of progressive innovations attempted in the school. For example: 'The P&C began to lobby politicians and the Education Department against the provision of open plan classrooms in Riverton. The basis of the P&C protest was disapproval of "open" educational practices' (p.262). Members of the P&C were also vocal in public meetings. The upshot was the installation of partitions and the continuation of one teacher–one class teaching at Riverton. (For a similar ethnographic account of middle class parental resistance to 'progressive' educational practices, see Miles and Gold 1981.) More generally Hatton reports that 'children of high status parents, through the intervention of their parents, achieve the best conditions, for example stable, competent staff.' Writing with striking prescience Hatton (1985) concludes that:

> As articulations approximate the market relationship the scope of situated autonomy [for teachers] reduces, and when tensions develop between teachers' pedagogic judgements and decisions and parents' beliefs about what is legitimate and appropriate, interventions are likely to follow.
>
> (p.270)

Bowe, Ball and Gold, 1992 (pp.50–3) cite another example, at Flight-path School, where parents directly challenged mixed ability grouping, and thus the teachers' right to decide on best practice. Again, as indicated in earlier examples, the senior management saw their handling of the dispute as 'accelerated by the whole gathering realization that we were in the marketplace' (senior deputy, quoted p.52). However, such instances of collective parental resistance to school policy are relatively unusual. We would also like to draw attention to the more everyday practices of monitoring and intervention which middle-class parents deploy. These may be conducted in homes without direct reference to the school (helping with homework, arranging after-school activities and so on), indeed they may 'by-pass' the school altogether (arranging private tution for example). However, there are also occasions when parental 'vigilance' (Allatt, 1993) leads parents to initiate 'conversation' with the school. ('Bypass' and 'conversation' are terms used by Martin, Ranson and Vincent in the 'Little Polities' project to describe parental strategies of communication with the school. Other possibilities include 'storming', 'exit' and 'silence'.)

We draw here on data collected for the 'Little Polities' project (for more details, see Martin and Vincent, 1999), exploring the expression and formulation of parental voice in schools, to develop this point. As part of the on-going analysis a group of 76 parents interviewed across two case study schools, Willow and Carson, were divided into three groups: high, intermediate and low interveners. The high interveners group of about 27 families were overwhelmingly those with at least one parent in professional or managerial occupations (21 out of 27). This group can be described as 'risk managers'. They are not willing to leave education, seen as a key determinant of their child's future, to the school. They are 'driven' by an awareness of the congested labour market, the need for their child to achieve to a high level if they are going to reproduce their class advantages, a strong feeling of parental responsibility for their children's welfare and achievement, and a sense of interconnection between the home and school on the aims and purposes of education (if that sense is not present, these parents will look to exit the school and search for another more in tune with their beliefs). Not all these characteristics are exclusive to this group, the first two – awareness of the congested labour market and feelings of parental responsibility for the children's achievement and welfare – are shared by many other respondents. However, this group have both the 'inclination and the capacity' (Gewirtz *et al.*, 1993) to act on their values and perceptions by interacting with the school. Having an active relationship with the school is part of their habitus, how 'people like us' behave. This manifests itself in a variety of, largely individual, strategies – attending parent forums and annual parents meetings in some cases, and bringing up issues (such as, in one school, the standard of maths teaching) which concerned them, writing to or ringing and visiting teachers on specific points arising from their tracking of the child's progress and/or welfare (such as requesting that their child be moved into a higher set). A group of parents who were regular attendees at a parents forum at one school, Willow, were there largely for the benefits they hoped their attendance might bring for their own individual children (stated reasons were getting information about school processes and events, building relationships with teachers and being seen to be interested).

An example is provided by Claire, one of the regulars at Willow's parents' forum. Her daughter failed the entrance exam for a nearby selective school, so attended Willow, a comprehensive, instead. Claire explains her attendance at meetings as being informed by her perception of 'the shortcomings of any ordinary comprehensive in London' and the concomitant need to monitor provision,

> I don't really agree with [selective schooling] but yeah I did do that [sit her child for entrance exam].... I was quite naïve really because I didn't really know that you should tutor them...so she didn't get in.... I mean, it's just that you end up wanting the very best for your children.... The thing is one of the reasons why I go to the [Willow parents' forum] is so that I know what's happening in the school and I feel reassured you know, I know about all the problems, like the fact that there aren't enough maths and science teachers nation-wide and in London, it's acute. It's a problem at Willow...I mean you've got to

be aware of all these things and try and, if necessary, to get a tutor for your child or whatever. But if your child gets into one of those [selective] schools you don't have to bother. I'd be surprised if I went to many PTA meetings if my child was in a school like that...I would go to some things obviously, I'd support the school [but] you wouldn't have to bother. I mean they don't have any trouble recruiting anyone.... So from that point of view you could just think 'oh, phew. Sit back and relax' You wouldn't have to worry.

(Claire, white mother)

Regular attendees at the parents' forum also employed less particularist language, focusing on 'giving something back' to the school, or offering support to the school, which ran alongside the more individualistic reasons for attendance, but was muted in comparison.

In one or two cases, 'risk manager' parents at the two schools, Willow and Carson, were from intermediate class groupings. These people were concerned more with what Diane Reay refers to as the transformation of habitus rather than its reproduction (1998 p.164). Their efforts and anxieties were directed towards ensuring that their children had more opportunities than they did, particularly the opportunity to go on into higher education, and to acquire a well-paid and secure job.

It is easy to characterize *all* middle class parents as effective in both articulating their agendas and in imposing them. The willingness to respond to the institution is one obvious dimension mediating effectiveness; although as noted already the 'pressures' of competition may encourage responsiveness. Even so in the 'Little Polities' project, the researchers found no examples of parents sucessfully persuading the schools to make major changes in policy or organization (although attempts were made to effect change, taking up issues such as mixed ability grouping, mathematics teaching styles, and uniform policies). There are a number of possible explanations for this apparent collapse into silence, spanning from parental deference to professional expertise and feelings of loyalty to what were generally perceived as 'good' schools, to the class fractions to which the parents belonged (for an example of a more vocal and determined parental group see Reay 1998 as well as the examples given above).

In various ways then what we are presenting here is what Jordon *et al.*, (1994) refer to as 'putting the family first' in their study of middle-class decision making: 'The interviewees used the repertoires of individualism to construct identities that bore the hallmarks of a distinctive culture – one that prioritized the family as a private, self-responsible setting for the pursuit of self-making in clearly gendered roles' (pp.5–6). This is in effect a culture of self interest or in Nagel's (1991) terms the morality of the 'personal standpoint'. There are changes both in the 'standpoint' perspectives of the middle class, in response to increases in uncertainty and reproduction risks, and the discursive climate (individualism/competition), and the policy context (markets, choice, consumerism/ empowering the parent) which makes certain strategies possible and indeed legitimate. We are in no way suggesting that these middle-class strategies are new. What we are suggesting is that the changing labour market context and policy context have encouraged and made possible, respectively, an increase in the use of such strategies.

Conclusions

We have four points in conclusion. First, we must acknowledge the importance of attending to differences within the middle classes both in terms of ideologies and practices in relation to education. The importance is a very material one. As Blackburn (1998) demonstrates 'the probability of entering university varies with father's occupation, with a huge difference between the top and bottom of the top class, and comparatively little difference between the bottom of this class and the bottom of the lowest class [at least prior to the recent expansion]' (p.737–8).

There have been many theoretical and empirical attempts to explore differentiation within the middle class(es). Dunleavy (1980) and Perkin (1989) argue that the most significant cleavage within the middle class as a whole is not between the asset basis of occupational groups (that is professionals, managers and entrepreneurs) but rather between public and private sectors of employment. Featherstone (1991) and Lee (1993) explore a further development of, and division within, the middle class; that is the class fraction that Featherstone refers to as 'the intellectuals and specialists in symbolic [as oppose to material] production' (pp.34–5). Another dimension has been suggested by Massey (1995), that of spatial mobility – the ease and flexibility of travel. Massey focuses mainly on inter-class differences but also poses the question of potential intra-class variations. A detailed understanding of the connections between the social location of different class fractions and their relationships with the education system, as students and then later perhaps as parents, is still required.

Our second point is that we are not seeking to pathologize individual middle-class parents. The discursive construction of a 'good' or 'responsible' parent is one which stresses individual parental responsibility (see for example the UK government's introduction of home–school agreements setting out 'approved' parental behaviour and the similar, though much wider attempt, to do the same thing in the New Zealand Code of Social and Family Responsibility, (Department of Social Welfare, 1998). 'Wanting the best' for one's children is constructed as a natural parental impulse with the caveat 'potentially at the expense of someone else's child' being rendered invisible. 'Working to preserve status' starts early (Papenek, 1979, cited in Beck and Beck-Gernsheim, 1995, p.131). As Beck and Beck-Gernsheim (1995, p.131–2) argue, 'Where people feel compelled to protect their place in society by their own exertions, this drive is bound to reach the nursery. Having a child is not enough, it has to be brought up, and parents find themselves contending with fears of sliding down the social scale as well as aspirations to climb up it.'

The degree of individualism and competition built into efforts to 'put the family first' lies hidden within a discourse privileging the necessary virtues of family responsibility, self-reliance and containment. This may lead to situations where individuals find themselves in a dilemma when their espoused principles conflict with their idea of what is 'best' for their child (as in the case of some of the mothers quoted above). There is certainly no simple relationship between principles and practice when it comes to familial interests as Ball (1997b) found when looking at the choice between state and private schooling. The relationships between principles and practice were fragile. Some principles may also be weakly held. Brantlinger, Majd-Jabbari and Guskin (1996) found in their inter-view study of middle-class mothers that those mothers who pronounced themselves committed to equity and tolerance also proceeded (under questioning) to become far more passionate in dismissing these very ideals when it came to the advantages they thought their own children should receive. It is the aggregate of individual decisions, strategies and actions which is of concern in policy terms. The effects, not only on the larger collectivity, but also for individuals (congestion means that the outcomes of parental investments in education are not guaranteed, Jordan 1996) is unplanned, inefficient and most of all inequitable.

Third, it is disproportionately middle-class mothers rather fathers who take the lead in maintaining 'vigilance' in respect to their chil-dren's welfare and achievement at school. Both parents may attend formal events such as parents' evenings, but it is overwhelmingly mothers who are involved in parents' forums and associations, who monitor homework, talk to their children about the details of their day, make contact with the teachers and arrange extra-curricular activities (Reay 1998, Vincent, 1996). The burden of discharging the responsibilities of a 'good' parent in respect to education, therefore falls on the mother.

Finally, we suggest here that as state education takes on more of the commodified characteristics of business and business practices *and* the risks of reproduction become more immediate then parents, and particular parents with certain skills and capitals will increasingly deploy, and feel able to make use of, their 'market position and rights and powers over productive resources' (Crompton, 1998 p.226). Brown (1997) refers to this as a change in the 'rules of engagement' in education from 'that based on "merit" to "the market"' (p.745). We are suggesting that the changing economic conditions of education make the middle classes more *alert* to their competitive interests in this field and that the changing political (and economic conditions) of, and in, education make them more *able* to pursue their competitive interests. Despite changes to, and the increasing fluidity and complexity of social relations in high modernity and the decline of traditional class politics, social class position still goes a long way towards determining life chances, although as Crompton argues 'increasingly societal fragmentation may render these facts more opaque' (Crompton, 1998, p.227).

10

Missing: A Sociology of Educating the Middle Class

Sally Power

Writing over 20 years ago, Patrick Hutber identified the 1970s as 'a time of crisis for the middle classes, who are subjected to unprecedented pressures and...unprecedented denigration' (1976: ix). His book *The Decline and Fall of the Middle Class and How It Can Fight Back* argues that the middle-class has not only sacrificed the economic basis for its continued prosperity, it has also lost the battle of ideas. Crippled by a self-inflicted drive for egalitarianism and a related 'middle class sense of guilt', Hutber claims that 'never has a section of society more enthusiastically co-operated in its own euthanasia'.

More recently, however, Diane Reay (1998a) claimed that the middle class is not only in the ascendancy, but is squeezing out the interests of other social groups. She argues that 'the triumph of individualism' evident in recent policies is a 'consequence of the universalism of a media controlled by middle-class' (p.263) and 'represents the almost universal acceptance of middle-class perspectives in society'. Indeed, she argues that 'working-class groupings in society under siege from aggressive legal actions to augment the advantages of the middle classes are both in retreat and in denial'.

In this chapter, I want to argue that the conflicts over the status of the middle class arise in part from the absence of a sociology of the middle class in general and of a sociology of educating the middle class in particular. As Butler and Savage point out (1995:vii), 'traditionally, the social scientific gaze has been directed either downwards, to the working classes, the poor and the dispossessed, or upwards, to the wealthy and powerful'. This is particularly true in relation to education and has, I shall argue, created an empirical gap which has grown ever more glaring as the number of people deemed to be 'middle class' grows and as the conventional indicators of success and failure shift upwards and become harder to define. I also want to argue that this gap has in turn contributed to some analytical difficulties and distortions.

While we are some way short of Blair's vision of a one class Britain in which the 'old establishment' is replaced by 'a new, larger, more meritocratic middle class . . . that will include millions of people who traditionally see themselves as working class' (Jones 1999), there is little doubt that the middle class has expanded. When Hutber was writing, only 14 per cent of the adult population were classed as professional/ managerial groups (ABs) and 36 per cent of the population were in non-manual occupations (Punt, 1975). More recent figures show that half the population is now middle class with about 30 per cent in managerial or professional jobs (Mills 1995).

For sociologists of education, this expansion is likely to be especially significant for our understanding of the relationship between schooling and social reproduction. Unlike the very few 'wealthy and powerful', whose assets are such that privilege can be passed down irrespective of external accreditation, members of the middle class largely depend upon the credentials bestowed by the education system in order to acquire or hold on to their position. Indeed, Giddens (1973) argues that the middle class is defined by education inasmuch as its market power is based principally upon educational qualifications. And just as the hard line distinguishing 'white collar' and 'blue collar' workers is blurring, or at least is becoming less relevant, as the principal means of classifying social differences, so the expansion of educational qualifications has rendered what counts as educational success and educational failure more opaque.

There was a time when obtaining any qualifications and staying on beyond the legal school leaving age indicated educational success. But the expansion of credentials, together with the limited number of employment opportunities for unskilled school-leavers, has raised the age of the critical branching points with the majority of school leavers obtaining some form of qualification. Analysis of the 9000 young people still remaining in the 1970 British Cohort Study shows that 64 per cent obtained GCSEs and 21 per cent went on to get degrees (Bynner *et al.*, 1997).

A sociology of educating the middle class is important not only because of demographic changes such as these, it is also important analytically. The absence of a visible presence for the middle class reflects the extent to which it has been 'normalized' within the field. In much the same way as 'whiteness' has only recently been granted the same attention as 'blackness' and gender studies focus on masculinity as well as 'women's issues', I want to argue that issues of class cannot be properly illuminated without looking at the middle class as well as the working class. Sociological exploration of the middle class as a social category will not only extend our understanding of the reproduction of an increasingly large section of the population, but also that it will enrich our understanding of the processes of social and cultural reproduction overall.

Representations of the middle class

In claiming that sociologists have largely overlooked the education of the middle class, I am not suggesting that the middle class is absent from sociological accounts. It has, however, rarely been the *focus* of the investigation – but rather the background against which the perspectives and experiences of the working class have been contrasted. The middle class exists in many studies predominantly as the symbol of success against which the structural disadvantages of others are compared. Because of this, its representation is often inadequate and based on sometimes spurious assertions. I want to examine four of these in particular that relate to (a) middle class homogeneity; (b) the nature of schools; (c) inevitable educational success; and (d) middle class attributes and orientations.

The assumed homogeneity of the middle class

Because middle-class students are often only points of contrast against which the various experiences of working-class students are set, they are typically seen as much of a muchness. Bernstein is one of the first, and still few, people working in education to recognize the significance of internal variation within the middle class. In 1975, he argued that the effects of differentiated schooling 'on the internal structure and culture of this class is something worthy of a prolonged study'. However, there have been very few empirical investigations – with notable exceptions including Delamont's (1984a and b) work at St Luke's and Aggleton's (1987) study of FE students at Spatown College.

Studying the internal structure and culture of the middle class is now long overdue. As the middle class has expanded it has become increasingly internally differentiated to the extent that many now agree that it is more appropriate to use the term middle *classes*. Although most classificatory systems differentiate vertically between upper and lower levels of occupational status, Savage *et al.* (1992) argue that there are also lines of horizontal differentiation that are based upon the ownership of distinctive types of asset. They identify three distinct middle classes; the petits bourgeoisie or entrepreneurs holding property assets, managers holding organizational assets and professionals holding cultural capital.1 The first of these, the petite bourgeoisie, has been relatively unimportant in terms of class formation in the UK, but the divide between the managerial and professional class is, they argue, fundamental to any understanding of the middle classes. Indeed, Hanlon (1998) argues that we are currently seeing a struggle between the managerial and the professional classes.

Others have claimed to identify other sources of division. Dunleavy (1980) and Perkin (1989) argue that one main cleavage in the middle class is based on the sector of employment. Those in the public sector derive their economic and ideological support from the state while those in the private sector derive their support from the market. As both the state and the market compete for resources, the economic and ideological positionings of each group remain distinctive and conflictual. A similar, but rather different, cleavage has been identified in terms of the field of production. In 1987, Berger commented that '[c]ontemporary Western societies are characterized by a protracted conflict between two classes, the old middle class (occupied in the production and distribution of material goods and services) and a new middle class (occupied in the production and distribution of symbolic knowledge)'. Indeed, it is this distinction upon which much of Bernstein's (1975, 1990, 1996) analyses of class and pedagogy is premised.

The implications of these divisions for education may be profound. In our recent project *'Destined for Success?'* which explored the biographies of a largely middle-class group of students, my colleagues and I argued that schools may feed into the middle class along a number of directions (see Power *et al.* 2000, Power 2000). First, some schools, notably those that are private and academically selective, feed a greater proportion of their students into high status universities and out into high status occupations. Schools also seemed to have contributed to horizontal differentiation of our middle-class respondents in terms of whether they took up employment in the public or private sector. If these tentative conclusions were supported with further analyses and further studies, they would suggest a relationship between school and occupational identity that extends beyond vertical differentiation. They might suggest varying allegiances to private and public forms of educational provision that influence sectors of employment and political preferences that may in turn contribute to more sophisticated understandings of school choice and occupational destination.

Schools as middle-class institutions

Another common assertion which relates to the assumed homogeneity of the middle class and the assumed success of middle-class students (considered next) is the often made claim that schools are 'middle-class institutions'. Reay (1998c: 52) for instance, talks about working class women being silenced through 'not being able to speak the language of middle-class institutions'. Inasmuch as teachers are, by definition, middle class then it can be argued that they are middle-class institutions. But then so are virtually *all* institutions. It is the case that the middle class gets more out of schools than the working class – but then it does out of every organization – whether they be hospitals or shops. It is hard to see what it is specifically about schools, as *schools*, that makes them middle class.

Calling schools 'middle-class institutions' also glosses over the differences between them. Willis' (1977) Hammertown Boys and Corrigan's (1979) Cullingham Secondary and Municipal Comprehensive do not feel particularly middle class and are certainly very different from Delamont's (1984a and b) St Luke's or even Lacey's (1970) Hightown Grammar. Even within those schools that might be seen to cater specifically for the middle class, there is huge variation. Bernstein comments on the:

> spectrum of British public schools, which over the last hundred years has created a range of social types out of the beatings of Harrow and the subtle spontaneity of Summerhill. The British middle class can not only ensure its privileged position in education, but through the public school system it can select which social type. In a way the British public school system is a system for generating not a finite range of sentences, but *social types*. I know of no other middle class which has the possibility of such a differentiated form of socialization.
>
> (1975:18, his emphasis)

The statement that schools are 'middle class' is therefore fairly meaningless unless we know precisely how and in what ways. Schools are institutions that have their own cultures and their own rules which are, as Bernstein's body of work argues, underpinned by complex relations to social class. It may be that there is greater congruence of values between some homes and some schools, but this cannot be presumed.

Referring back to our *'Destined for Success?'* biographies again, the schools our middle-class respondents attended had very different cultures. Using Bernstein *et al.*'s (1966) distinction between the expressive order (to do with conduct, character and manner) and the instrumental order (concerned with the acquisition of specific skills and bodies of knowledge) we were able to map out the dimensions of variation and how different schools were 'open' or 'closed' with social relations that were respectively 'differentiated' or 'stratified' (Power *et al.*, 1998a). Through mapping these properties against family attributes, we were able to show how middle-class children grew to be variously 'committed', 'detached', 'estranged' or 'alienated' throughout their educational careers. These complex responses help us to begin to undermine another commonly held assumption about the middle class – that success is guaranteed.

The inevitability of middle-class success

There is often an implicit assumption within the sociology of education that for the middle-class student academic progress is painless and a successful path through higher education into a prestigious occupation assured. That this is not always so, and the implications of this 'failure', is one of the most neglected areas of sociological research. There is no doubt that proportionately middle-class children do better than working-class children – but the extent of middle-class 'underachievement' is larger than is often assumed. For instance, even if we look back to the tripartite system which was seen to sanction class advantages institutionally, we find sizeable middle-class failure. Comparison of 11+ pass rates from two LEAs (Swift, 1965), shows that while it is the case that only 2 per cent of children from social class VI passed the test, it is also true that 46 per cent of those from Social Class I failed the test. If we look at Social Class II, the majority of children (61 per cent) failed the test. In connection with staying-on rates, one fifth (22 per cent) of boys from Social Class I and nearly two thirds (61 per cent) from Social Class II left school at 15 years of age or before (obtained from the 1961 census cited in Meighan 1981).

Although the significant benchmarks of success have changed since then, middle-class 'failure' is by no mean uncommon. Our respondents' profiles revealed high levels of success during the 1980s – but many achieved less than had been predicted. Even though the large majority of respondents appear 'successful', some of their retrospective accounts communicate disappointment, regret and even outright hostility towards their schools. The translation of educational promise into educational success is rarely easy or straightforward – irrespective of socio-economic background or kind of school attended. Half the interviewees had some form of 'troubled' or 'broken' progression, even though the majority 'got there' in the end. A significant minority had to retake their

A-levels to achieve required entry qualifications, dropped out of their initially chosen degree programme, entered or returned to higher education after an unplanned period of casual employment, or failed to find the kind of employment which they believed their graduate qualifications merited. Of course, it could be argued that middle-class failure does not merit significant attention because it is less of a 'problem' than working class failure. And certainly this is true on a societal level, even if on an individual level middle-class failure can be extremely wounding. But, I think there are analytical reasons which make exploration of middle-class failure imperative, even apart from broadening our understanding.

Studies which concentrate on socio-structural explanations have no way of accounting for middle-class failure – and ignoring such exceptionality (which, as we have just seen, is perhaps less exceptional than is often assumed) makes such explanations vulnerable. In particular, it opens the door to those who would claim that while social background *does* matter, individual attributes are at least as important. 'Exceptionality' then gets celebrated as evidence of indeterminacy or voluntarism. The construction of the 'bright' working-class and the 'dull' middle-class student (Saunders, 1996) actually endorses the assumptions of ability and intelligence and works against sociology as the prevailing source of explanation. Far better than either downplaying or celebrating such exceptionality, we should surely, as sociologists, be attempting to unravel it.

Middle-class attributes

Another by-product of using the middle class as a backdrop to studies of the working class is that they take on characteristics only in contrast to those attributed to the working class. This raises some interesting inconsistencies. At times the middle class is seen to be strategic and calculating. This is particularly so in relation to parental interactions with their children's schools and is most pronounced within many of the recent studies from King's College London. In the study of parents and school choice (for example Gewirtz *et al.*, 1995), middle-class parents are presented as 'successful strategists' – the 'skilled choosers' who are able to operate in the market place to advantage their children. In their study of post-16 strategists (Macrae *et al.*, 1996), the middle class students are 'calculating'.

In these studies, middle-class parents are portrayed in a manner which is often pejorative. Their strategicness is seen as an example of selfishness. Reay (1998c:145) claims that 'In monopolizing scarce resources within the state sector, deploying financial resources to secure children's educational advantage and drawing on useful social networks which excluded working class mothers, many of the middle-class women were ensuring that the outcome of the educational competition was resolved in their children's favour.' Not only does the empirical evidence suggest that there is no such thing as 'ensuring' educational success, but her account also indicates a thinly disguised hostility towards the middle class. Reay again, for instance, notes that:

> ... the white middle-class women queried neither the *status quo* nor the inequalities it produced. There was an unexplored assumption, underlying most of the white middle-class women's words, that the educational system should be working to secure their ambitions for their offspring without any contextualization of what that implied in terms of the opportunities for other people's children.
>
> (Reay 1998c:132)

Working-class parents are seen as less selfish. In relation to school choice, for instance, '[t]here is a collectivity to choosing, in contrast to the individuality of the child-matching strategies of the privileged' (Gewirtz *et al.*, 1995: 48). They are 'disconnected' from the market and tend to choose local schools 'partly as a result of a positive attachment to the locality and to going to school with friends and family' (183).

However, it is not just that their attributes are different, but that working-class values and practices are *better*. While the working class is described warmly in terms of community and solidarity, the middle class is seen as calculating and competitive. The working class thinks and acts collectively, whereas the middle class is individualistic. Because the middle class is defined in opposition, however, other accounts present them differently. Where the working class are attributed with 'savvy', the middle class are not presented as percipient strategists, but as blinkered conformists. In Willis' account, for instance, it is the working-class 'lads' whose understandings:

> ... involve a partial penetration of the really determining conditions of existence of the working class which are definitely superior to those official versions of their reality which are proffered through the school and various state agencies.
>
> (Willis 1977: 3)

Although Willis acknowledges that these penetrations work against rather than for the success of individual students, it is the working-class students who gain the respect of the ethnographer.[2] The disdain with which the largely middle-class conformists are held is apparent in the following passage:

> the term 'ear'ole' itself connotes the passivity and absurdity of the school conformists for 'the lads'. It seems that they are always listening, never *doing*: never animated with their social internal life, but formless in rigid reception.
>
> (ibid.14)

Like Reay, Ball, Gewirtz and their colleagues at King's College, Willis holds that the working class act and think collectively. Indeed, he claims that their grasp of the difference between *individual* and *group* logic leads them to understand that conformism has no rewards for the working class as a whole – 'a profound critique of the dominant ideology of individualism in our society' (1977: 129). While the distinction between an individualistic middle class and a collective working class has the attraction of analytical simplicity, it is often hard to identify. I find it difficult to know what the difference is between 'collective' and 'individual' practice – as most social practices are inevitably comprised of the latter even if they arise out of, or have consequences for, the former. Moreover, the distinction is often difficult to support empirically. Willis himself concedes that working-class 'collectivism' is only partial – in that 'individuals are still behaving perhaps individualistically and competitively in some things and in the private spheres of their lives' (129). Conversely, Reay found middle-class mothers were very effective at networking and working together (for example, organizing a petition) to achieve their ends. Indeed she goes so far as to claim that 'contemporary *collective* middle-class action has led to increasing class and racial segregation' (Reay 1998c, 161, my emphasis).

Inadequate, inconsistent and partial representation of the middle class may result from an attempt to value and validate the accounts and experiences of the disadvantaged. As Gillborn (1998b) argues, there is a frequent misreading of Becker's (1967, Becker cited in Verhoeven 1989) 'Whose side are we on?', which suggests that sociologists have a 'kind of sentimental and quasi-political imperative . . . to side with "the underdog" '. This appears to have led to a situation in which acknowledging that the working class are unfairly disadvantaged also means casting the middle class as the perpetrators of this unfairness. Indeed, in the accounts of parental choice, middle-class parents are seen to be the *cause* of recent policies which have further damaged educational equity. Gewirtz *et al.*, (1995), for instance, claim that the education market is a 'middle-class strategy' designed to preserve middle-class advantages that had been eroded over recent years. They claim that their research shows that the market is a middle-class mode of social engagement and that schools are increasingly oriented towards meeting the perceived demands of middle-class parents.

However, while the middle class clearly has more power, as conventionally defined, than the working class, this does not mean that they are all powerful. The position of the middle class is problematic. As Mann (1993) argues, the 'problem' of the middle class is usually seen as a subset of a different class 'problem' – that of the relationship between the capitalist and working classes. Orthodox Marxism would place members of the middle class within the working class. It is somewhat surprising then that the sociology of education terms to place them within what Mann (1993: 547) refers to as 'an occasional pessimistic Marxian response' and make them part of the ruling bourgeoisie or capitalist class. It is perhaps more accurate to see them as occupying an ambiguous, contradictory class location.

Conclusion

This chapter has sought to argue that the absence of a sociology of education of the middle class has created a number of absences and analytical inconsistencies within the sociology of education as a whole. Examining the intimate relationship between education and the middle class and the complex way in which schools foster differentiated middle-class identities can throw light on some of the enduring issues within the sociology of education. In particular, it can help illuminate how 'success' is constructed and distributed and how this success contributes to social and cultural reproduction. The picture may become more complex, but it is surely an important task for the sociology of education to unravel such complexity rather than to ignore it or to use it to celebrate indeterminacy.

Notes

1. These are somewhat similar to Mann's (1993, 549) three-fold division of the middle class into the petite bourgeoisie (proprietors of small, familial business), careerists (employees moving up corporate and bureaucratic hierarchies) and professionals ('learned', collectively organized occupations licensed by the state).
2. Although Willis does distance himself from the 'lads' on occasions, at others his allegiance is, at least implicitly, given to them.

11
Vultures and Third Ways: Recovering Mannheim's Legacy for Today

Geoff Whitty

Chris Woodhead (1998), until recently Her Majesty's Chief Inspector of Schools, used a review of the reissued sociology of education volumes in the International Library of Sociology, founded by Karl Mannheim in the 1940s, to attack contemporary education research in general and the sociology of education in particular and to call for a return to the traditions of Mannheim's time. In response, while pointing to some obvious limitations and contradictions in Woodhead's analysis, Michael Young (1998, p.31) conceded that 'education research has certainly got to ask some hard questions about its methodology, concepts and priorities and...its links with teachers and policymakers'. In this chapter, I consider how far the legacy of Karl Mannheim, after whom my former chair at the Institute of Education, University of London, is named, might still be of use to the sociology of education and to contemporary education research and policy.

Background

Karl Mannheim left his native Hungary for Heidelberg in 1918 and became Professor of Sociology at Frankfurt in 1930. He moved to England from Germany in 1933 (staying briefly in Amsterdam on the way) and worked in exile as a lecturer at the London School of Economics. He took up British citizenship and was eventually appointed to the Chair of Education at the Institute of Education in 1946, but unfortunately died only a year later. Although Mannheim is best known for his work in social theory and the sociology of knowledge, he devoted much of his time in England to work on the sociology of education and social education (Kudomi, 1996).

Prior to Mannheim's appointment to the Institute, Sir Fred Clarke, who was its Director during the Second World War, had argued the case for a professor versed in sociological aspects of education in the following terms:

> The case for a professorship to work in terms of the sociological approach may be related to the uneasy awareness, now so widespread and yet so ill-defined, that great changes in the social order and the inter-play of social forces are already in progress – and that educational theory and educational policy that take no account of these will be not only blind but positively harmful.
>
> (Sir Fred Clarke, Director, Institute of Education, 18 March 1943)

Mannheim, of course, was an ideal choice to introduce such a perspective in the 1940s. And as Clarke (1967) said, in his memoir of Mannheim, 'the best tribute we can pay to him is to follow up and develop the inspiration he gave' (p.169). In my view, the argument for taking the wider view in the study of education is at least as strong now as it was when Clarke was arguing the case for Mannheim's appointment over 50 years ago. There is a similar widespread sense today that significant but ill-defined changes in the nature of the social order are in progress, as intimated – but inadequately characterized – by concepts such as high, late and postmodernity.

A graphic, though perhaps unfortunate, metaphor for Clarke's notion that educational researchers should take account of this broader context, and use wider social theories to help to 'make sense' of it, is a 'vulture's-eye view' of education. Apparently a vulture is always able to keep the background landscape in view while enlarging its object of immediate interest. However, useful as it may be, the analogy may not quite capture the significance of the notion of the 'bigger picture' in the social world. Arguably, the bigger picture is not just 'out there' in the background. As Britain's leading contemporary social theorist, Anthony Giddens (1994a), says of globalization, it is not something that takes place beyond the local, it 'is an "in here" matter, which affects, or rather is dialectically related to, even the most intimate aspects of our lives' (p.95). Education is similarly infused with, and dialectically related to, the bigger picture.

Making these sorts of connections involves understanding the intersection between biography and history, between identity and structure and between personal troubles and public issues – what C. Wright Mills (1961) termed the exercise of the 'sociological imagination'. For Mills, the exercise of the sociological imagination was certainly not a feature of the work of all sociologists nor was it necessarily restricted to signed-up members of that profession. But, for me, it is certainly a feature of good educational research, whether or not it is undertaken by sociologists. Thus, understanding changes in modern societies, educational reform and the development of new identities – and the connections between them – requires the exercise of the sociological imagination, even if we do not choose to call it that.

The importance of the bigger picture

Martyn Hammersley (1996) has implied that explicit sociologizing about education is now less common and, indeed, less necessary than it used to be because something like Giddens' 'double hermeneutic' (Giddens 1984) has taken a sociological way of thinking about the world into the common sense of other educators and educational researchers. But even in the context of supposed 'reflexive moderniza-tion' (Beck *et al.*, 1994), there is little evidence of the sociological imagin-ation being exercised liberally in contemporary institutional and political life: certainly not in whole swathes of politics and education in Britain where research that is not empiricist or instrumental is under severe attack for being irrelevant and self-serving. Yet, for a proper understanding of the nature of what is happening in education the vulture's-eye view is essential and the more cynical among us might feel that is exactly why some of our politicians prefer us to take a more myopic approach to our research.

Campbell Stewart, who knew Mannheim well and prepared his papers on sociology of education for publication (Mannheim and Stewart 1962), remarked in the 1960s that 'before long we shall need again to call on the kind of perspective which Karl Mannheim could command and which for the moment we seem to be too committed [to other priorities] to realize we have lost' (Stewart 1967, p.37). Stewart was particularly concerned about empiricism and an argument is now gain-ing strength among policymakers in Britain that the only sort of educa-tional research that is of any value is experimental research, based on the medical model of Randomized Control Trials (RCTs). While I per-sonally have no objection whatsoever to RCTs being part of the portfolio of educational research methods, to define them as the only worthwhile form of educational research is to trivialize the activity in potentially damaging ways. Yet, today, just as in the days of Mannheim, too much education policy and a great deal of contemporary educational research has lost sight of Clarke's important insight that education policy needs to be informed by a sensitivity to the nature of the wider society. Mannheim's own concern about 'a tendency in democracies to discuss problems of organization rather than ideas [and] techniques rather than aims' (Mannheim, 1951, p.199) also remains pertinent today.

Although these concerns may seem less relevant to contemporary sociology of education than some other aspects of educational research, some work that is much closer to the sociology of education than RCTs can have similar dangers. For example, classroom ethnographies, policy evaluations, action research and life histories, even where they identify themselves as critical, sometimes fail to take account of the 'bigger picture' (Goodson, 1997). Gerald Grace has long argued for the importance of the 'bigger picture' on the grounds that ' . . . too many . . . education reformers have been guilty of producing naive school-centred solutions with no sense of the structural, the political and the historical as constraints' (Grace 1984, p. xii). Work on school effectiveness and school improvement, which has attracted a number of prominent sociologists of education in Britain, has often been among the worst offenders, as one of its leading advocates, the previous Director of the Institute, Peter Mortimore, has acknowledged (Mortimore and Whitty 1997).

Far too much research, as well as education policy, remains stubbornly decontextualized. An Australian sociologist of education, Lawrence Angus (1993), rightly criticizes much of the school effectiveness research for failing 'to explore the relationship of specific practices to wider social and cultural constructions and political and economic interests' (p.335). Thus, he says, the apparent message in some of the work 'that all children can succeed at school provided teachers have expectations, test them regularly, etc, shifts attention away from the nature of know-ledge, the culture of schooling and, most importantly, the question of for whom and in whose interests schools are to be effective' (p.342). Certainly the more optimistic versions of work in this genre tend to exaggerate the extent to which local agency can challenge structural inequalities. Angus also suggests that a lack of engagement with socio-logical theory can mean that such work is trapped in 'a logic of common sense which allows it . . . to be appropriated into the Right's hegemonic project' (Angus, 1993, p.343). Thus, it sometimes seems that not only neo-liberal rhetoric, but also some forms of research, take the discursive repositioning of schools as autonomous self-improving agencies at its face value rather than recognizing that, in practice, the atomization of schooling too often merely allows advantaged schools to maximize their advantages. This only becomes clear when school-level reforms are studied in their broader context.

I now want to draw on my own area of research on the sociology of education policy to consider how we might understand the reforms that are going on in that field through looking at both the detail and the bigger picture. I explore a number of distinct but loosely interrelated issues. The first is to what extent the broader developments – sometimes of global proportions – are, in Giddens' sense, 'in there' in the politics of contemporary education reform. Second, I discuss ways of researching the impact of reform at societal and individual levels. Third, I examine the relationship between diagnosis and intervention and the extent to which the work of sociologists of education might usefully inform education policy. Finally, I consider how far what I am advocating relates to contemporary notions of a 'third way'. As in the case of Mannheim's writings, my explorations of these issues do not yet constitute a coherent whole. There are disjunctions, and possibly even inconsistencies, between them. Hopefully, though, generous readers will regard them as part of a 'dynamic totality' – the euphemism Mannheim's intellectual biographer (Loader, 1985) used to characterize the less than systematic nature of his works!

In what follows, I shall not be adopting a Mannheimian perspective as such, even insofar as it is possible to discern a consistent one in his own corpus. I do not share some of Mannheim's own assumptions about the nature of society and social order, nor (hardly surprisingly) is my immediate focus of interest the same as his. But, as Loader (1985, p.189) puts it, 'if many of [Mannheim's] answers can be rejected, the questions he raised...cannot'. I shall, therefore, be following what I take to be the spirit of his approach in seeking to make connections and think relationally.

Understanding education reform

It is clear that, in many parts of the world, there is a move away from the 'one best system' of state-funded and state-provided education. Recent reforms have sought to dismantle centralized bureaucracies and create in their place devolved systems of schooling with an emphasis on consumer choice by parents and competition between increasingly diversified types of schooling. Sometimes, alongside these elements of deregulation, there have also been new systems of inspection and accountability.

Although these developments are sometimes described as 'privatization', and in some cases do include elements of privatization, it is difficult to argue that education has actually been privatized on any significant scale. If we look strictly at the issue of funding, or even at provision in most countries, marketization is a better metaphor for what has been happening in relation to education. This most often refers to the development of 'quasi-markets' in state-funded and/or state-provided services, involving a combination of increased parental choice and school autonomy, together with a greater or lesser degree of public accountability and government regulation (Levacic, 1995). However, if mass education systems have not usually been privatized in the strictly economic sense, there is more evidence of 'privatization' in the ideological sense of transferring decisions that might formerly have been made by the state and its professional employees to the private decisionmaking sphere of individuals and their families (Whitty and Power, 2000).

Most advocates of choice and school autonomy base their support on claims that competition will enhance the efficiency and responsiveness of schools and thus increase their effectiveness. Many hope that market forces will overcome a levelling-down tendency which they ascribe to bureaucratic systems of mass education, while others see them as a way of giving disadvantaged children the sorts of opportunities hitherto available only to those who can afford to buy them through private schooling or their position in the housing market (Moe, 1994; Pollard, 1995). Even the political rhetoric of parties of the left places an increasing emphasis on diversity and choice in education, as in the case of New Labour in Britain.

However, my own reading of the evidence (Whitty, 1997a; Whitty *et al*, 1998) suggests that the more optimistic claims for such policies are unlikely to be realized in the absence of broader policies that challenge deeper social and cultural inequalities. As the new discourse of choice, specialization and diversity replaces the previous one of common and comprehensive schooling, there is a growing body of evidence that, rather than benefiting the disadvantaged, the emphasis on parental choice and school autonomy is further disadvantaging those least able to compete in the market (Gewirtz *et al*., 1995; Lauder *et al*., 1994; Smith and Noble 1995). At the same time, it is increasing the differences between popular and less popular schools on a linear scale – reinforcing a vertical hierarchy of schooling types rather than producing the promised horizontal diversity. For most members of disadvantaged groups, as opposed to the few individuals who escape from schools at the bottom of the status hierarchy, the new arrangements seem to be just a more sophisticated way of reproducing traditional distinctions between different types of school and between the people who attend them. It is too easy to accuse the perpetrators of such policies of bad faith. Even if there is some plausibility in the argument that handing decision making down to schools and parents is a clever way of 'exporting the crisis', it is the misrecognition of the context that is more significant. As Amy Stuart Wells (1993) points out, the economic metaphor that schools will improve once they behave more like private, profit-driven corporations and respond to the demands of 'consumers' ignores critical sociological issues that make the school consumption process extremely complex. Her own research in the USA suggests that escape from poor schools will not necessarily emerge from choice plans because 'the lack of power that some families experience is embedded in their social and economic lives' (p.48). Similarly, Gewirtz, Ball and Bowe (1992) suggest that, in the case of England, the new arrangements for school choice discriminate against those who have more pressing immediate concerns than being an educational 'consumer'. In their subsequent work (Gewirtz, Ball and Bowe 1995), they draw upon the theories of Bourdieu and Passeron (1977) to explore 'the logic that informs the economy of cultural goods', which helps explain the class-related patterns of advantage and disadvantage they identify. Contrary to Woodhead's dismissal of such work as being irrelevant to an understanding of what goes on in schools and to raising standards, it helps us to make sense of the (often) unintended consequences of reform.

Sociology of education can thus help us to understand why, whatever the advocates of school choice might believe, the provision of new choices to individual families is unlikely to overcome deep-rooted patterns of structural and cultural disadvantage. Some of this work has clear resonances with Mannheim's. Not surprisingly, Mannheim favoured some forms of selection in education, but he also questioned the view that 'struggle and social competition always foster and select those who are the best according to an absolute standard of worth'. In doing so, he contrasted 'objective abilities' with 'social abilities' including 'pulling strings and discovering influential patrons' (Mannheim, 1957, p.85). While not dismissing the importance of competition, he saw the dangers of it going too far and stressed the necessity of co-operation. He also contrasted what he called 'the new democratic personalism' with 'the atomized individualism of the *laissez-faire* period' and emphasized the need to break down 'the frustration which comes from isolation, exaggerated privacy and sectarianism' and sought to mobilize instead 'the forces of group living in the service of a social ideal' (Mannheim, 1943, p.52).

Atomized decision making in a highly stratified society may appear to give everyone equal opportunities, but transferring responsibility for decision making from the public to the private sphere may remove the possibility of collective action to improve the quality of education for all. Since educational disadvantage has multiple causes, tackling it requires strategies that bring different groups and agencies together rather than expecting individual families to seek their own salvation. Indeed, significant and sustainable improvement is only likely to be achieved as part of a broader strategy of social and economic change. Indeed, Jean Anyon (1995) may even be right to argue that the real 'solution to educational resignation and failure in the inner city is the ultimate elimination of poverty and racial degradation' (p.89).

This means that there must be limits to the extent to which individual schools and their teachers can be expected to overcome these problems. Yet recent governments, of both political hues in Britain, as well as the former Chief Inspector of Schools, have too often felt that the solution lies in the 'naming and shaming' of schools and teachers that do not live up to their expectations. Many of the strategies for 're-forming' the teaching profession can be seen when examined through the lenses of sociology of education as sometimes cynical, but more often misguided, attempts to 'shift the blame' for educational failure and growing inequality from the state to individual school managers and teachers.

As indicated earlier, similar reforms can now be found in many parts of the world. They are partly a response by nation states to the impact of globalization and their need to confront perceived threats to stability and competitiveness – both from within and without. However, as Weiss (1993) argues, it is likely that policies of devolution and choice can provide only a temporary solution. Green (1996) suggests that even the current degree of responsibility taken by national governments for public education may not be enough 'as the social atomization induced by global market penetration becomes increasingly dysfunctional. With the decline of socially integrating institutions and the consequent atrophy of collective social ties, education may soon again be called upon to stitch together the fraying social fabric' (p.59). While the demise of some forms of national solidarity may be long overdue, the general atrophy of collective ties and consequent loss of notions of citizenship which Green predicts must surely be cause for concern. The issue then becomes one of establishing how education might best help reconstruct the social fabric and new conceptions of citizenship and who shall influence its design. These questions are reminiscent of Mannheim's concerns with social reconstruction in Europe following the upheavals of the 1930s and 1940s and with his own concern to develop social education for democratic citizenship (Mannheim, 1943).

Researching the impact of education reform

The impact of recent reforms on coming generations can only be a matter of conjecture, but it does seem clear that the very structures of education systems and their associated styles of educational decision-making impinge upon modes of social solidarity and forms of political consciousness. In this way, education reform is, indeed, both an 'in-here' matter, as well as a national and global phenomenon. This, of course, raises classic questions concerning the relationship between structure and agency and the extent to which they are either distinct but interrelated aspects of social reality or one is ultimately reducible to the other (Giddens, 1984; Willmott, 1999). Either resolution of the structure–agency issue would indicate the limitations of the analogy of the vulture's eye, but it remains a useful heuristic device for indicating the need to combine different methods and analytic practices.

Stephen Ball (1994, p.14) writes of the need in policy analysis for a 'toolbox of diverse concepts and theories'. In doing so, he cites approvingly Ozga's (1990) plea to 'bring together structural macro-level analysis of education systems and education policies and micro-level investigation, especially that which takes account of people's perceptions and experiences' (p.359). Such a toolbox of concepts and theories is necessary to explore the different levels of analysis and the interconnections between them that have been outlined above. Rather like using the different lenses in the vulture's eye, it is necessary to employ a variety of methods to explore the different elements of the picture at the same time.

This is something we tried to do in a study of the impact of different forms of selection for secondary education in England. In this study (Power *et al*, 2000), we traced the careers of a cohort of 350 students who were all assessed as of high academic ability at age 11 in the early 1980s. Some attended elite private schools as fee-payers, while some from poorer families received government assistance under the terms of what was arguably the Thatcher government's first 'marketising' measure (Edwards *et al.*, 1989). Others went to selective or non-selective state schools in the same localities. Surveying them in their early teens and mid-twenties, we were able to explore their experiences of schooling, their higher education and their initial entry into the labour market.

In one sense, our sample lent itself to a political arithmetic approach in the tradition of the Oxford Mobility Studies (Goldthorpe, 1980; Halsey *et al.*, 1980). We were certainly interested in how the numbers stacked up to reveal potential structural continuities and discontinuities between the different groups, and between them and their parents' generation. Our survey data yielded many tables demonstrating a clear and apparently consistent influence of types of schooling on subsequent experiences, outcomes and orientations. Yet when we used our interview data to look beyond the aggregate statistics, the situation proved to be a great deal more complicated.

Although political arithmetic could provide a useful picture of the general landscape, it could not capture the problematic nature of many transitions or the instances of unexpected success or failure (Power *et al.*, 1998a). Like Jackson and Marsden (1966, p.26) in *Education and the Working Class*, we have tried to 'go behind the numbers... into the various human situations they represent'. We have, therefore, tried to reconstruct biographies, but not just for their immediate human interest, absorbing as that has often been. The exercise has helped to highlight that, even for middle-class and academically able pupils, transitions which may appear 'smooth' in aggregate figures can be anything but smooth for some individuals; indeed one of our more counterintuitive findings was that as many as half of the transitions were 'interrupted' in some way even though the overall picture suggested a fairly unproblematic reproduction of middle-class careers and middle-class identities. This might seem to raise questions about the value of the 'bigger picture' as it appears in the less powerful lens.

But there is also a danger of over-individualising biographies to the extent that each one is exceptional with little way of grasping the extent or dimensions of exceptionality. We have, therefore, used them to try to understand the cultural interplay between home and school and to try to theorize the processes through which individuals 'construct' their careers. So, although we have focused in from the aggregate statistics to the individual cases, we have then tried to refine the 'bigger picture'. By digging beneath the surface of its landscape, we have sought to understand how its sedimented histories 'get in' to those individual biographies as well as how those individual biographies contribute to a more complex bigger picture.

In attempting to go beyond both the structural dimensions of the political arithmetic approach and the sheer individuality of biographies as they are 'lived out', we have rubbed the data up against various theories. Recent work in class analysis based on rational action theory (Breen and Goldthorpe, 1997) addresses some of the issues about why some people choose one pathway and others avoid it and we found it particularly helpful in explaining the careers of our most successful young women in comparison with those of their mothers. However, such theories seemed to underplay the cultural context in which decisions are made. Although it may appear that the majority of our students had acted 'rationally' in choosing their careers, school and family expectations were often at least as important as, and sometimes overrode, explicit or even implicit calculation of the odds of future material or status gains.

We therefore found ourselves increasingly drawn back to some currently rather unfashionable theories. In exploring how people navigate pathways or forge careers, and the role of the culture of institutions in shaping aspirations, we have found Bourdieu and Passeron's (1977) work, and potentially even their concept of 'habitus', rather more useful than John Goldthorpe (1996) (or, indeed, Chris Woodhead) suggests. We have also revisited the work of an earlier holder of the Karl Mannheim Chair of Sociology of Education, Basil Bernstein, and found some of his 1970s work particularly useful in understanding the complexity of the middle classes, and their symbolic resources (Power *et al.*, 1998b).

From diagnosis to intervention

At the end of that particular study we concluded that, although it was relevant to policy and practice, it could not lead to straightforward policy prescriptions. However, I now want to consider whether there might be any legitimate role for sociologists of education in moving beyond diagnosis to prescription about possible interventions, as Mannheim clearly did in his later years. Jean Floud (1959) has argued that he would have done better to continue 'to try to understand and diagnose, rather than to plan and legislate' (p.62). But, although Mannheim developed a now unfashionable faith in what he called 'planning for freedom', it is arguable that, after the experience of neo-liberal deregulation, his concern to counter the damaging effects of atomization and a *laissez-faire* society once again has considerable pertinence. Madeleine Arnot (1998) has certainly suggested that it is salutory to re-read Mannheim in the current context of 'heightened individualism and atomism in society'.

So, nothwithstanding a proper caution about the difficulties of controlling anything in today's 'runaway world' (Shilling 1993), we should not assume that *laissez faire* is the only, or the best, way of confronting our present 'troubles'. I would argue that sociology of education can still play a role here, at least in so far as it can help to make sense of the broader context of educational reform and demonstrate its immense complexity. Beyond that, the role of the sociologist becomes less distinctive and more hazardous. Mannheim himself said of political sociology that 'it must teach what alone is teachable, namely, structural relationships; the judgements themselves cannot be taught but we can become more or less adequately aware of them and we can interpret them' (Mannheim, 1936, p.146).

This might seem to suggest that, in order to avoid the hazards, sociologists should confine themselves to what Stephen Ball terms studies *of* education policy rather than studies *for* policy (Ball, 1994). But, although it follows from what I said earlier that work which recognizes the bigger picture is to be preferred to the myopia and narrow instrumentality of much official activity in education, I am *not* myself arguing for an ivory tower or blue skies approach to sociology of education and I do not claim that our work should be entirely isolated from policy and practice. Nor, despite its attractions, do I think our relationship to policy should consist only of the 'semiotic guerrilla warfare' implied by a post-structuralist and deconstructionist view of the role of theory (Ball, 1995). Like Mannheim, I am still committed to a version of the 'modernist' project in social research, though hopefully somewhat more reflexive about its own limits and possibilities than he was, particularly in his later work. Certainly, as Mannheim recognized, different lenses give different takes on social reality. Even vultures come at the same object from different angles and are sometimes blinded by the sun. But I do want to claim that, at the present time, some lenses are more powerful than others in helping us to see what is at stake in education and the limits and possibilities of professional and political interventions.

Furthermore, while British sociology of education itself seems to have become more isolated in the academy in recent years and somewhat disengaged from wider social movements, grander theorists such as Anthony Giddens seem to be taking social theory back to its wider concerns and showing a willingness to go beyond diagnosis and try to address the political challenges posed by the changing social order they are studying. Giddens notes that 'on each side of the political spectrum today we see a fear of social disintegration and a call for a revival of community', and argues for the development of a 'dialogic democracy' in keeping with his analysis of the nature of the age and its attendant dangers (Giddens, 1994b, p.124). Though he may not recognize it, this is a truly Mannheimian project, albeit one shorn of its confidence and certainty.

In my own book, *Sociology and School Knowledge*, I suggested that 'the practical implications of [sociological] work for...political and educational practice [are] as much concerned with the ways in which policy is made as with specific substantive policies' (Whitty, 1985, p.82). Given the limitations of recent marketising reforms, which have atomized education decisionmaking, I shall conclude here with some observations concerning alternative modes of decisionmaking that could be more democratic and inclusive.

Whatever the rhetoric of devolution may suggest, it is quite clear that, in many countries, significant constituencies have remained excluded from education policy and decisionmaking either intentionally or, just as often, as an unintended consequence of decisions made with the best of intentions but without the benefit of the vulture's-eye view. The result, as I implied earlier, is that recent market-oriented reforms have often led to advantaged schools and advantaged families increasing their advantage, certainly in the initial stages of reform (Gorard and Fitz, 1998). Yet, even a cursory examination of the social processes involved in choice would have identified this as a likely outcome.

If equity and social cohesion are to remain important considerations within education policy, there is an urgent need to balance consumer rights with a new conception of citizen rights to give voice to those excluded from the benefits of both social democratic and neo-liberal policies. Insofar as social relations are becoming increasingly accommodated in the notion of the strong state and the free economy (Gamble, 1988), neither the state nor civil society is currently much of a context for active democratic citizenship through which social justice can be pursued. Foucault (1988) pointed out that what he called new forms of association, such as trade unions and political parties, arose in the 19th century as a counterbalance to the prerogative of the state and that they acted as a seedbed of new ideas on governance. The reassertion of citizenship rights in education would now seem to require the development of a new public sphere somehow between the state and a marketized civil society, in which new forms of collective association can be developed. But the real challenge is how to move away from atomized decisionmaking to the reassertion of collective responsibility for education, without recreating the sort of overcentralized planning favoured by Mannheim, and whose shortcomings in the social democratic era have helped to legitimate the current tendency to treat education as a private good rather than a public responsibility.

If new approaches to collective decisionmaking are to be granted more legitimacy than previous ones, careful consideration will need to be given to the composition, nature and powers of new institutional forms if they are to prove an appropriate way of reasserting democratic citizenship rights in education in the 21st century. They will certainly need to respond to critiques of conventional forms of political association in modern societies. While market forms are part of a social text that helps to create new subject positions which undermine traditional forms of collectivism, those forms of collectivism themselves often failed to empower many members of society, including women and minority ethnic groups.

A new politics of education will therefore need to reflect a conception of citizenship that entails creating unity without denying specificity (Mouffe 1989). In Nancy Fraser's (1997a) terms, it will have to combine the politics of recognition with the politics of redistribution if it is really to put social justice back at the heart of the educational agenda. Even if the social democratic era looks better in retrospect – and in comparison with neo-liberal policies – than it did at the time, that does not remove the need to rethink what might be progressive policies for the next century. If we do not take the opportunity to do this, we may even find the policy agenda dominated by those radical rightist commentators who will foster the very forms of individualism and competition that Mannheim saw as such a threat to the future of liberal democracies (Tooley, 1996).

Outside the sociology of education, there is rather more consideration of alternatives to markets as a response to the challenge of 'post' or 'high modernity'. Indeed, there is currently a great deal of discussion among social and political theorists in Britain and elsewhere about ways of democratising the state and civil society. In the USA, Joshua Cohen and Joel Rogers (1995) take the view that it is possible to improve the practical approximation, even of market societies, to egalitarian democratic norms. They argue that, by altering the status of 'secondary associations' within civil society, associative democracy can 'improve economic performance and government efficiency and advance egalitarian–democratic norms of popular sovereignty, political equality, distributive equity and civic consciousness' (p.9). It may even be that, especially on a global scale, the Internet has a role to play here, though I am by no means as convinced as some that it is a democratic medium and we would need to be as alert as Mannheim (1943) was in the case of other media to its totalising and totalitarian possibilities. He was concerned about the growth of 'social techniques' that penetrate deep into our private lives and subject 'to public control psychological processes which were formerly considered as purely personal'.

Third ways?

In the context of the confrontation between fascism and Stalinism in Europe in the 1930s and 1940s, Mannheim was suspicious of the totalising narratives and social techniques employed by both left and right. Recently, and in another parallel with Mannheim – though with no reference to him – Giddens (1998) has written about a 'Third Way' in politics. But, while Mannheim's (1943) 'Third Way' lay between a *laissez-faire* approach and totalitarianism, Giddens' own version of the notion is an alternative to conventional social democracy and neo-liberalism. He suggests it is time to move beyond the old dualism of left and right, so perhaps the metaphorical vulture's role here is not so much to provide analytic lenses as to pick over and finally dispose of the corpses of outdated ideologies.

Giddens' Third Way claims to be not just a mid-point between two old political ideologies, but the creation of a new and heterodox alignment of ideas which recognizes that our new times may render many former political certainties obsolete. The focus is thus on 'what works', rather than on ideologies and utopias. This also gives greater scope than in grand narrative politics for a recognition of diverse and flexible local identities typical of high or late modernity. Giddens believes New Labour is already moving in the direction of his Third Way and looks to Tony Blair's leadership in Britain for a new approach to government that will renew civil society through greater transparency and experiments with democracy. This could revive the notion of community, as well as creating a new mixed economy through the synergies of public, private and voluntary sectors. In doing so, it would transcend both the egalitarianism of the old Left and the acceptance of inequality by the new right and replace these with the concept of social inclusion.

It is certainly possible to argue that at least one of New Labour's policies, Education Action Zones (EAZs), prefigures a new, more inclusive politics of education and fulfils Giddens' (1998, p. 79) vision of Third Way politics working at community level to provide practical means of fostering social inclusion and furthering the social and material refurbishment of local areas (Power and Whitty, 1999). This policy entails public, private and voluntary sectors working together to improve education in areas of multiple social disadvantage and persistent underachievement. In theoretical terms, it might be located within the currently fashionable 'social capital' theories (for example Putnam, 1993), which suggest that interventions that increase 'social capital' can lead to consequent improvements in the educational achievement and economic prosperity of disadvantaged communities. And, at least in theory, the Education Action Forums, which are intended to bring different groups together to run EAZs, could be used to facilitate those 'experiments with democracy' envisaged by Giddens as part of the way forward in the 21st century.

However, New Labour has hitherto seemed far keener to encourage the involvement of private enterprise in EAZs, and to deregulate education within them, than it has been to foster new forms of civic association among local residents. Therefore, I remain sceptical about the extent to which the reality, as opposed to the rhetoric, of this particular policy lives up to its claims to be the harbinger of a distinctive new Third Way in the politics of education. Furthermore, when we look across the whole range of New Labour's policies for a 'world-class' education system, there can be little doubt that Tony Blair's version of the 'Third Way' is skewed heavily to the right. It is, of course, too early to predict with any confidence the longer term impact of New Labour's programme of educational reform, but the record so far suggests that those who want a genuinely alternative reform agenda to supersede the neo-liberal response to globalization and changes in modern societies may have to look elsewhere.

Interestingly, Chris Woodhead even calls for a 'third way' for the sociology of education, as an alternative to what he characterizes as 'the ethnomethodological road' and the 'macro-explanatory' route. This involves, among other things, a return to the subject's 'classical terrain' in an effort to regain the 'intellectual high ground it occupied when Karl Mannheim began putting his library together' (Woodhead, 1998, p. 52). I have tried to show that, as the former Chief Inspector might have realized had he not 'given up' reading the journals, such a tradition is not entirely dead. Indeed, my own view is that his dichotomous characterization of the field applies more to the 1970s and 1980s than to the 1990s. Nor, as will be clear from this chapter, do I accept that contemporary sociology of education is entirely irrelevant to education policymaking. However, further application of Mannheim's legacy to the contemporary educational scene would not necessarily lead to research findings that Woodhead himself would wish to see, any more than it would necessarily lead to the policies of New Labour.

Acknowledgement

This chapter draws on work carried out with Tony Edwards, Sharon Gewirtz, David Halpin and Sally Power, but they do not necessarily subscribe to the conclusions I have drawn from it here.

Bibliography

Abercrombie, N., S. Hill and B.S. Turner (1994) (3rd edn) *Penguin Dictionary of Sociology*. London: Penguin Books.

Acker, J. (1989) 'The problem with patriarchy', *Sociology*, 23:2.

Acker, S. (1981) 'No woman's land: British sociology of education', *Sociological Review*, 29:1.

Acker, S. (1994) *Gendered Education: Sociological Reflections on Women, Teaching and Feminism*. Buckingham: Open University Press.

Acker, S. and G. Feurverger (1997) 'Doing good and feeling bad: The work of women university teachers', *Cambridge Journal of Education*, 26:3.

Aggleton, P. (1987) *Rebels without a Cause*: London: Falmer Press.

Ahmed, M. (1997) 'Education For All', in W.K. Cummings and N.F. McGinn 1997 (eds) *International Handbook of Education and Development: Preparing Schools, Students and Nations for the Twenty-First Century*. Oxford: Pergamon Press.

Allatt, P. (1993) 'Becoming Privileged', in I. Bates and G. Riseborough (eds) *Youth and Inequality*. Buckingham: Open University Press.

Almond, G.A. and S. Verba (1965) *The Civic Culture: Political Attitudes and Democracy in Five Nations*. Boston: Little Brown.

Altbach, P.G. (1991) 'Student Political Activism', in P.G. Altbach (ed.) *International Higher Education: An Encyclopedia*. New York: Garland Publishing.

Altbach, P.G. (1991) 'Trends in Comparative Education', *Comparative Education Review*, 35:3.

Angus, L. (1993) 'The Sociology of School Effectiveness', *British Journal of Sociology of Education*, 14:4.

Anyon, J. (1983) 'Intersections of gender and class: accommodation and resistance by working class and affluent females to contradictory sex role ideologies', in L. Barton and S. Walker (eds) *Gender, Class and Education*. Lewes: Falmer Press.

Anyon, J. (1995) 'Race, Social Class and Educational Reform in an Inner-city School', *Teachers' College Record*, 97:1.

Apple, M. and J. Beane (eds) (1999) *Democratic Schools: Lessons from the Chalk Face*. Buckingham: Open University Press.

Archer, M. (1995) *Realist Social Theory: the morphogenetic approach*. Cambridge: Polity Press.

Armer, M. and R. Youtz (1971) 'Formal education and individual modernity in an African society', *American Journal of Sociology*, 76:4.

Arnot, M. (1981) 'Culture and political economy: dual perspectives in the sociology of women's education', *Educational Analysis*, 3:1.

Arnot, M. (1982) 'Male hegemony, social class and women's education', *Journal of Education*, 164:1

Arnot, M. (1985) 'Current developments in the sociology of women's education', *British Journal of Sociology of Education*, 6:1.

Arnot, M. (1998) 'Respondent: "Distressed worlds": social justice through educational transformations', in D. Carlson and M.W. Apple (eds) *Power/Knowledge/*

Pedagogy: The Meaning of Democratic Education in Unsettling Times. Boulder: Westview Press.

Arnot, M., M. David and G. Weiner (1999) *Closing the Gender Gap: postwar educational and social change.* Cambridge: Polity Press.

Arnot, M. and J. Dillabough (l999) 'Feminist Politics and Democratic Values in Education', *Curriculum Inquiry*, 29:2.

Arnot, M. and J. Dillabough (eds) (2000) *Challenging Democracy: International feminist perspectives on gender, citizenship and education.* London: Routledge.

Arnot, M., J. Gray, M. James, J. Rudduck with G. Duveen (1998) *A Review of Recent Research on Gender and Educational Performance.* Ofsted Research Series. London: The Stationery Office.

Ball, S. and S. Gewirtz (1997) 'Girls in the education market: choice, competition and complexity', *Gender and Education*, 9:2.

Ball, S.J. (1993) 'Education Markets, Choice and Social Class: the market as a class strategy in the UK and the USA', *British Journal of Sociology of Education*, 14:1.

Ball, S.J. (1994) *Education Reform: A critical and post- structural approach.* Buckingham: Open University Press.

Ball, S.J. (1995) 'Intellectuals or technicians: The urgent role of theory in educational studies', *British Journal of Educational Studies*, 43:3.

Ball, S.J. (1997a) 'Markets, Equity and Values in Education', in R. Pring and G. Walford, (eds) *Affirming the Comprehensive Ideal.* London: Falmer.

Ball, S.J. (1997b) 'On the Cusp: Parents Choosing between state and private schools', *International Journal of Inclusive Education*, 1:1.

Barber, B. (1994) *Strong Democracy.* Berkeley: University of Cailifornia Press.

Barrett, M. (1980) *Women's Oppression Today: Problems in Marxist Feminist Analysis.* London: Verso.

Bates, I. (l993a) 'A job which is right for me? Social class, gender and individualisation', in I. Bates and G. Riseborough (eds) *Youth and Inequality.* Buckingham: Open University.

Bates, I. (l993b) 'When I have my own studio ... The making and shaping of designer careers', in I. Bates and G. Riseborough (eds) *Youth and Inequality.* Buckingham: Open University.

Bates, I. and G. Riseborough (1995) 'Deepening Divisions, Fading Solutions', in U. Beck, and E. Beck-Gernsheim (1995) *The Normal Chaos of Love.* Cambridge: Polity Press.

Beck, U. (1992) *Risk Society: towards a new modernity.* London: Sage.

Beck, U., A. Giddens and S. Lash (1994) *Reflexive Modernization: Politics, Tradition and Aesthetics in the Modern Social Order.* Cambridge: Polity Press.

Becker, H.S. (1967) 'Whose side are we on?', *Social Problems*, 12.

Belenky, N.S., B.M. Clinchy, N.R. Goldberger and J.M. Tarule (1986) *Women's Ways of Knowing.* New York: Basic Books.

Benavot, A. (1996) 'Education and Political Democratization: Cross-National and Longitudinal Findings', *Comparative Education Review*, 40:4.

Bennell, P. (1996) 'Using and abusing rates of return: a critique of the World Bank's 1995 Education Sector Review', *International Journal of Educational Development*, 16:3.

Bennell, P. (1999) 'Education for All: How attainable is the DAC Target in Sub-Saharan Africa?'. A paper presented at the Oxford International Conference *Poverty, Power and Partnership*, September.

Berger, P. (1987) *The Capitalist Revolution*. Aldershot: Wildwood House.

Bernstein, B. (1966) 'Sources of consensus and disaffection in education', *Journal of the Association of Assistant Mistresses*, 17.

Bernstein, B. (1975) *Class, Codes and Control Volume 3: Towards a Theory of Educational Transmissions*. London: Routledge and Kegan Paul.

Bernstein, B. (1990) *Class, Codes and Control Volume 4: The structuring of pedagogic discourse*. London: Routledge.

Bernstein, B. (1990) *The Structuring of Pedagogic Discourse: Class, Codes and Control Volume Four*. London: Routledge.

Bernstein, B. (1996) *Pedagogy, Symbolic Control and Identity: Theory, Research, Critique*. London: Taylor and Francis.

Bernstein, B., L. Elvin, and R. Peters (1966) 'Ritual in education', *Philosophical Transactions of the Royal Society of London*, Series B, 251, number 772.

Bhatti, G. (1999) *Asian Children at Home and at School: An Ethnographic Study*. London: Routledge.

Bird, J. (1996) *Black Students and Higher Education: Rhetorics and Realities*. Buckingham: Open University Press.

Birenbaum-Carmeli, D. (1999) 'Parents who get what they want: on the empowerment of the powerful', *Sociological Review*, 47:1.

Blackburn, R.M. (1998) 'A New System of Classes: But what are they and do we need them?', *Work, Employment and Society*, 12:4.

Blackmore, J. (1996) 'Doing emotional labour in the education market place: stories from the field of women in management', *Discourse*, 17:3.

Blackmore, J. (1999) *Troubling Women: feminism, leadership and educational change*. Buckingham: Open University Press.

Blair, M. (1995) 'Race, class and gender in school research', in J. Holland, M. Blair and S. Sheldon (eds) *Debates and Issues in Feminist Research and Pedagogy*. Clevedon: Multilingual Matters in association with the Open University.

Blair, M. and J. Holland with S. Sheldon (eds) (1995) *Identity and Diversity: gender and the experience of education*. Clevedon: Multilingual Matters in association with the Open University.

Blaug, M. (1985) 'Where are we now in the economics of education?', *Economics of Education Review*, 4:1.

Bourdieu, P. (1986) *Distinction: a social critique of the judgement of taste*. London: Routledge.

Bourdieu, P. and L. Boltanski (1981) 'The Education system and the Economy: Titles and Jobs', in C. Lemert (ed.) *French Sociology: Rupture and Renewal since 1968*. New York: Columbia University Press.

Bourdieu, P. and J.C. Passeron (1977) *Reproduction in Education, Society and Culture*. London: Sage.

Bowe, R., S.J., Ball, and A. Gold (1992) *Reforming Education and Changing Schools: case studies in policy sociology*. London: Routledge.

Bowles, S. and H. Gintis (1976) *Schooling and Capitalist America*. London: Routledge and Kegan Paul.

Brah, A. and R. Minhas (1985) 'Structural racism or cultural difference: Schooling for Asian girls', in G. Weiner (ed.) *Just a Bunch of Girls: Feminist Approaches to Schooling*. Milton Keynes: Open University.

Brantlinger, E., M., Majd-Jabbari and S.L. Guskin (1996) 'Self-Interest and Liberal Educational Discourse: How Ideology Works for Middle-Class Mothers', *American Educational Research Journal*, 33.

Braungart, R.G. and M.M. Braungart (1997) 'Political Socialization and Education', in L.J. Saha (ed.) *International Encyclopedia in the Sociology of Education*. Oxford: Pergamon Press.

Breen, R. and J. Goldthorpe (1997) 'Explaining educational differences: towards a formal rational action theory', *Rationality and Society*, 9:3.

Brehony, K.B. and R. Deem (1999) 'Rethinking Sociologies of Education'. Unpublished paper, School of Education, University of Reading.

Brine, J. (1999) *underEducating Women: Globalising Inequality*. Buckingham: Open University Press.

Broaded, C.M. (1993) 'China's Response to the Brain Drain', *Comparative Education Review*, 37:3.

Brown, P. (1997) 'Cultural Capital and Social Exclusion: some observations on recent trends in education, employment and the labour market', in A.H. Halsey, H., Lauder, P. Brown, and A. Stuart Wells, (eds) *Education: Culture, Economy and Society*. Oxford: Oxford University Press.

Budge, D. (1998) 'Ability grouping under fire', *Times Educational Supplement*, 4 December.

Burstall, C. (1989) 'Boffin passes new IQ test', *Guardian*, 15 August.

Butler, J. (1990) *Gender Trouble: Feminism and the Subversion of Identity*. New York and London: Routledge.

Butler, T. and M. Savage (eds.) (1995) *Social Change and the Middle Classes*. London: UCL Press.

Bynner, J., E. Ferri and P. Shepherd (eds) (1997) *Twenty-Something in the 1990s: Getting On, Getting By, and Getting Nowhere*. Aldershot: Ashgate Books.

Byrne, E. (1978) *Women and Education*. London: Tavistock Press.

Carby, H. (1982) 'Schooling in Babylon', in Centre for Contemporary Cultural Studies *The Empire Strikes Back: race and racism in 70s Britain*. London: Hutchinson.

Carnoy, M. and H. Levin (1985) *Schooling and Work in the Democratic State*. California: Stanford University Press.

Carr, W. and A. Hartnett, (1996) *Education and the Struggle for Democracy*. Buckingham: Open University Press.

Carrington, B., A. Bonnett, J. Demaine, A. Nayak, D. Pearce, G. Short, C. Skelton, F. Smith, and R. Tomlin (1999a) *Ethnic Minorities and Teaching: A Survey of Postgraduate Certificate in Education Students in England and Wales (1998/9)*. Report Number One to the Teacher Training Agency.

Carrington, B., A. Nayak, R. Tomlin, A. Bonnett, J. Demaine, G. Short, and C. Skelton, (1999b) *Policy and Practice in Sixteen English Initial Teacher Training Institutions*. Report Number Two to the Teacher Training Agency.

Carrington, B., A. Bonnett, J. Demaine, A. Nayak, G. Short, C. Skelton, F. Smith, and R. Tomlin, (1999c) *The Perceptions and Experiences of Ethnic Minority PGCE Students*. Report Number Three to the Teacher Training Agency.

Carrington, B., A. Bonnett, J. Demaine, I. Hall, A. Nayak, G. Short, C. Skelton, F. Smith, and R. Tomlin, (2000) *Ethnicity and the Professional Socialisation of Teachers*. Final Report to the Teacher Training Agency.

Carter, J. (1997) 'Post-Fordism and the Theorisation of Educational Change: what's in a name?', *British Journal of Sociology of Education*, 18:1.

Carter, E., J. Donald and J. Squires (eds) (1993) *Space and Place: Theories of Identity and Location*. London: Lawrence and Wishart.

Chisholm, L. and M. Du Bois-Reymond (1993) 'Youth transitions, gender and social change', *Sociology*, 27:2.

Chodorow, N. (1979) 'Feminism and difference: gender, relation and differences in psychoanalytic perspective', *Socialist Review*, 46.

Chubb, J. and T. Moe (1992) *A Lesson in School Reform from Great Britain*. Washington, DC: Brookings Institution.

Clarke, F. (1967). 'Karl Mannheim at the Institute of Education', Appendix B in F. W. Mitchell, *Sir Fred Clarke: Master-Teacher 1880–1952*. London: Longmans.

Clegg, S. (1979) 'The Sociology of Power and the University Curriculum', in M.R. Pusey and R.E. Young (eds) *Control and Knowledge: The Control of Knowledge in Institutional and Educational Settings*. Canberra: Australian National University Press.

Coffield, F. and A. Vignoles, (1997) 'Widening participation in higher education by ethnic minorities, women and alternative students', in *The National Committee of Enquiry into Higher Education, Higher Education in the Learning Society* (The Dearing Report). London: HMSO.

Cohen, J. and J. Rogers (1995) *Associations and Democracy*. London: Verso.

Collins, R. (1986) *Sociological Theory*. New York: Basic Books.

Commission for Racial Equality (1986) *Black Teachers: the challenge of increasing the supply*. London: Commission for Racial Equality.

Commission for Racial Equality (1986) *Black Teachers: the Challenge of Increasing the Supply*. London: CRE.

Commission for Racial Equality (1998) *Education and Training in Britain*. London: CRE.

Commission on Social Justice (1994) *Social Justice: Strategies for National Renewal*. London: Vintage Books.

Connell, R.W. (1987) *Gender and Power*. Cambridge: Polity Press.

Connell, R.W. (1995) *Masculinities*. Cambridge: Polity Press.

Connolly, P. (1998) *Racism, Gender Identities and Young Children: Social Relations in a Multi-Ethnic, Inner-City Primary School*. London: Routledge.

Coombs, P.H. (1968) *The World Educational Crisis: A Systems Analysis*. New York: Oxford University Press.

Coombs, P.H. (1985) *The World Crisis in Education: The View From the Eighties*. New York: Oxford University Press.

Corrigan, P. (1979) *Schooling the Smash Street Kids*. London: Macmillan.

Crompton, R. (1998) *Class and Stratification: An Introduction to Current Debates*. Cambridge: Polity Press.

Dale, R. (1989) *The State and Education Policy*. Milton Keynes: Open University Press.

Dale, R. (1992) 'Recovering from a Pyrrhic victory? Quality, relevance and impact in the sociology of education', in M. Arnot and L. Barton (eds) *Voicing Concerns: Sociological Perspectives on Educational Reforms*. Wallingford: Triangle Books.

Dale, R. (1994) 'Applied Education Politics or Political Sociology of Education?' in B. Troyna and D. Halpin (eds) *Researching Education Policy: Ethical and Methodological Issues*. London: Falmer Press.

Dale, R. (1996) 'The State and the Governance of Education: an Analysis of the Restructuring of the State–Education Relationship', in A.H. Halsey, H. Lauder,

P. Brown, and A.S. Wells, (eds) *Education: Culture, Economy, Society.* Oxford: Oxford University Press.

Dale, R. (1997) 'Alternative Forms of Governance in Education'. A paper presented to the conference of American Educational Research Association, Chicago.

Dale, R. (1999a) 'Globalisation and Education: a Focus on the Mechanisms', *Journal of Education Policy,* 14:1.

Dale, R. (1999b) 'Globalisation: A New World for Comparative Education', in J. Schriewer, (ed.) *Discourse and Comparative Education.* Berlin: Peter Lang.

Dale, R. (1999c) 'A Common World Education Culture or a Globally Structured Agenda for Education?', *Educational Theory,* Winter.

Dale, R. (1999d) 'Education Markets and Legitimacy'. A paper presented to a conference titled 'A Decade of Reform in New Zealand Education – Where to Now?' University of Waikato, 11 June.

Dale, R. and S. Robertson, (1999) 'The competitive contractual state settlement and the new educational agenda'. A paper presented to the International Sociology of Education Conference, Sheffield, 2–4 January.

David, M. (1980) *Women, Family and Education,* London: Routledge.

David, M. (1993) *Parents, Gender and Education Reform.* Cambridge: Polity Press.

David, M. and G. Weiner, (1997) 'Keeping balance on the gender agenda', *Times Educational Supplement,* 23 May.

David, M., A. West, and J. Ribbens (1994) *Mothers' Intuition? Choosing Secondary Schools.* London: Falmer Press.

Davies, B. (1989) *Frogs and Snails and Feminist Tales: Pre- school Children and Gender.* Sydney: Allen and Unwin.

Davies, L. (1984) *Pupil Power: Deviance and Gender in School.* London: Falmer Press.

Davies, L. (1990) *Equity and Efficiency? School Management in an International Context.* London: Falmer Press.

Davies, L. (1993) 'Teachers as implementers or subversives', *International Journal of Educational Development,* 12:4.

Davies, L. (1999a) 'Comparing definitions of democracy in education', *Compare* 29:2.

Davies, L. (1999b) 'The Meanings and Indicators of Internationalisation', *The Development Education Journal,* 5:3.

Davies, L. (1999c) *A Review of Citizenship and Human Rights Education in Key Countries.* Report to British Council.

Davies, L. (1999d) *Education in Kosova.* Report to British Council

Davies, L. and G. Kirkpatrick, (2000) *The EURIDEM Project: A Review of Pupil Democracy in Europe.* London: Children's Rights Alliance.

Davis, A. (1983) *Women, Race and Class.* New York: Random House.

Dawtrey, L., J. Holland, M. Hammer, and S. Sheldon, (eds) (1995) *Equality and Inequality in Education Policy.* Clevedon: Multilingual Matters in association with the Open University.

Dearing Report (1997) The National Committee of Enquiry into Higher Education, *Higher Education in the Learning Society.* London: HMSO.

Deem, R. (1978) *Women and Schooling,* London: Routledge and Kegan Paul.

Deem, R. (1996) 'Border territory: a journey through sociology, education and women's studies', *British Journal of Sociology of Education,* 17:1.

Deem, R. (ed.) (1980) *Schooling for Women's Work.* London: Routledge and Kegan Paul.

Delacroix, J. and C. Ragin, (1978) 'Modernizing Institutions, Mobilization, and Third World development', *American Journal of Sociology*, 84:1.

Delamont, S. (1980) *Sex Roles and the School*. London: Methuen.

Delamont, S. (1984a) 'Debs, Dollies, Swots and Weeds: Classroom Styles at St. Luke's', in G. Walford, (ed.) *British Public Schools*. London: Falmer Press.

Delamont, S. (1984b) 'The Old Girl Network', in R.G. Burgess, (ed.) *Fieldwork in Educational Settings*. London: Falmer Press.

Delhi, K. (1996) 'Between "Market" and "State"? Engendering education in the 1990s', *Discourse*, 17:3.

Demack, S., D. Drew and M. Grimsley (1998) 'Myths about underachievement: gender, ethnic and social class differences in GCSE results 1988–93'. A paper presented at the British Educational Research Association annual conference, Belfast.

Demaine, J. (1981) *Contemporary Theories in the Sociology of Education*. London and New York: Macmillan and The Humanities Press.

Demaine, J. (1989) 'Race, Categorisation and Educational Achievement', *British Journal of Sociology of Education*, 10:2.

Demaine, J. (1999) (ed.) *Education Policy and Contemporary Politics*. London: Macmillan.

Demaine, J. and H. Entwistle, (eds) (1996) *Beyond Communitarianism: Citizenship, Politics and Education*. London and New York: Macmillan and St Martin's Press.

Department for Education and Employment (1997) *Excellence in Schools*. (Cmnd. 3681) London: HMSO.

Department for Education and Employment (1998) *Teachers: Meeting the Challenge of Change*. London: HMSO.

Department of Social Welfare (1998) *New Zealand Code of Social and Family Responsibility: a discussion document*. Wellington: Department of Social Welfare.

Dietz, M. (1985) 'Citizenship with a feminist face: The problem with maternal thinking', *Political Theory*, February.

Dillabough, J. (1999) 'Gender Politics and conceptions of the modern teacher; women, identity and professionalism', *British Journal of Sociology of Education*, 29:2.

Dore, R.J. (1976) *The Diploma Disease: Education, Qualifications and Development*. London: Allen and Unwin.

Drew, D. (1995) *'Race', Education and Work: The Statistics of Inequality*. Aldershot: Avebury Books.

Drew, D., B. Fosam, and D. Gillborn (1995) ' "Race", IQ and the Underclass: Don't Believe The Hype', *Radical Statistics*, 60.

Drew, D., J. Gray and N. Sime (1992) *Against the Odds: The Education and Labour Market Experiences of Black Young People*. England and Wales Youth Cohort Study, (Report Number 68). Sheffield, Employment Department.

Dronkers, J. and S.W. van der Ploeg (1997) 'Educational Expansion: Sociological Perspectives', in L.J. Saha (ed.) *International Encyclopedia of the Sociology of Education*. Pergamon Press: Oxford.

Duncan, J. (1992) 'Elite landscapes as cultural (re)productions: the case of Shaughnessy Heights', in K. Anderson and F. Gale (eds) *Inventing Places: Studies in Cultural Geography*. Melbourne: Longman Cheshire.

Dunleavy, P. (1980) 'The political implications of sectoral cleavages and the growth of state employment, part 2: cleavages structures and political alignment', *Political Studies*, 28.

Eade, D. (1998) *Development and Rights*. Oxford: Oxfam, Great Britain.

Easton, P. and S. Klees (1990) 'Education and the economy: considering alternative perspectives', *Prospects*, 20:4.

Ebert, T. (1991) 'Political Semiosis in/of American Cultural Studies', *American Journal of Semiotics*, 8:1 and 2.

Edwards, T., J. Fitz and G. Whitty (1989) *The State and Private Education: An Evaluation of the Assisted Places Scheme*. Lewes: Falmer Press.

Ehrenreich, B. (1989) *Fear of Failing: The Inner life of the Middle Class*. New York: Pantheon.

Ellsworth, E. (1989) 'Why doesn't this feel empowering? Working through the oppressive myths of critical pedagogy', *Harvard Educational Review*, 59.

Ellsworth, E. (1998) *Teaching Positions: difference, pedagogy and the power of address*. New York: Teachers' College Press.

Epp, J.R. and A. Watkinson (1996) (eds) *Systemic Violence: How Schools Hurt Children*. London: Falmer Press.

Epstein, D. and R. Johnston (1998) *Schooling Sexualities*. Buckingham: Open University Press.

Epstein, D., J. Elwood, V. Hey and J. Maw (eds) (1998) *Failing Boys? Issues in Gender and Achievement*. Buckingham: Open University Press.

Epstein, E.H. (1994) 'Comparative and International Education: Overview and Historical Development', in T.N. Postlethwaite and T. Husén, (eds) *The International Encyclopedia of Education* (second edition). Oxford: Pergamon Press.

Ersson, S. and J. Lane (1996) 'Democracy and Development: A Statistical Exploration', in A. Leftwich (ed.) *Democracy and Development*. Cambridge: Polity Press.

Etzioni, A. (1996) 'The Responsive Community: A Communitarian Perspective', *American Sociological Review*, 61:1.

Evans, D.R. (1997) 'Conscientization and Mobilization', in L.J. Saha (ed.) *International Encyclopedia in the Sociology of Education*. Oxford: Pergamon Press,.

Eve, R., S. Horsfall, and M. Lee (eds) (1997) *Chaos, Complexity and Social Theory*. Thousand Oaks, California: Sage.

Eysenck, H.J. (1994) 'Much ado about IQ', *Times Higher Education Supplement*, 11 November.

Fagerlind, I. and L.J. Saha (1989) *Education and National Development: A Comparative Perspective* (2nd edn). Oxford: Pergamon Press.

Featherstone, M. (1991) *Consumer Culture and Postmodernism*. London: Sage.

Featherstone, M. (1991) Consumer Culture and Postmodernism. London: Sage.

Floud, J. (1959) 'Karl Mannheim', in A.V. Judges (ed.) *The Function of Teaching*. London: Faber and Faber.

Ford, J. (1969) *Social Class and the Comprehensive School*. London: Routledge and Kegan Paul.

Foster, M. (1993) '"Othermothers": Exploring the educational philosophy of black American women teachers', in M. Arnot and K. Weiler (eds) *Feminism and Social Justice in Education: International Perspectives*. London: Falmer Press.

Foster, P., R. Gomm and M. Hammersley (1996) *Constructing Educational Inequality: an Assessment of Research on School Processes*. London: Falmer Press.

Foster, V. (2000) 'Is female educational "success" destablising the male learner-citizen', in M. Arnot and J. Dillabough (eds) *Challenging Democracy: International feminist perspectives on gender, education and citizenship*. London: Routledge.

Foucault, M. (1974) 'Human nature: Justice versus power', in F. Elders (ed.) *Reflexive Water: The Basic Concerns of Mankind*. London: Souvenir Press.

Foucault, M. (1988) *Politics, philosophy, culture: interviews and other writings* (edited by Lawrence D. Kritzman). New York: Routledge.

Franklin, J. (1998) 'Introduction: Social Policy in Perspective', in J. Franklin (ed.) *Social Policy and Social Justice*. Oxford: Polity Press in association with IPPR.

Fraser, N. (1997a) *Justice Interruptus: Critical Reflections on the 'Post-socialist' Condition*. New York and London: Routledge.

Fraser, N. (1997b) 'A rejoinder to Iris Young', *New Left Review*, 223.

Freeland, J. (1991) 'Dislocated Transitions: Access and Participation for Disadvantaged Young People', in The Australian Education Council Review Committee, *Young People's Participation in Post-compulsory Education and Training*. Volume 3, Appendix 2.

Freeland, J. (1996) 'The Teenage Labour Market and Post- Compulsory Curriculum Reform'. A paper presented at a conference titled 'Making it Work: Vocational Education in Schools', Melbourne: March.

Friere, P. (1970) *Pedagogy of the Oppressed* New York: Herder and Herder.

Friere, P. (1973) *Education for Critical Consciousness*. NewYork: Seabury Press.

Gamble, A. (1988) *The Free Economy and the Strong State*. London: Macmillan.

Gaskell, J. (1983) 'The reproduction of family life: perspectives of male and female adolescents', *British Journal of Sociology of Education*, 4:1.

Gewirtz, S. (1998) 'Conceptualizing social justice in education: mapping the territory', *Journal of Social Policy*, 13:4.

Gewirtz, S., S.J. Ball and R. Bowe (1992) 'Parents, Privilege and the Educational Marketplace'. A paper presented at the Annual Conference of the British Educational Research Association in Stirling.

Gewirtz, S., S.J. Ball and R. Bowe (1993) Parents, Privilege and the Education Market, *Research Papers in Education*, 9:1.

Gewirtz, S., S.J. Ball and R. Bowe (1995) *Markets, Choice and Equity in Education*. Buckingham: Open University Press.

Giddens, A. (1973) *The Class Structure of Advanced Societies*. London: Hutchinson.

Giddens, A. (1984) *The Constitution of Society*. Cambridge: Polity Press.

Giddens, A. (1990) 'Structuration Theory and Sociological Analysis', in J. Clark, C. Modgil and S. Modgil (eds) *Anthony Giddens: consensus and controversy*. Lewes: Falmer Press.

Giddens, A. (1994a) 'Living in a post-traditional society', in U. Beck, A. Giddens and S. Lash (eds) *Reflexive Modernization: politics, tradition and aesthetics*. Cambridge: Polity Press in association with Blackwell.

Giddens, A. (1994b) *Beyond Left and Right: The Future of Radical Politics*. Cambridge: Polity Press.

Giddens, A. (1997) *Sociology* (3rd edn). Polity Press: Cambridge.

Giddens, A. (1998) *The Third Way: The Renewal of Social Democracy*. Cambridge: Polity Press.

Gilbert, R. and P. Gilbert (l998) *Masculinity goes to School*. London: Routledge.

Gillborn, D. (1990) *'Race', Ethnicity and Education: Teaching and Learning in Multi-Ethnic Schools*. London: Unwin Hyman.

Gillborn, D. (1997) 'Race and Ethnicity in Education 14–19', in S. Tomlinson (ed.) *Education 14–19: Critical Perspectives.* London: Athlone Press.

Gillborn, D. (1998a) 'Racism, selection, poverty and parents: New Labour, old problems?', in *Journal of Education Policy*, 13:6.

Gillborn, D. (1998b) 'Racism and the politics of qualitative research: learning from controversy and critique', in P. Connolly and B. Troyna (eds) *Researching Racism in Education: Politics, Theory and Practice.* Buckingham: Open University Press.

Gillborn, D. (1999) 'Fifty years of failure: "race" and education policy in Britain', in A. Hayton (ed.) *Tackling Disaffection and Social Exclusion: Education Perspectives and Politics.* London: Kogan Page.

Gillborn, D. and C. Gipps, (1996) *Recent Research on the Achievements of Ethnic Minority Pupils.* Report for the Office for Standards in Education. London: HMSO.

Gillborn, D. and D. Youdell (2000) *Rationing Education: policy, practice, reform and equity.* Buckingham: Open University Press.

Gilligan, C. (1982) *In a Different Voice: Psychological Theory and Women's Development.* Cambridge, MA: Harvard University Press.

Goacher, B. (1984) *Selection post-16: the role of examination results.* London: Methuen.

Goldthorpe, J.H. (1980) *Social Mobility and Class Structure in Modern Britain.* Oxford: Clarendon Press.

Goldthorpe, J.H. (1996) 'Class analysis and the reorientation of class theory: the case of persisting differentials in educational attainment', *British Journal of Sociology, 47*:3.

Goodson, I. (1997) 'Educational Study and Teachers' Life and Work'. A paper presented to the Mid-Term Conference of the Sociology of Education Research Committee of the International Sociological Association, University of Joensuu, Finland, 16–18 June.

Gorard, S. and J. Fitz, (1998) 'The more things change . . . the missing impact of marketisation', *British Journal of Sociology of Education*, 19:3.

Gordon, T., J. Holland and E. Lahelma (2000) 'From Pupil to Citizen: a gendered route', in M. Arnot and J. Dillabough (eds) *Challenging Democracy: International feminist perspectives on gender, education and citizenship.* London: Routledge.

Gould, S.J. (1995) 'Curveball', in S. Fraser (ed.) *The Bell Curve Wars.* New York: Basic Books.

Gouldner, A. (1971) *The Coming Crisis of Western Sociology.* New York: Basic Books.

Grace, G. (ed.) (1984) *Education and the City: Theory, History and Contemporary Practice.* London: Routledge and Kegan Paul.

Graduate Teacher Training Registry (1997) Annual Statistical Report, Autumn 1996 Entry (GTTR: Cheltenham).

Graduate Teacher Training Registry (1998) Annual Statistical Report – Autumn 1997 Entry (GTTR: Cheltenham).

Gramsci, A. (1971) *Selection from the Prison Notebooks*, in Q. Hoare and G. Smith (trans) New York: International Publishers.

Green, A. (1996) 'Education, Globalization and the Nation State'. A paper presented at a conference titled, 'Education, Globalization and the Nation State: Comparative Perspectives. World Congress of Comparative Education Societies', University of Sydney.

Green, P.A. (1983) 'Male and female created He them', *Multicultural Teaching*, 2:1.

Gusfield, J. (1967) 'Tradition and modernity: misplaced polarities in the study of social change', *American Journal of Sociology*, 72:4.

Haddad, W.D., M. Carnoy, R. Rinaldi and O. Regel (1990) *Education and Development: Evidence For New Priorities*. World Bank Discussion Paper Number 95. Washington DC: The World Bank.

Hahn, C.L. (1998) *Becoming Political: Comparative Perspectives on Citizenship Education*. Albany, New York: SUNY Press.

Hall, S. (1988) 'New Ethnicities', in *ICA Document 7*. London: ICA

Hallam, S. (1999) 'Set to see a rise in standards', *Times Educational Supplement*, 23 July.

Hallam, S. and I. Toutounji (1996) *What Do We Know About the Grouping of Pupils by Ability? A Research Review*. London: University of London Institute of Education.

Halpin, D., S. Power and J. Fitz (1997) 'Opting into the Past? Grant-Maintained Schools and the Reinvention of Tradition', in R. Glatter, P.A. Woods and C. Bagley (eds) *Choice and Diversity in Schooling: Perspectives and Prospects*. London: Routledge.

Halsey, A.H., J. Floud and C.A. Anderson (1961) *Education, Economy and Society*. New York: The Free Press.

Halsey, A.H., A.F. Heath and J.M. Ridge (1980) *Origins and Destinations*. Oxford: Clarendon Press.

Hammersley, M. (1996) 'Post Mortem or Post Modern? Some reflections on British sociology of education', *British Journal of Educational Studies*, 44:4.

Hanlon, G. (1998) 'Professionalism as enterprise: service class politics and the redefinition of professionalism', *Sociology*, 32:1.

Harber, C. and L. Davies (1997) *School Management and Effectiveness in Developing Countries: The post-bureaucratic school*. London: Cassell.

Harber, C.R. (1984) 'Development and Political Attitudes: the Role of Schooling in Northern Nigeria', *Comparative Education*, 20:3.

Harber, C.R. (1994) 'Ethnicity and education for democracy in Subsaharan Africa', *International Journal of Educational Development*, 14:3.

Harber, C.R. (1997) *Education, Democracy and Political Development in Africa*. Brighton: Sussex Academic Press.

Harvey, D. (1993) 'Class Relations, Social Justice and the Politics of Difference', in J. Squires (ed.) *Principled Positions: Postmodernism and the Rediscovery of Value*. London: Lawrence and Wishart.

Hatcher, R. (1997) 'New Labour, school improvement and racial inequality', *Multicultural Teaching*, 15:3.

Hatcher, R. (1998) 'Social justice and the politics of school effectiveness and improvement', *Race, Ethnicity and Education*, 1:2.

Hatton, E.J. (1985) 'Equality, Class and Power: a case study', *British Journal of Sociology of Education*, 6:3.

Haywood, C. and M. Mac an Ghaill (1996) 'What about the boys? Regendered labour markets and recomposition of working class masculinities', *British Journal of Education and Work*, 9:1.

Hearnshaw, L.S. (1990) 'The Burt Affair: A Rejoinder', *The Psychologist*, 3:2.

HEFCE (1999) *Widening participation in higher education – Request for initial statements of plans and Invitation to bid for special funds: 1999–2000 to 2001–02* (Circular 99/33). Bristol: HEFCE

Herrnstein, R.J. and C. Murray (1994) *The Bell Curve: Intelligence and Class Structure in American Life*. New York: The Free Press.

Hewitt, R. (1996) *Roots of Racism: the Social Basis of Racist Action*. Stoke-on-Trent: Trentham Books.

Hey, V. (1997) *The Company She Keeps: an ethnography of girls' friendships*. Buckingham: Open University Press.

Higher Education Funding Council for England (1995) *Special Initiative to Encourage Widening Participation of Students from Ethnic Minorities in Teacher Training*. Bristol: Higher Education Funding Council for England.

Higher Education Funding Council for England (1995) *Special Initiative to Encourage Widening Participation of Students from Ethnic Minorities in Teacher Training*. Bristol: HEFCE.

Higher Education Funding Council for England (1999) *Widening Participation in Higher Education: Request for initial statements of plans and invitation to bid for special funds: 1999–2000 to 2001–02* (Circular 99/33) Bristol: HEFCE.

Hill-Collins, P. (1990) *Black Feminist Thought: Knowledge, Consciousness, and the Politics of Empowerment*. Boston: Unwin Hyman.

Himmelstrand, U. (ed.) *The Multiparadigmatic Trend in Sociology: A Swedish Perspective*. Uppsala: Acta Universitatis Uppsaliensis: Studia Sociologica Uppsaliensis, 25.

Hirsch, F. (1977) *Social Limits to Growth*. London: Routledge and Kegan Paul.

Holms, B. (1965) *Problems in Education: A Comparative Approach*. London: Routledge and Kegan Paul.

Holsinger, D. B. (1974) 'The elementary school as modernizer: a Brazilian study', *International Journal of Comparative Sociology*, 24.

Honneth, A. (1992) 'Integrity and Disrespect: Principles of a Conception of Morality Based on the Theory of Recognition', *Political Theory*, 20:2.

hooks, b. (1989) *Talking Back, Thinking Feminism, Thinking Black*. Boston, Massachusetts: Southend Press.

Hughes, G. and Mooney, G. (1998) 'Community' in G. Hughes (ed.) *Imagining Welfare Futures*. London: Routledge.

Husén, T. (1997) ' Research Paradigms in Education', in L.J. Saha (ed.) *International Encyclopedia in the Sociology of Education*. Oxford: Pergamon Press.

Hutber, P. (1976) *The decline and fall of the middle class and how it can fight back*. London: Associated Business Programmes.

Ichilov, O. (1991) 'Political Socialization and Schooling Effects among Israeli Adolescents', *Comparative Education Review*, 35:3.

Ichilov, O. (1994) 'Political Education', in T.N. Postlethwaite and T. Husén (eds) *The International Encyclopedia of Education* (second edition). Oxford: Pergamon Press.

Ichilov, O. (ed.) (1990) *Political Socialization, Citizenship Educationand Democracy*. New York: Teachers College Press.

Inglehart, R. (1996) 'Generational Shifts in Citizenship Behaviours: The Role of Education and Economic Security in the Declining Respect for Authority in Industrial Society', *Prospects*, 25:4.

Inkeles, A. (1983) *Exploring Individual Modernity*. New York: Columbia University Press.

Inkeles, A. (1999) 'Psychological and Psychocultural Factors Influencing the Establishment, Maintenance and Development of Democracy'. Paper presented at the 34th World Congress of the International Institute of Sociology, Tel Aviv, Israel.

Inkeles, A. and D.H. Smith (1974) *Becoming Modern*. London: Heinemann Education Books.

Jackson, B. and D. Marsden (1966) *Education and the Working- Class*. Harmondsworth: Pelican Books.

Jensen, A.R. (1969) 'How much can we boost IQ and scholastic achievement?', *Harvard Educational Review*, 39:1.

Johnson, P. (1994) 'Gone is the time when Americans led the world in saying what they thought', *Spectator*, 26 November.

Jones, C., M. Maguire and B. Watson (1997) 'The school experiences of some minority ethnic students in London schools during initial teacher training', *Journal of Education for Teaching*, 23:2.

Jones, G. (1999) 'We're all middle class, says Blair', *Daily Telegraph*, 15 January.

Jonsson, J.O. (1998) 'Class and the Changing Nature of Work: testing hypotheses of deskling and convergence among Swedish employees', *Work, Employment and Society*, 12:4.

Jordan, B. (1996) *A Theory of Poverty and Social Exclusion*. Cambridge: Polity Press.

Jordon, B., M. Redley and S. James (1994) *Putting the Family First: identities, decisions and citizenship*. London: UCL Press.

Joseph Rowntree Foundation (1995) *Inquiry into Income and Wealth*. York: Joseph Rowntree Foundation

Joynson, R.B. (1989) *The Burt Affair*. London: Routledge.

Kahl, J.A. (1968) *The Measurement of Modernism: A Study of Values in Brazil and Mexico*. Austin: The University of Texas Press.

Kamin, L.J. (1974) *The Science and Politics of IQ*. Harmondsworth: Penguin.

Kamin, L.J. (1981) Contributions in H.J. Eysenck versus L.J. Kamin *Intelligence: The Battle for the Mind*, London: Pan Books.

Kamin, L.J. (1999) 'Review of Steven Selden's *Inheriting Shame*', *Race, Ethnicity and Education*, 2:2.

Karabel, J. and A. H. Halsey (eds) (1977) *Power and Ideology in Education*. Oxford: Oxford University Press.

Kearns, G. and C. Philo (1993) *Selling Places: the city as cultural capital, past and present*. Oxford: Pergamon Press.

Keeves, J.P. (1988) 'The Unity of Educational Research', *Interchange*, 19:1.

Keeves, J.P., and D. Adams (1994) 'Comparative Methodology in Education', in T.N. Postlethwaite and T. Husén (eds) *The International Encyclopedia of Education* (second edition). Oxford: Pergamon Press.

Keith, M. and S. Pile (eds) (1993) *Place and the Politics of Identity*. London and New York: Routledge.

Kelly, A. (1981) 'Gender roles at school and home', *British Journal of Sociology of Education*, 3:3.

Kenway, J. (1990) 'Class, Gender and Private Schooling', in D. Dawkins (ed.) *Power and Politics in Education*. Lewes: Falmer Press.

Kenway, J. (1995) 'Maculinities in schools: under siege, on the defensive and under reconstruction', *Discourse*, 16:1

Kenway, J. (1996) 'Having a postmodernist turn or postmodernist angst: a disorder experienced by an author who is not yet dead or even close to it', in

R. Smith and P. Wexler (eds) *After Postmodernism: Education, Politics and Identity*. London: Falmer Press.

Kenway, J. (1999) 'Change of Address?: Educating economics and vocational education and training', *International Journal of Work and the Economy*, 12:2.

Kenway, J. and D. Epstein (eds) (1996) *Discourse* (Special Edition), 17:3.

Kenway, J. and P. Kelly (2000) 'Local/global labour markets and the restructuring of gender, schooling and work', in N. Stromquist and K. Monkman (eds) *Globalisation Influences in Education*. Maryland: Roman and Littlefield.

Kenway, J. and D. Langmead (2000) 'Cyber-feminism and citizenship? Challenging the political imaginary', in M. Arnot and J.-A. Dillabough (eds) *Challenging Democracy: International feminist perspectives on gender, education and citizenship*. London: Routledge.

Kenway, J., S. Willis, J. Blackmore and L. Rennie (1998) *Answering Back: girls, boys and feminism in schools*. London: Routledge.

Kenway, J., K. Tregenza and P. Watkins (eds) (1997) *Vocational Education Today*. Geelong, Australia: Deakin University Centre for Education and Change.

Klees, S.J. (1989) 'The economics of education: a more than slightly jaundiced view', in F. Caillods (ed.) *The Prospects For Educational Planning*. Paris: Unesco, IIEP.

Kohn, A. (1998) 'Only for My Kid: How Privileged Parents Undermine School Reform', *Phi Delta Kappan*, 79:8.

Kudomi, Y. (1996) 'Karl Mannheim in Britain: An interim research report', *Hitotsubashi Journal of Social Studies*, 28:2.

Labarea, D. (1997) *How to Succeed in School without really Learning: The Credentials Race in American Education*. New Haven: Yale University Press.

Labour Party (1997) *New Labour: Because Britain Deserves Better* (The Labour Party Manifesto). London: The Labour Party.

Lacey, C. (1970) *Hightown Grammar*. Manchester: Manchester University Press.

Lane, C. (1999) 'The tainted sources of *The Bell Curve*', in A. Montagu (ed.) *Race and IQ* (expanded edition). New York: Oxford University Press.

Lash, S. (1994) 'Reflexivity and its Doubles: Structure, Aesthetics, Community', in U. Beck, A. Giddens and S. Lash (eds) *Reflexive Modernization: Politics, Tradition and Aesthetics in the Modern Social Order*. Cambridge: Polity Press.

Lash, S. and J. Urry, (1994) *Economies of Signs and Spaces*. London: Sage.

Laslett, B., J. Brenner, and Y. Arat (eds) (1996) *Rethinking the Political: Gender, Resistance and the State*. Chicago: University of Chicago Press.

Lather, P. (1991) *Getting Smart: Feminist Research and Pedagogy Within the Postmodern Classroom*. New York: Routledge.

Lauder, H., D. Hughes, S. Waslander, M. Thrupp, J. McGlinn, S. Newton, and A. Dupuis (1994) 'The Creation of Market Competition for Education in New Zealand'. A paper presentation at the Smithfield Project, Victoria University of Wellington.

Lee, M.J. (1993) *Consumer Culture Reborn: The cultural politics of consumption*. London: Routledge.

Lees, S. (1986) *Losing Out: sexuality and adolescent girls*. London: Hutchinson.

Leftwich, A. (1996) 'On the Primacy of politics in Development', in A. Leftwich (ed.) *Democracy and Development*. Cambridge: Polity Press.

Leonard, P. (1997) *Postmodern Welfare: Reconstructing an Emancipatory Project*. London: Sage.

Lerner, D. (1964) *The Passing of Traditional Society: Modernizing the Middle East*. New York: The Free Press.

Levacic, R.(1995) *Local Management of Schools: Analysis and Practice*. Milton Keynes: Open University Press.

Leys, C. (1996) *The Rise and Fall of Development Theory*. London: James Currey.

Lipman, P. (1998) Race, Class and Power in School Restructuring. Albany: SUNY.

LLamas, I. (1994) 'Education and Labor Markets in Developing Countries', in T.N. Postlethwaite and T. Husén (eds) *The International Encyclopedia of Education* (2nd edn). Oxford: Pergamon Press.

Loader, C. (1985) *The Intellectual Development of Karl Mannheim*. Cambridge: Cambridge University Press.

Lockheed, M.E., D.T. Jamison and L.J. Lau (1980) 'Farmer Education and Farm Efficiency: A Survey', in T. King (ed.) *Education and Income*. Staff Working Paper Number 402. Washington DC: The World Bank.

Lovell, T. (1990) *British Feminist Thought: A Reader*. Oxford: Basil Blackwell.

Lowe, M. (1993) 'Local Hero! An Examination of the Role of the Regional Entrepreneur in the regeneration of Britain's Regions', in G. Kearns and C. Phillo (eds) *Selling Places: The City as Cultural Capital, Past and Present*. Oxford: Pergamon.

Luke, C. (1989) 'Feminist politics in radical pedagogy', in C. Luke and J. Gore (eds) *Feminisms and Critical Pedagogy*. New York: Routledge.

Luke, C. and J. Gore (eds) (1989) *Feminisms and Critical Pedagogy*. New York: Routledge.

Lukes, S. (1972) *Power: A Radical View*. London: Macmillan.

Luttrell, W. (1997) *Schoolsmart and Motherwise*. New York: Routledge.

Lynch, K. (1995) 'The Limits of Liberalism for the Promotion of Equality in Education'. Keynote address at the Association for Teacher Education in Europe, 20th Annual Conference, Oslo, 3–8 September.

Lyons, N. (1990) 'Dilemma's of knowing: Ethical and epistemological dimensions of teachers' work and development', *Harvard Educational Review*, 60:2

Mac an Ghaill, M. (1988) *Young, Gifted and Black: Student- Teacher Relations in the Schooling of Black Youth*. Milton Keynes: Open University Press.

Mac an Ghaill, M. (1994) *The Making of Men*. Milton Keynes: Open University Press.

Mac an Ghaill, M. (ed.) (1996) *Understanding Masculinities*. Milton Keynes: Open University Press.

Mac an Ghaill, M. (1998) Review of Hey – *The company She Keeps: an ethnography of girls' friendships*, in the *British Journal of Sociology of Education*, 19:1.

Maccoby, E.E. and C.N. Jacklin (1974) *The Psychology of Sex Differences*. Stanford: Stanford University Press.

MacDonald, M. (1980) 'Schooling and the reproduction of class and gender relations', in L. Barton, R. Meighan and S. Walker (eds) *Schooling, Ideology and the Curriculum*. Barcombe: Falmer Press.

Macey, D. (1993) *The Lives of Michel Foucault*. London: Vintage Books.

Macpherson, Sir William (1999) *The Stephen Lawrence Inquiry*. Cm. 42621. London: HMSO.

Macrae, S., M. Maguire, and S.J. Ball (1996) 'Opportunity Knocks: Choice in the Post-16 Education and Training Market', *Proceedings of Markets in Education: Processes and Practices*. University of Southampton 4–5 July.

Mahony, P. (1983) 'How Alice's chin really came to be pressed against her foot: sexist processes of interaction in mixed sexed classrooms', *Women's Studies International Forum*, 16:1.

Mahony, P. (1985) *Schools for the Boys: coeducation reassessed* London: Hutchinson.

Malcolm, N. (1998) *Kosovo: A Short History*. London: Macmillan.

Manji, F. (1998) 'The depoliticization of poverty', in D. Eade (ed.) *Development and Rights*. Oxford: Oxfam Great Britain.

Mann, M. (1993) *The Sources of Social Power Volume II: The rise of classes and nation-states, 1760–1914*. Cambridge: Cambridge University Press.

Mannheim, K. (1936) *Ideology and Utopia: An Introduction to the Sociology of Knowledge*. London: Kegan Paul.

Mannheim, K. (1943) *Diagnosis of Our Time: Wartime Essays of a Sociologist*. London: Routledge and Kegan Paul.

Mannheim, K. (1951) *Freedom, Power and Democratic Planning*. London: Routledge and Kegan Paul.

Mannheim, K. (1957) *Systematic Sociology: An Introduction to the Study of Society*. London: Routledge and Kegan Paul.

Mannheim, K., and W.A.C. Stewart (1962) *An Introduction to the Sociology of Education*. London: Routledge and Kegan Paul.

Marchand, M.H. and J.L. Parpart (eds) (1995) *Feminism/Postmodernism/Development*. London: Routledge.

Marshall, G. (ed.) (1997) *Repositioning Class*. London: Sage.

Marshall, G., and A. Swift (1997) 'Social class and social justice', in G. Marshall (ed.) *Repositioning Class*. London: Sage.

Martin, J. and C. Vincent (1999) 'Parental Voice: an exploration', *International Studies in Sociology of Education*, 9:2.

Mason, D. (1990) 'A rose by any other name? Categorisation, identity and social science', *New Community*, 17:1.

Massey, D. (1995) 'Reflections on Gender and Geography', in T. Butler and M. Savage, (eds) *Social Change and the Middle Classes*. London: UCL Press.

McFadden, M. (1995) 'Resistance to Schooling and Educational Outcomes: questions of structure and agency', *British Journal of Sociology of Education*, 16:3.

McGinn, N.F. (1996) 'Education, Democratization, and Globalization: A Challenge for Comparative Education', *Comparative Education Review*, 40:4.

McLaren, A.T. (1996) 'Coercive invitations: how young women in school make sense of mothering and waged labour', *British Journal of Sociology of Education*, 17:3.

McRobbie, A. (1978) 'Working-class girls and the culture of femininity', in Centre for Contemporary Cultural Studies (eds) *Women take Issue: aspects of women's subordination*. London: Hutchinson Educational.

Measor, L. and P. Sikes (1992) *Gender and Schooling*. London: Cassell.

Meighan, R. (1981) *A Sociology of Educating*. London: Holt, Rhinehart and Winston.

Meyer, J. (1986) 'Types of Explanation in the Sociology of Education', in J. Richardson (ed.) *Handbook of Theory and Research for the Sociology of Education*. Westport: Greenwood Press.

Middleton, S. (1987) 'The sociology of women's education as a field of academic study', in M. Arnot and G. Weiner (eds) *Gender and the Politics of Schooling*. London: Open University Press.

Middleton, S. (1993) 'A post modern pedagogy for the sociology of women's education', in M. Arnot and K. Weiler (eds) *Feminism and Social Justice in Education*. London: Falmer Press.

Middleton, S. (l998) *Disciplining sexuality: Foucault, life histories, and education*. Teachers College Press: New York.

Miles, M. and B. Gold (1981) *Whose School is it Anyway?* New York: Praegar Publishing.

Miller, D. (1976) *Social Justice*. Oxford: Clarendon Press.

Millet, K. (1977) *Sexual Politics*. London: Virago.

Mills, C. (1995) 'Managerial And professional work histories' in T. Butler and M. Savage (eds) *Social Change and the Middle Classes*. London: UCL Press.

Mills, C.W. (1961) *The Sociological Imagination*. Harmondsworth: Penguin.

Mirza, H.S. (1992) *Young, Female and Black*. London: Routledge.

Mirza, H.S. (1993) 'The social construction of black womenhood in British educational research: Towards a new understanding', in Arnot, M. and Weiler, K. (eds) *Feminism and Social Justice in Education: International Perspectives*. London: Falmer Press.

Mirza, H.S. (ed.) (1997) *Black British Feminism*. London: Routledge.

Mirza, H.S. and D. Reay, (2000) 'Redefining citizenship: black women educators and 'the third space', in M. Arnot and J. Dillabough (eds) *Challenging Democracy: feminist perspectives on gender, education and citizenship*. London: Routledge.

Modood, T. and A. Shiner (1994) *Ethnic Minorities and Higher Education*. London: Policy Studies Institute/UCAS.

Modood, T. and A. Shiner (1994) *Ethnic Minorities and Higher Education*. London: Policy Studies Institute/UCAS.

Modood, T., R. Berthoud, J. Lakey, J. Nazroo, P. Smith, S. Virdee and S. Beishon (1997) *Ethnic Minorities in Britain: Diversity and Disadvantage*. London: Policy Studies Institute.

Moe, T. (1994) 'The battle for choice', in K.L. Billingsley (ed.) *Voices on Choice: The Education Reform Debate*. San Francisco: Pacific Institute for Public Policy.

Moock, P.R. and H. Addou (1997) 'Agricultural Productivity and Education', in L.J. Saha (ed.) *International Encyclopedia in the Sociology of Education*. Oxford: Pergamon Press.

Moore, R. (1988) 'The correspondence principle and the Marxist sociology of education', in M. Cole (ed.) *Bowles and Gintis Revisited* Lewes: Falmer Press.

Moore, R. (1996) 'Back to the Future: the problem of change and the possibilities of advance in the sociology of education', *British Journal of Sociology of Education*, 17:2.

Mortimore, P. and G. Whitty (1997) *Can school improvement overcome the effects of disadvantage?* London: Institute of Education.

Mouffe, C. (1989) 'Toward a radical democratic citizenship', *Democratic Left*, 17:2.

Murphy, P. and J. Elwood (1998) 'Gendered experiences, choices and achievement: exploring the links', *International Journal of Inclusive Education*, 2:2.

Nagel, T. (1991) *Equality and Partiality*. Oxford: Oxford University Press.

Nathan, J.A. and R.C. Remy (1977) 'Comparative Political Socialization: A Theoretical Perspective', in S.A. Renshon (ed.) *Handbook of Political Socialization: Theory and Research*. New York: The Free Press.

Nehaul, K. (1996) *The Schooling of Children of Caribbean Heritage*. Stoke-on-Trent: Trentham Books.

New Zealand Department of Social Welfare (1998) *Towards a Code of Social and Family Responsibility: public discussion document*. Wellington: Department of Social Welfare.

Niemi, R.G. and J. Junn (1996) 'What Knowledge for a Reinforced Citizenship in the United States of America?', *Prospects*, 24:4.

Noddings, N. (1988) An ethic of caring and its implication for instructional arrangements'. *American Journal of Education*, 96: 2.

Oakley, A. (1972) *Sex, Gender and Society*. London: Temple Smith.

Ofsted (1999) *Raising the Attainment of Minority Ethnic Pupils*. London: Office for Standards in Education.

Ohrn, E. and L. Davies (1999) 'Power, Democracy and Gender in Schools'. A paper presented at the 1999 *Women's Worlds Conference*, Tromso.

Osler, A. (1997) *The Lives and Careers of Black Teachers: Changing Identities, Changing Lives*. Buckingham: Open University Press.

Ozga, J. (1990) 'Policy Research and Policy Theory: a comment on Fitz and Halpin', *Journal of Education Policy*, 5:4.

Pakulski, J. and M. Waters (1996) *The Death of Class*. London: Sage.

Parker, C.S. and E.H. Epstein (1998) 'Cumulative Index'. *Comparative Education Review*, 42 (Supplement).

Pateman, C. (1992) 'Equality, difference and subordination: the politics of motherhood and women's citizenship' in G. Bock and S. James (eds) *Beyond Equality and Difference: citizenship, femimist politics, female subjectivity*. New York: Routledge.

Pateman, C. (l988) *The Sexual Contract*. Cambridge: Polity Press.

Paulston, R.G. (1994) 'Comparative and International Education: Paradigms and Theories', in T.N. Postlethwaite and T. Husén (eds) *The International Encyclopedia of Education* (2nd edn). Oxford: Pergamon Press.

Payne, J. (1995) *Routes Beyond Compulsory Schooling. England and Wales Youth: Cohort Study Report Number 31*. Sheffield: Department of Employment.

Perkin, H. (1989) *The Rise of Professional Society: England since 1800*. London: Routledge.

Pheonix, A. (1987) 'Theories of gender and black families', in G. Weiner and M. Arnot (eds) *Gender Under Scrutiny: New Inquiries in Education*. London: Hutchinson.

Philips, A. (1997) 'From Inequality to Difference: A Severe Case of Displacement?', *New Left Review*, 224.

Pollard, S. (1995) *Schools, Selection and the Left*. London: Social Market Foundation.

Power, S. and G. Whitty (1999) 'New Labour's education policy: first, second or third way? *Journal of Education Policy*, 14:5.

Power, S. (2000) 'Educational Pathways into the Middle Class(es), *British Journal of Sociology of Education*, 21:2.

Power, S., G. Whitty, T. Edwards and V. Wigfall (1998a) 'Schools, families and academically able children: contrasting modes of involvement in secondary education', *British Journal of Sociology of Education*, 19:2.

Power, S., T. Edwards, G. Whitty and V. Wigfall (l998b) Schoolboys and schoolwork: gender identification and academic achievement, *Journal of Inclusive Education*, 2:2.

Power, S., G. Whitty, T. Edwards and V. Wigfall (2000) 'Destined for Success: Educational Biographies of Academically Able Pupils', *Research Papers in Education.*

Preston, P.W. (1996) *Development Theory: An Introduction.* Oxford: Blackwell.

Price, B. (1997) 'The Myth of Postmodern Science' in R. Eve, S. Horsfall and M. Lee (eds) *Chaos, Complexity and Social Theory.* Thousand Oaks, California: Sage.

Probert, B. (1995) *The Transformation of Work: Social, Cultural and Political Contexts,* in J. Spierings, I. Voorendt, and J. Spoehr. (eds) *Jobs for Young Australians.* Adelaide: Jobs for Young Australians Conference Organising Committee in association with Social Justice Research Foundation Inc.

Psacharopoulos, G. (1985) 'Returns to education: a further international update and implications', *Journal of Human Resources*, 20.

Psacharopoulos, G. (1994) 'Returns to investment in education: a global update', *World Development*, 22:9.

Punt, T. (1975) 'Social Pressures' in J. Morrell (ed) *Britain in the 1980s.* London: The Henley Centre for Forecasting.

Putnam, R.D. (1993a) *Making Democracy Work: Civic Traditions in Modern Italy.* Princeton: Princeton University Press.

Putnam, R.D. (1993b) 'The Prosperous Community: Social Capital and Public Life', *The American Prospect*, 13, Spring.

QCA (1998) *Education for Citizenship and the teaching of democracy in schools* (Report of the Advisory Group on Citizenship). London: Qualifications and Curriculum Authority.

Rabinow, P. (1986) 'Introduction', in P. Rabinow (ed.) *The Foucault Reader.* Harmondsworth: Penguin Books.

Raftery, A.E. and M. Hout (1993) 'Maximally Maintained Inequality: Expansion, Reform, and Opportunity in Irish Education', *Sociology of Education*, 66:1.

Rampton Report (1981) *West Indian Children in Our Schools* (Interim Report). Cmnd. 8273. London: HMSO.

Rawls, J. (1972) *A Theory of Justice*, Oxford: Clarendon Press.

Reay, D. (1998a) 'Rethinking Social Class: Qualitative Prespectives on Class and gender', *Sociology*, 32:2.

Reay, D. (1998b) 'Setting the Agenda: The growing impact of market forces on pupil grouping in secondary schooling', *Journal of Curriculum Studies*, 30.

Reay, D. (1998c) *Class Work: Mothers' Involvement in their Children's Primary Schooling.* London: UCL Press.

Reay, D., J. Davies, M. David and S.J. Ball (1999) 'Choices of Degree and Degrees of Choice: a report from work in progress'. Paper presented at the BERA Annual meeting in Brighton.

Renshon, S.A. (ed.) (1977) *Handbook of Political Socialization.* The Free Press: New York.

Rich, A. (1980) 'Compulsory heterosexuality and lesbian existence', reprinted in A. Rich (ed.) (1984) *Blood, Bread and Poetry.* New York: Norton Books.

Richardson, R. and A. Wood (1999) *Inclusive Schools, Inclusive Society: race and identity on the agenda.* Stoke-on- Trent: Trentham Books.

Roberts, K., S.C. Clark and C. Wallace (1994) 'Flexibility and individualisation: a comparison of transitions into employment in England and Germany', *Sociology*, 28:1.

Robertson, S. (1999) 'Risky Business: Market Provision, Community Governance, and the Individualization of Risk in New Zealand Schooling', *International Studies in the Sociology of Education*, 9:3.

Robertson, S. (2000) *A Class Act: Changing Teachers' Work, Globalization and the State*. New York: Garland-Falmer.

Roland M.J. (1982) 'Excluding women from the educational realm', *Harvard Educational Review*, 52: 2.

Roman, L. (1992) 'The political significance of other ways of narrating ethnography: a feminist materialist approach', in M.D., Lecompte, W. Milroy and J. Priessle (eds) *The Handbook of Qualitative Research in Education*. San Diego, California: Academic Press.

Roman, L. (1993) 'Double exposure: the politics of feminist materialist ethnography', *Educational Theory*, 43.

Rust, V.D., A. Soumare, O. Pescador and M. Shibuya (1999) 'Research Strategies in Comparative Education', *Comparative Education Review*, 43:1.

Sadler, D. (1993) 'Place marketing, Competitive Places and the Construction of hegemony', in G. Kearns and C. Phillo (eds) *Selling Places: The City as Cultural Capital, Past and Present*. Oxford: Pergamon.

Sadovnik. A.R. (1995) 'Basil Bernstein's theory of pedagogic practice: A structuralist approach', in A.R. Sadovnik (ed.) *Knowledge and Pedagogy: The Sociology of Basil Bernstein*. Norwood, New Jersey: Ablex.

Saha, L.J. (1995) 'Two decades of education and development: some reflections', in H. Daun, M. O'Dowd and S. Zhao (eds) (1995) *The Role of Education in Development: From Personal to International Arenas*. Stockholm: University Institute of International Education.

Said, E.F. (1979) *Orientalism*. New York: Pantheon.

Salmi, J. (1999) 'Violence, Democracy and Education: An Analytical Framework'. A paper presented at the Oxford International Conference on Education and Development, September.

Saunders, P. (1996) *Unequal but Fair? A Study of Class Barriers in Britain*. London: Institute of Economic Affairs, Choice and Welfare Unit.

Savage, M., J. Barlow, P. Dickens and A. J. Fielding (1992) *Property, Bureaucracy and Culture: middle class formation in contemporary Britain*. London: Routledge.

Savage, M., and T. Butler (1995) 'Assets and the middle classes in contemporary Britain', in T. Butler and M. Savage (eds) *Social Change and the Middle Classes*. London: UCL Press.

Savage, M. and M. Egerton (1997) 'Social Mobility, Inidividual Ability and the Inheritance of Class Inequality', *Sociology*, 31:4.

Schrag, F. (1999) 'Why Foucault Now?', *Journal of Curriculum Studies*, 31:4.

Scott, J. (1994) 'Deconstructing equality versus difference: or the uses of postculturalist theory for feminism', in S. Seidman (ed) *The Postmodern Turn: new perspectives on social theory*. Cambridge: Cambridge University Press.

Selden, S. (1999) *Inheriting Shame: The Story of Eugenics and Racism in America*. New York: Teachers College Press.

Sewell, T. (1997) *Black Masculinities and Schooling: How Black Boys Survive Modern Schooling*. Stoke-on-Trent: Trentham Books.

Sewell, T. (1998) 'Loose canons: exploding the myth of the "black macho" lad', in D. Epstein, J. Elwood, V. Hey and J. Maw (eds) *Failing Boys? Issues in Gender and Achievement*. Buckingham: Open University Press.

Sharpe, S. (l994) *Just Like a Girl* (2nd edn). Harmondsworth: Penguin

Shilling, C. (1992) 'Reconceptualising structure and agency in the sociology of education: structuration theory and schooling', *British Journal of Sociology of Education*, 13:1.

Shilling, C. (1993). 'The demise of sociology of education in Britain?', *British Journal of Sociology of Education*, 14:1.

Sibley, D. (1992) 'Outsiders in society and space', in K. Anderson and F. Gale (eds) *Inventing Places: Studies in Cultural Geography*. Melbourne: Longman Cheshire.

Siraj-Blatchford, I. (1991) 'A study of black students' perceptions of racism in initial teacher education', *British Educational Research Journal*, 17, pp.35–50.

Skeggs, B. (l997) *Formations of Class and Gender*. London: Sage.

Sklar, R. (1996) 'Towards a Theory of Developmental Democracy', in A. Leftwich (ed.) *Democracy and Development* Cambridge: Polity Press.

Smith, D.H. (1974) *Becoming Modern*. London: Heinemann.

Smith, T. and M. Noble (1995) *Education Divides: Poverty and Schooling in the 1990s*. London: Child Poverty Action Group.

Smolicz, J.J. (1998) 'From Tradition to Modernity: Higher Education in an Era of Global Change', *Education and Society*, 16:1.

Spender, D. (1980) *Man Made Language*. London: Routledge and Kegan Paul.

Spender, D. (1982) *Invisible Women: The Schooling Scandal*. London: Writers' and Readers' Publishing Collective.

Spender, D. (1987) 'Education: the patriarchal paradigm and the response to feminism', in M. Arnot and G. Weiner (eds) *Gender and the Politics of Schooling*. London: Hutchinson.

Sternberg, R.J. (1998) 'Abilities are forms of developing expertise', *Educational Researcher*, 27:3.

Stewart, W.A.C. (1967) *Karl Mannheim on Education and Social Thought*. London: George G Harrap for the University of London Institute of Education.

Stone, L. (ed.) (1994) *The Education Feminism Reader*. New York: Routledge.

Stromquist, N. P. (1990) 'Women and Illiteracy: The Interplay of Gender Subordination and Poverty', *Comparative Education Review*, 34:1.

Stuart Wells, A. (1993) 'The sociology of school choice' in E. Rasell and R. Rothstein (eds) *School Choice: Examining the Evidence*. Washington DC: Economic Policy Institute.

Stuart Wells, A. and J. Oakes (1996) 'Potential Pitfalls of Systemic Reform: Early Lessons from Research on Detracking', *Sociology of Education*, 69.

Stuart Wells, A., and I. Serna (1997) 'The Politics of Culture', in A. H. Halsey, H. Lauder, P. Brown and A. Stuart Wells (eds) *Education: Culture, Economy and Society*. Oxford: Oxford University Press.

Sukhnandan, L. and B. Lee (1998) *Streaming, Setting and Grouping by Ability*. Slough: NFER.

Sweet, R. (1995) *All of their talents? Policies and programs for fragmented and interrupted transitions*. Melbourne: Dusseldorp Skills Forum.

Swift, D. (1965) 'Meritocratic and social class selection at age 11', *Educational Research*, 8:1.

Taylor, C. (1992) *Multiculturalism and the Politics of Recognition*. Princeton: Princeton University Press.

Teacher Training Agency (1998) *Initial Teacher Training: Performance Profiles*. London: TTA.

Thatcher, M. (1993) *The Downing Street Years*. London: HarperCollins.

Thompson, J. (1983) *Learning Liberation: women's response to men's education*. London: Croom Helm.

Thurow, L.C. and R.E.B. Lucas (1972) 'The American Distribution of Income: A Structural Problem' US Congress Joint Economic Committee, in P. Berger (1987) *The Capitalist Revolution*. Aldershot: Wildwood House.

Tong, R. (1989) *Feminist Thought*. Sydney: Unwin and Hyman.

Tooley, J. (1995a) 'Can IQ tests liberate education?', *Economic Affairs*, 15.

Tooley, J. (1995b) 'A measure of freedom', *The Times Higher*, 7 July.

Tooley, J. (1996) *Education without the State*. London: Institute of Economic Affairs.

Tooley, J. and D. Darby (1998) *Educational Research: a critique*. London: Office for Standards in Education (Ofsted).

Torney-Purta, J. and J. Schwille (1986) 'Civic values learned in school: policy and practice in industrialized nations', *Comparative Education Review*, 30:1.

Tueros, M. (1994) 'Education and Informal Labor Markets', in T.N. Postlethwaite and T. Husén, (eds) *The International Encyclopedia of Education* (2nd edn). Oxford: Pergamon Press.

Turner, F. (1997) 'Forward', in R. Eve, S. Horsfall and M. Lee (eds) *Chaos, Complexity and Social Theory*. Thousand Oaks, California: Sage.

United Nations Development Programme (1995) *Human Development Report 1995*. New York: UNDP.

Urry, J. (1995) *Consuming Places*. London: Routledge.

Vanhanen, T. (1996) *Prospects of Democracy: A Study of 172 countries*. London: Routledge.

Verba, S., N.H. Nie and J. Kim (1978) *Participation and Political Equality*. London: Cambridge University Press.

Verhoeven, J.C. (1989) *Methodological and Metascientific Problems in Symbolic Interactionism*. Leuven: Departement Sociologie, Katholicke Universitet Leuven.

Vincent, C. (1996) *Parents and Teachers: Power and Participation*. London: Falmer Press.

Vincent, C., and J. Martin (1999) '"The Committee People": school-based parents' groups – a politics of voice and representation?' Paper presented at the Parental Choice and Market Forces Seminar, King's College London.

Volman, M. and G. ten Dam (1998) 'Equal but different: contradictions in the development of gender identity in the 1990s', *British Journal of Sociology of Education*, 19: 4.

Wagner, D.A. and A. Lofti (1980) 'Traditional Islamic Education in Morocco: Socio-historical and Psychological Perspectives', *Comparative Education Review*, 24.

Wagner, D.A. (1985) 'Islamic Education: Traditional Pedagogy and Contemporary Aspects', in T. Husen and T.N. Postlethwaite (eds) *International Encyclopedia of Education* (Volume 5). Oxford: Pergamon Press.

Waldrop, M. (1992) *Complexity: the emerging science at the edge of order and chaos* London: Penguin Books.

Walford, G. (1987) *Doing Sociology of Education*. London: Falmer Press.

Walker, J. (1993) 'Cultural perspectives on work and schoolwork in an Australian inner-city boys' high school', in L. Angus (ed.) *Education, Inequality and Social Identity*. London: Falmer Press.

Walkerdine, V. (1987) 'Femininity as performance', *Oxford Review of Education*, 15:3.

Walkerdine, V. (1990) *School Girl Fictions*. London: Verso.

Weiler, H.N. (1978) 'Education and development from the age of innocence to the age of scepticism', *Comparative Education*, 14:3.

Weiner, G. (1994) *Feminism(s) in Education: An Introduction*. Buckingham: Open University.

Weiner, G., M. Arnot and M. David (l998) 'Is the future female? Female success, male disadvantage and changing gender relations in education', in A.H. Halsey, H. Lauder, P. Brown and A. Stuart Wells (eds) *Education: Culture, Economy and Society*. Oxford: Oxford University Press.

Weis, L. (l990) *Working Class without Work: high school students in a de-industrialising economy*. New York: Routledge.

Weiss, M. (1993) 'New Guiding Principles in Education Policy: The Case of Germany', *Journal of Education Policy*, 8:4.

Wexler, P. (1987) *The Social Analysis of Education*. London: Routledge.

Whelehan, I. (1995) *Modern Feminist Thought*. Edinburgh: Edinburgh University Press.

Whitty, G. (1985). *Sociology and School Knowledge: Curriculum Theory, Research and Politics*. London: Methuen.

Whitty, G. (1997a) 'Creating quasi-markets in education: a review of recent research on parental choice and school autonomy in three countries', in M.W. Apple (ed.) *Review of Research in Education: Volume 22*. Washington, DC: American Educational Research Association.

Whitty, G. (1997b) *Social Theory and Education Policy: The Legacy of Karl Mannheim*. London: Institute of Education.

Whitty, G. (1998) 'New Labour, Education and Disadvantage', *Education and Social Justice*, 1:1.

Whitty, G. and S. Power (2000) 'Marketization and privatization in mass education systems', *International Journal of Educational Development*, 20.

Whitty, G., S. Power and D. Halpin (1998) *Devolution and Choice in Education: the school, the state and the market*. Buckingham: Open University Press.

Williamson, Bill (1974) 'Continuities and Discontinuities in the Sociology of Education', in M. Flude and J. Ahier (eds) *Educability, Schools and Ideology*. London: Croom Helm.

Willis, P. (1977) *Learning to Labour*. Farnborough: Saxon House.

Willis, S. and P. McClelland (1997) 'Reading the region', in P. Jeffery (ed.) *Proceedings of the Australian Association for Research in Education Conference*. Melbourne: Australian Association for Research in Education and published at www.swin.edu.au/aare/97pap/MACCJ97328.html

Willmott, R. (1999) 'Structure, Agency and the Sociology of Education: rescuing analytical dualism' *British Journal of Sociology of Education*, 20:1.

Wollstonecraft, M. (1992) (first published in 1792) *Vindication of the Rights of Women*. London: Penguin.

Wolpe, A.M. (1988) ' "Experience" as analytical framework: Does it account for girls' education', in M. Cole (ed.) *Bowles and Ginties Revisited*. Lewes: Falmer Press.

Woodhead, C. (1998) 'Academia gone to seed', *New Statesman*, 20 March.

Woods, P., C. Bagley and R. Glatter (1998) *School Choice and Competition*. London: Routledge.

World Bank (1994) *Enhancing Women's Participation in Economic Development*. Washington DC: The World Bank.

World Bank (1995) *Priorities and Strategies for Education*. Washington, DC: The World Bank.

Wright, C. (1986) 'School processes – an ethnographic study', in J. Eggleston, D. Dunn and M. Anjali (1986) *Education for Some: The Educational and Vocational Experiences of 15–18 year old Members of Minority Ethnic Groups*. Stoke-on-Trent: Trentham Books.

Wright, C. (1992) *Race Relations in the Primary School*. London: David Fulton.

Wright, C., D. Weekes, A. McGlaughlin and D. Webb (1998) 'Masculinised Discourses within Education and the Construction of Black Male Identities amongst African Caribbean Youth', *British Journal of Sociology of Education*, 19:1.

Young, I. (1997) 'Unruly categories: a critique of Nancy Fraser's dual systems theory', *New Left Review*, 222.

Young, I.M. (1995) 'Gender as seriality: Thinking about women as a social collective', in L. Nicholson and S. Seidman (eds) *Social Postmodernism*. Cambridge: Cambridge University Press.

Young, I.M. (1990) *Justice and the Politics of Difference*, Princeton: Princeton University Press.

Young, M. (1998) 'Right questions, wrong answers'. Letter to the *New Statesman*, 3 April.

Young, M.F.D. (ed) (1971) *Knowledge and Control: New Directions for the Sociology of Education*. London: Macmillan.

Young, M.F.D. (1988) *Curriculum and Democracy: Lessons from a Critique of the 'New Sociology of Education'*. Centre for Vocational Studies, University of London Institute of Education.

Yuval-Davis, N. (1997) *Gender and Nation*. London: Sage.

Zagefka, P. (1993) 'The Sociology of Education in Seven European Countries: Theoretical Trends and Social Contexts', *Innovation*, 6:2.

Zukin, S. (1991) *Landscapes of Power: from Detroit to Disney World*. California: University of California Press.

Index